WHISPERS OF GOD

FROM HIS HEART TO YOURS

By
MARY R. BOLTON

PRESS

Whispers of God
From His Heart to Yours
By Mary R. Bolton

Printed in the United States of America

ISBN 9781628712353

Unless otherwise indicated, Bible quotations are taken from The New King James Version (NKJV). Copyright © 1982 by Thomas Nelson, Inc.

www.xulonpress.com

INTRODUCTION

❦

"And after the earthquake a fire but the Lord was not in the fire;
and after the fire a still small voice."
I Kings 19:12

S ince 1974, when my relationship with and my commitment to
the Lord became alive and personal, I have kept a journal. I
would ask the Lord questions, and then I would write down what
I understood Him to be saying to me. Like Elijah, the most powerful of those times was when His answer would come in a "small,
still voice."

You know the story in I Kings 18. Elijah had confronted the
prophets of Baal. They had built an altar to their god and called upon
him. Nothing happened. Elijah built an altar to Jehovah God, dug
a trench around the altar and filled the trench with water to overflowing. He then called on the Lord God Jehovah, and He responded
mightily with fire that licked up all the water and blazed until the
sacrifice on the altar was gone! Elijah then killed the prophets of
Baal with a sword. Fearing Jezebel, Elijah ran off and sat under
a Juniper tree and prayed that he would die. The Lord answered
Elijah, not in the wind, not in the earthquake, not in fire; but He
answered him with a small, still voice!

The Lord responds to us in many ways, but one of the most
intriguing ways that He responds to us is in a small, still voice – a
whisper! I wrote a daily devotional, which was published in 1999.
Many people have asked me when I would write another book, and
I would tell them, "When the Lord tells me."

In late August 2012, I was walking through my house, and I heard a "small, still voice" that said, "Whispers of God." I asked the Lord, "What does that mean?" He told me that was to be the title of my next book. Recently in reading I Kings 19:12 in the New Living Translation, I saw that verse 12b is translated, "And after the fire, there was the sound of a gentle whisper." That confirmed to me the title of this book.

Whispers of God is a daily word from the Lord to each of us to encourage us in our walk with Him. As we hear and respond to God's whispers to us, our lives are changed. When He whispers, He is bidding us to know and understand the depth of His love. He is helping us to understand the wonder of Who He is and how He sees us. He wants us to know His purpose and destiny for us here on earth. As He draws us into His presence, He is giving us discernment to understand the times in which we are living – that we may be a reflection of Him wherever we go.

My desire is that this prophetic devotional will touch your heart with the heart of God! May you be greatly blessed as He speaks to you just where you are, each day, to show you the length, width, depth and height of His love for you.

I would like to dedicate this book to My fun-loving and delightful husband, John. Over the many years that we have been married, I have learned to lighten up, laugh a lot and to have fun. The Lord has used him to turn a very serious person in to someone that enjoys life. I so appreciate all the support and encouragement that is so much a part of who he is, and I am grateful for our growing together in the Lord over these many years together.

ACKNOWLEDGMENTS

I would like to express my deep and heartfelt gratitude to my dear friend, Beth Arnurius, who spent many hours editing this book for me. She and her husband, Don, are the pastors of Care and Nurture at New Covenant Church in Knoxville, Tennessee, and they have touched the lives of many.

My life has been greatly impacted by the friendship and prayers of my two prayer partners, Maxine Raines and Pastor Sharon Welch. We have prayed weekly (when we are all in town) for approximately sixteen years, and we have had the most wonderful times with our Jesus!

My husband and family have been a constant source of love and encouragement. I am grateful to the Lord for my children, their spouses and my grandchildren. They keep inspiring me as I see how the Lord is using each one of them in very special ways. Family times are filled with love and laughter!

My eternal gratitude, thanksgiving and praise goes to My heavenly Father, Who has been shaping and molding me for many years now. I love Him more each day, and I am so grateful for His presence growing moment-by-moment and day-by-day in my life! I cannot wait to see what He has ahead for myself and for all of you that are reading *Whispers of God!*

JANUARY

1 JANUARY

COME, MY BELOVED

Come, My beloved and let Me whisper to you those things that are in My heart. I long to share My heart, My very being, with you. I long to show you those things about yourself that I am drawing out, that I am strengthening. I am doing a work within you to fulfill My purpose in your precious life, for you are My beloved. My love for you is great, and I long for the times when you seek Me, when you seek My face. Our fellowship together is precious to Me.

My beloved, I am calling you forth. My anointing is upon you, and more and more doors will be open for you to go forth. As you seek Me and as I send you forth, it will be My words, My power and My Spirit within you that will come forth and minister to those that I bring to you. Always seek Me and My word as I send you forth.

My beloved spoke, and said to me:
"Rise up, my love, my fair one, and come away."
Song of Solomon 2:10

2   JANUARY

THE DEPTH OF GOD'S LOVE

Come closer, move into that realm with Me where you know the depth of My love for you. Let Me pour out My love upon you in such a way that you will not doubt My love for you – yes, you! Some of you are having trouble receiving My love, but I want you to know, understand and experience the length, depth, width and height of My love. I want you to believe that it is My desire to pour out My love upon you exceedingly, abundantly beyond all that you can ask or imagine. Reach out for Me. Receive from Me, and My love will transform you in such a way that you will wonder at the changes you begin to experience.

You will find yourself boldly sharing Me and My love with others. You will see people saved, healed, delivered and set free! I am pouring out My abundant love upon you so you can go forth and pour out My love upon those who need Me and those who have never experienced Me. I am calling you to reveal that I am alive and real in this world. Go forth in My power, in My might and in My love, and see the lives of multitudes transformed.

That Christ may dwell in your hearts through faith; that you, being rooted and grounded in love may be able to comprehend with all the saints what is the width and length and depth and height – to know the love of Christ which passes knowledge; that you may be filled with all the fullness of God.
Ephesians 3:17-19

3   JANUARY

REBUILDING SPIRITUALLY

Dear Ones, My anointing is upon you to rebuild. I will show you step by step how to rebuild – not physical things, but spiritual rebuilding – as you draw close to Me, loving Me, growing in My likeness and loving as I love, accepting as I accept. Do not rush out ahead of Me, but allow My anointing to flow. Stay close to Me as I direct you and as I teach you. Receive My wisdom that I hold out to you. And as you do, you will be experiencing My love and My compassion afresh and anew. As you draw close, as you receive from Me, you will find yourself walking in obedience to Me.

But we all, with unveiled face, beholding as in a mirror the glory of the Lord, are being transformed into the same image from glory to glory, just as by the Spirit of the Lord.
II Corinthians 3:18

4 JANUARY

A MIGHTY, ROARING FIRE

As My presence surrounds you, step out into the places that I show you. Step into righteousness, holiness, humility and purity! Seek My will, My way and My timing. As you take a step towards Me, I will pour forth My Sprit (the oil of My Spirit) upon the fire that is ignited within you. As My oil mixes with the fire within you, a mighty, roaring fire will blaze through you wherever you go. No water can quench this fire – this is My consuming fire that will burn away all the debris and empower you to blaze for Me!

In speaking of the angels, He says, "He makes His angels
spirits and His servants flames of fire."
Hebrews 1:7 NIV

5   JANUARY

STAND FAST IN FAITH

Come, come, come and listen. Listen to My words of wisdom that I speak to you. I have you in this place for this time. You are not here by chance. You did not just happen by – you are here for a purpose! Submit your will to My purpose, and you will know pure joy. At first, you will think "I cannot do this," but as you decide to submit to My will regardless of what you think, you will know pure joy. I have called you for such a time as this. Gather together and pray. Gather together and seek Me. Gather together and enter into My presence in such a way that you KNOW that you are truly in the presence of the Great I AM. You will KNOW that there is no other place to be but where I am. Enter into My Holy of holies and experience My holiness in such a way that you are completely transformed. I am changing you – I am changing you from glory-to-toglory into My image! Reflect Me wherever I send you. It is time for change. I am changing you. Watch and stand fast in faith. Be brave and be strong. Let all that you do be done with love.

Watch, stand fast in the faith, be brave, be strong.
Let all that you do be done with love.
I Corinthians 16:13-14

6 JANUARY

THE HARVEST OF THE LORD IS RIPE

I am preparing you for the coming of the Lord. I am preparing you for the tumultuous days that are ahead. I am strengthening you with My strength. I am placing My wisdom within you to walk in My peace in the midst of chaos. You will stand strong and be a shining light as many are looking for comfort and assurance. I have been preparing you for years to be My vessel during this time and during the days that are ahead. Keep your eyes focused on Me. Keep your ears tuned to Me as you listen for the sound that will bring redemption to multitudes. Listen for the sound that will bring deliverance to those that are in deep bondage, and listen for the sound that will stir the hearts of the desolate.

There has never been a time on earth as that which is about to come forth. Look up and rejoice, for it is a time of harvest. It is a time to see the multitudes running, racing into My arms as they recognize the sound of heaven reverberating upon and throughout the earth. Listen for the sound – listen for My voice and rejoice, for I am coming! I am coming!

Put in the sickle, for the harvest is ripe. Come, go down; for the winepress is full, the vats overflow – for their wickedness is great. Multitudes, multitudes in the valley of decision! For the day of the Lord is near in the valley of decision.
Joel 3:13-14

7   JANUARY

ACKNOWLEDGE MY WAYS

I say to you, "Acknowledge My ways." To acknowledge My ways, you must first know My ways. To know My ways means to know Me. Draw close and know Me. Know that I am God – a mighty, powerful God, a loving, merciful God. As you draw close and know Me, you will know My ways and as you know My ways, acknowledge My ways in your life. Watch the fruit of the Spirit – My ways – grow in your life. Spend time in My presence, listening to Me. Experience My love permeating your very being. Share that love with others, and grow in My wisdom and understanding. Hear My direction for your life. Yes, I am doing a new thing. Do not be led by the ways of the past, but be led by My Spirit.

In all your ways acknowledge Him, and He shall direct your paths.
Proverbs 3:6

8 JANUARY

RESURRECTION LIFE

This is a time that you need to be living a resurrected life. The things that sufficed in the past will not in these days. This is a time that it is imperative that making Jesus Lord of your life becomes a reality and not just words that you speak. It is time to die to the things that are of the flesh and have seemed "not so bad" in the past. "Good things" must give way to My best. As you die to yourself – your desires and the things of the flesh – you are resurrected to glorious life that brings fulfillment and joy in loving and being with Me. And you will discover that I am greater than any earthly pleasure. To die is to live! It is only when you die that you find what life is all about – being in My presence, living and moving and having your being in Me!

Then He said to them all, "If anyone desires to come after Me, let him deny himself, and take up his cross daily and follow Me."
Luke 9:23

9   JANUARY

LIFE MORE ABUNDANT

I have come that they might have life and life more abundant. Walk in obedience to Me as I direct you step by step. I will take you to heights that you have yet to know. I will use you to bring forth My glory and My purpose. I will direct your steps as you reach out to others and lead them into the heights of My presence, My glory and My love. This is a time that I am revealing Myself. This is a time to seek Me as you choose to walk closer and closer to Me. This is a time to know Me better – it is a time to seek My face as I pour forth My light upon you. Lead others to Me! Take them by the hand, and show them the way to My presence. Show them the importance of knowing Me with deep commitment and closeness. Lead them to Me, for I AM all and everything that each one needs!

The thief does not come except to steal, and to kill,
and to destroy. I have come that they may have life,
and that they may have it more abundantly.
John 10:10

10 JANUARY

ABIDE IN ME

The days of striving and performance are over. This is a time of total abandonment to Me. As you learn to rest in Me, My Spirit will burst forth in such power that those around you will see and know that you are Mine. I say to you, abandon yourself to Me – abide in Me. Let Me abide in you. Put away the old and prepare for the new. Prepare for the increase, for surely increase is coming. Just as death brings new life, abandonment brings increase. Picture a tree, big and full of fruit, beginning to wither and dry up. Then the rains begin to come, and new life begins to sprout upon the limbs of the tree. The tree grows stronger than before and produces a greater amount of fruit.

It is time for new life to spring forth. That which has seemed dead will be resurrected, and there will be a flourishing and an increase as you abide in Me!

Abide in Me, and I in you. As the branch cannot bare fruit of itself, unless it abides in the vine, neither can you, unless you abide in Me. I am the vine, you are the branches. He who abides in Me, and I in him, bears much fruit; for without Me you can do nothing.
John 15:4-5

11 JANUARY

SEND OUT LABORERS!

My might and My power are getting ready to blow across the earth. The inhabitants of earth will see and know that I am in their midst. Even so, there will be many that still will not accept Me. Great revival will come forth, and multitudes will come into My kingdom and take their place as a part of My family. There will be great rejoicing on earth and in heaven. Those that turn away from Me, reject Me and go their own way will enter into greater degrees of darkness. Much darkness is coming upon the earth; but as it comes, My light will shine brighter and brighter. Rejoice in My presence. Rejoice in the knowledge that I am greater than the deeds of darkness.

The day of reckoning is at hand. Prepare the way. Prepare the way, for the Lord is coming soon. The great day of the Lord is at hand. Seek Me, share Me and rejoice in the harvest that is coming. Be prepared to bring the harvest in. Call forth the laborers, for this labor is a labor that brings great joy. Prepare the way of the coming of the Lord.

Then He said to them, "The harvest truly is great, but the laborers are few; therefore pray the Lord of the harvest to send out laborers into His harvest."
Luke 10:2

12 JANUARY

SEEK ME WITH ALL THAT IS WITHIN YOU!

As you praise Me, something rises up within you. Joy, confidence, peace and power rises up within you. As you praise Me, you forget about yourself and your problems, and you focus on Me. You focus on Who I Am. You begin to seek Me in greater depth; and as you seek Me in greater depth, you begin to become aware of the depth of Who I Am. You are overcome with love for the greatness of Who I AM, and you find yourself being changed. You become aware of My glory, and My glory begins to rise upon you. You are being changed from glory to glory into My image. You begin to see people through My eyes. You begin to see situations through My eyes. No longer do you become discouraged, because you recognize that I Am truly Who I say that I Am. Nothing is too great for Me. Seek Me; seek Me with all that is within you. Draw close to Me as I reveal Myself in greater and greater measure. Spend precious time with Me, and My LIFE will rise up greater and greater within you.

One thing I have desired of the Lord, that will I seek: that I may dwell in the house of the Lord all the days of my life, to behold the beauty of the Lord, and to inquire in His temple.
Psalms 27:4

13 JANUARY

THE HARVEST IS RIPE

The days ahead will be tumultuous days. The dark is getting darker, but I am pouring out My Spirit, My living waters, in torrents. When I send torrential rain upon the earth, that is symbolic of the torrential rain of the Spirit that is coming. I am preparing and equipping My people for the harvest. As the darkness increases, many will be ready to turn to Me. Revival is at hand. Be prepared for the outpouring of My Spirit and My glory upon you and upon My people. Signs and wonders – the miraculous – will happen over and over again. But, My supernatural power will not become something that is considered an everyday occurrence, even though it will be every day.

Every time I reach out My hand to perform a miracle, My people and those that are unbelievers will both be in awe. Many of the unbelievers will become believers. The harvest is ripe! This is the time, and I am equipping My people to bring in the harvest.

Put in the sickle, for the harvest is ripe. Come, go down; for the winepress is full, the vats overflow – for their wickedness is great. Multitudes, multitudes in the valley of decision! For the day of the Lord is near in the valley of decision.
Joel 3:13-14

14 JANUARY

I WILL POUR FORTH MY LIFE!

I say to you to get ready. Get ready for My presence; My power and My glory are getting ready to break forth. You have looked in some places, and you have seen lethargy. You have looked in other places, and you have seen weariness. And then you look at even another place, and you see division. You look in many places, and you see rebellion. And sometimes you even see some that seem to be dead, but I have heard the cry of your heart. I say to you to get ready, for I will answer your heart's cry. I will pour forth My Life in your midst in such great measure that there will be no room for ungodliness. I will send forth purity of heart that will bring people together in a bond of love, caring and acceptance that all will look and know that it could only come in such great measure by the hand of God!

That you may love the Lord your God, that you
may obey His voice, and that you may cling to Him,
for He is your life and the length of your days.
Deuteronomy 30:20

15 JANUARY

AWAKE, ARISE!

I am coming soon! I am coming soon! Proclaim the Word! Speak truth into the hearts of people. Hold onto My truth, walk in My truth, be an example of My truth and proclaim the Word of the Lord, for I am coming soon. My church needs to be alive with My Spirit. My church needs to walk in godly zeal. I am saying to My church, "Awake. Arise, and walk in the life that I hold out to you. Walk with joy, walk with peace and walk with My life and light, as you become examples of Jesus to those around you." The world is waiting to see and to know that I am alive! I live in you! You are my hands and my feet on the earth. Rise up, and let the world see Who I am! Let them see Who I really am! Don't show them who you think I am, but let me shine My light so brightly through you that the world truly sees the greatness of My love for them!

Awake, you who sleep, arise from the dead,
and Christ will give you light.
Ephesians 5:14

16 JANUARY

I NEED WATCHMEN

I am using you in a way that requires that you listen to Me carefully. I am about to pour forth My Spirit in such a way that millions and even billions around the world will be changed. The harvest is already in the making. And yes, I need watchmen. Some of you have been functioning as watchmen in several different capacities, even though you did not completely understand the fullness of the call of watchman. I have been teaching you, and I will continue to teach you. Walk in the fullness of My presence – My healing presence – so that you can complete and fulfill My destiny for your life. Be prepared. Let My living waters bring LIFE into your life. Let the wind of My Spirit blow away the things that beset you. Let the fire of My Spirit refine and empower you for the days, months and years ahead. Rest in Me. Allow yourself to bask in My presence, where all the things of the world will melt away as you center upon Me – your strength, your life, your shield and strong tower. I am coming soon! Prepare the way of the coming of the Lord!

Your watchmen shall lift up their voices, with their voices
they shall sing together; for they shall see eye to eye when the
Lord brings back Zion. Break forth into joy; sing together, you
waste places of Jerusalem! The Lord has made bare His holy
arm in the eyes of all the nations; and all the ends of the earth
shall see the salvation of our God.
Isaiah 52:8-9a, 10

17 JANUARY

BREATH OF LIFE

Come unto Me and allow My breath of life to blow upon every area of your life. Yes, you have given much to me – as much as you know and are aware of to give to Me. But, I am going to show you more of yourself that needs to be given over to Me. Oh, it gives Me much joy to receive the releasing of areas of your life unto Me. It gives Me great joy to see you trust Me, and to see healing and wholeness come into your life in greater measure. As you yield more and more, you will see me more and more clearly. Come unto Me with greater surrender, for My love for you is eternal.

Again, He said to me, "Prophesy to these bones, and say to them, O dry bones, hear the word of the Lord!" Thus says the Lord God to these bones: "Surely I will cause breath to enter into you, and you shall live." Ezekiel 37:4-5

18 JANUARY

MY WORD IS TRUTH!

Hold on, hold on to My Truth for the day is coming, and it is coming very soon, where all that I have promised you and all that I have planned for you will begin to break forth. Yes, it will burst forth; and you will know that which I have told you, that which I have promised you will actually be a reality in the world in which you live. Do not doubt, do not waiver – but stand upon My word to you. I can do nothing less than fulfill My word. My word is set in concrete – it will not move. It is as sound as concrete – more sound than concrete. An earthquake can demolish concrete. A machine can demolish concrete; but nothing, no, nothing can demolish My word. Stand on My word. Believe My word, for it is truth!

For the word of God is living and powerful, and sharper than
any two-edged sword, piercing even to the division of soul
and spirit, and of joints and marrow, and is a discerner of the
thoughts and intents of the heart.
Hebrews 4:12

19 JANUARY

I AM ALL YOU NEED

Come into My presence with thanksgiving, come into My courts with praise and sing praises unto Me. Worship with your whole heart, for I inhabit the praises of My people. As you press into Me, I will be there for you, for I am your shield and your fortress. I am your strength and your high tower. I give you strength and boldness when you need it. I am the cleft of the rock, your hiding place when you need a place to hide. I am your hope and your mercy when you need it. I am your might and your power when you are weak. I am your forgiveness when no one else wants to forgive. I am the lily of the valley, the sweet rose of Sharon. I am the morning star, and I am the Prince of peace as well as the King of kings. When you press into Me, I become to you all that you need.

Make a joyful shout to the Lord, all you lands! Serve the Lord with gladness; come before His presence with singing. Know that the Lord, He is God; it is He who has made us, and not we ourselves; we are His people and the sheep of His pasture. Enter into His gates with thanksgiving, and into His courts with praise. Be thankful to Him, and bless His name. For the Lord is good; His mercy is everlasting, and His truth endures to all generations.
Psalm 100:1-4

20 JANUARY

MY MANIFEST PRESENCE AND POWER

Listen to Me. My love for you is everlasting. I will never leave you nor forsake you. You can always know that I am with you. You can always know that I hold you in the palm of My hand. My strength will uphold you. My power resides within you. You can do all things through Me, because I strengthen you. I enable you to walk in My ways. I enable you to walk in My ways, and I enable you to fulfill My will in your life. You are never alone – I am always with you. Trust Me; trust Me to work My will and way through you. The day is coming when you will see Me at work in you in such a way that you will be amazed. You have seen Me do much, but in the days ahead, you will see such a multitude of My power that you will fall down before Me in total worship and adoration. It brings Me great joy to bless you with My manifest presence and power.

O God, You are my God; early will I seek You; my soul thirsts for You; my flesh longs for You in a dry and thirsty land where there is no water. So I have looked for You in the sanctuary, to see Your power and Your glory.
Psalms 63:1-2

21 JANUARY

RECEIVE MY GLORY

I hear the cries of those today that want more of Me. I hear the cries, and I am responding. My Spirit is hovering over you even now. My Spirit longs to fulfill the longings of your hearts. I am opening up the windows of heaven, and I am pouring forth an abundance of the rain of My Holy Spirit. I am pouring forth a deluge of My rain, a deluge of My presence and a deluge of My glory! Receive My abundant outpouring upon you and a fresh outpouring upon the land. Get ready to move by My Spirit. Lift up your hands, lift up your faces, lift up your hearts and receive the abundance, the deluge of My rain, that is coming forth upon you. Get ready for the torrents of spiritual water that I will pour out upon you. Receive My Glory and shine forth My Glory! Go forth bathed, surrounded and immersed in My glory! I'm sending you forth with arms outstretched to receive the masses!

For it is the God who commanded light to shine out of darkness, who has shone in our hearts to give the light of the knowledge of the glory of God in the face of Jesus Christ.
II Corinthians 4:6

22 JANUARY

TRANSFORMED INTO THE IMAGE OF GOD

Come unto Me and offer up your praises, your prayers and your petitions. Open up your heart to Me. Allow Me to bless you with My presence as I walk with you, as I talk with you, as we fellowship together. Yes, it is My desire to reveal Myself to you in more and greater ways. As you come to know Me better and better, you will begin to reflect My ways more and more. You are being transformed daily into My image. My image is greater in you today than it was ten years ago and even one year ago. It will be greater in you next year than today. Stay close to Me. Allow Me to teach you, correct you, love you and draw you close. You are My precious one, and I have much to show you. My plan for you encompasses greatness in My kingdom. Walk in humility day by day. Prefer others to yourself, and watch My image grow within you.

For whom He foreknew, He also predestined to be conformed to the image of His Son, that He might be the first born among many brethren. Moreover whom He predestined, these He also called; whom He called, these He also justified; and whom He justified, these He also glorified.
Romans 8:29-30

23 JANUARY

COMFORT, O COMFORT MY PEOPLE

Comfort, O comfort My people with the comfort that I give to you. Learn from the distresses; learn from the hard times of My love for you and My comfort to you. Seek Me with all your heart. Lean upon Me, and trust Me to take this crisis and turn it around for My Glory. I am able; yes, I am able even in this, which looms so big before you, for I am a big God. My power is great. I bring you comfort, I bring you strength and I bring you all that you need to overcome the power of darkness that has been dealing blows to you. It is by My power, My strength and My Spirit that you overcome. I am with you always. I will never leave you or forsake you. My love is ever present with you.

"Comfort, yes, comfort My people!" says your God.
Isaiah 40:1

24 JANUARY

MY PRESENCE

Speak forth My truth and as My truth goes forth, I will see to it that it comes alive in the hearts of the hearers by My Spirit. Always seek for My Spirit to abide within you and to prevail over whatever you are doing, because it is by My Spirit that My work is accomplished. Seek Me with all your heart and yield yourself to Me with your whole being. Walk before Me with a humble heart and allow My love to flow through you. Enter into My presence each day with freshness and newness. Seek Me as you drive, as you work, as you go to school, as you go about your daily routine, and you will know that I am always with you. I give you the gift of My presence, and when you choose to give me your presence, that is a wonderful gift for me because I receive from your presence. I long for and enjoy the presence of My people.

And He said, "My Presence will go with you,
and I will give you rest."
Exodus 33:14

25 JANUARY

THE LORD SHINES HIS FACE ON YOU!

Trust in Me, and walk in obedience to Me. Walk in the path that I have placed before you. I have called you to a walk of righteousness, and it pleases Me when you respond in obedience. I am faithful to reveal the areas of weaknesses that need My strength. I am faithful to reveal to you how to overcome the opportunities and challenges that come your way. I am the Lord of all, and I bring My light, My truth and My goodness into your life in greater depths. I am the Lord your God, Who is your all-sufficiency. It pleases Me when you give Me a special time each day, for I love to fellowship with you. I desire to show you many things. It is My desire to bring My anointing upon you in greater measure. As you respond to Me in the areas I reveal to you, My anointing will increase. You have entered upon My holy mountain, and your life will never be the same again. Continue to seek Me with all your heart. Long after Me and receive the fullness of My presence as I shine My face upon you.

The Lord bless you and keep you. The Lord make His face shine upon you, and be gracious to you; the Lord lift up His countenance upon you, and give you peace.
Numbers 6:24-26

26 JANUARY

BY MY SPIRIT

I would say unto you to place yourself in My hands, for I am a mighty God. I am Mighty and powerful, and able to provide all that you need in every circumstance. It pleases Me for you to look to Me to receive victory in your life. It pleases Me for you to seek Me and trust Me for victory in every situation. I will give you wisdom, for it is My wisdom that dwells within you by My Spirit. It is My strength and My courage that dwells within you by My Spirit. Rise up and walk in My strength, in My wisdom, and in My might and power by My Spirit and with My anointing.

So he answered and said to me: "This is the word of the Lord to Zerubbabel: 'Not by might nor by power, but by My Spirit,' says the Lord of hosts."
Zechariah 4:6

27 JANUARY

REST IN ME – I AM ALL THAT YOU NEED!

My face is shining upon you, My beloved. The light of My countenance is upon you. You will go forth in My strength, My power, with My grace and mercy resting upon you. I am touching you this day, and you KNOW that I can do all things through you by My Spirit. Place your complete trust, faith and hope in Me, for I WILL accomplish My plan and purpose through you. The days ahead will be days full of My glory. You will come to understand My will and way in greater measure, and you will spread word of My will and way everywhere that I send you. Rest in Me – I am all that you need. Place your burdens in My hands – see My hands are outstretched and ready to take them. Rest in the joy of Who I am – not only Who I am to the world, but Who I am to you. Nothing is too difficult for Me, and you will see the impossible changed. You will see miracles, signs and wonders that could only happen through My hand. Get ready for the days ahead, for they are days of signs and wonders, miracles and My glory!

He gives power to the weak, and to those who have no might, He increases strength. Even the youths shall faint and be weary, and the young men shall utterly fall, but those who wait on the Lord shall renew their strength, they shall mount up with wings like eagles, they shall run and not be weary, they shall walk and not faint.
Isaiah 40:29-31

28 JANUARY

CONSUMING FIRE OF MY SPIRIT

Move out into the highways and byways. Listen to Me and find out what I am saying to you, and then obey My direction. I am empowering you to take your city, state and nation for My Kingdom! That will require intimacy with Me, listening and responding in obedience to what I tell you to do. Be so in love with Me that you are willing to do all that I show you to do. Be so in love with Me that you are willing to listen, hear and KNOW that I will provide all that you need. Be willing to lay down the things that hinder you from spending time with Me, for I want to be your first love always and in all things. I am prepared to answer the cries of your hearts – the only requirement is that you allow the fire of My Spirit to burn within you in such a way that you are consumed with Me!

Therefore, since we are receiving a kingdom, which cannot be shaken, let us have grace, by which we may serve God acceptably with reverence and godly fear. For our God is a consuming fire.
Hebrews 12:28-29

29 JANUARY

LOVE, OBEY AND CLING

I want to set you and those around you on fire with My *dunamis* power. I will strengthen you with My supernatural fire and power as you seek Me, as you leave those things that are not of Me, and as you choose to follow Me. I am calling you into a place of submission. I want you to submit to My way, My will and My purpose for you. As you do, you will see great and mighty changes occurring in your lives, in the lives of your loved ones, in the lives of your neighbors, your friends and your co-workers.

You have been asking Me for revival. I will tell you now that you do not want revival more than I do. I am chomping at the bit. I am ready. I am waiting for you to be ready. I am asking you even now to choose to receive My *dunamis* power, and move out wherever I send you with My presence, My power and My truth! I am giving you even now your marching orders! Say yes! Receive more of Me, and watch for the changes that come about through your love, obedience and clinging to Me! Never let go! Hold on tight, for I am ready for you to move with Me!

That you may love the Lord your God, that you may obey His voice, and that you may cling to Him, for He is your life and the length of your days.
Deuteronomy 30:20

30 JANUARY

COME TO THE LIVING WATERS

Come to the waters! Come to the waters – the cascades of waters that are flowing from heaven. I am pouring out My waters on you, over you, through you – drink of My waters! Drink of My waters, and you will never thirst again. I am pouring out a fountain – a large fountain of water that will cascade over and in you – so that wherever you go, My waters will flow from you. It is time for My waters to be poured out upon those that have a heart for Me! It is time for My waters to bring healing, wholeness and cleansing to My body. It is time for all the dirt and debris to be washed away as My church chooses to follow Me – to be obedient to My will and to bring glory to My name. I am preparing My church to prepare the way of My coming! Receive My living waters!

On the last day, that great day of the feast, Jesus stood and cried out, saying, "If anyone thirsts, let him come to Me and drink. He who believes in Me, as the Scripture has said, out of his heart will flow rivers of living water."
John 7:37-38

31 JANUARY

BASK IN MY PRESENCE

Come unto Me, My beloved, and bask in My presence. Allow Me to have My way in your life – in every area of your life. Allow Me full reign in your life as I show you the areas that need to be changed. Yield to Me as I correct you with My generous love. You are learning of My great love that brings chastisement and change. You are learning of the joy that comes from yielding to My correction. I am molding and remaking you after My will, and I am pouring forth My presence and the joy of being in My presence as we commune with one another.

Do not seek others' ways, but seek only Me and My ways, for I am truly life to you. I am freedom, victory and truth. I am peace – amazing peace that surpasses all understanding. Glory in My presence. Glory in the knowledge of My will as I reveal it to you. Glory in My ways and in the greatness of Who I am. Glory in the knowledge that I am always present with you. I am forever your Father – the great and mighty one, the merciful and compassionate one.

You will show me the path of life; in Your presence is fullness of joy; at Your right hand are pleasures forevermore.
Psalm 16:11

FEBRUARY

1   FEBRUARY

MY ANOINTING IS STRONG UPON YOU

Come, My beloved, I am going to take you up on My holy mountain. I will tell you things as we walk hand in hand together. You are My beloved, and you are able to accomplish My purposes – not by your strength, but by My Spirit. I have placed My Spirit within you to do a mighty work. Yes, I said, "A mighty work." Do not doubt My Spirit within you, for My anointing is strong upon you. Walk in faith and walk in obedience. Trust Me, and watch and see what I will accomplish through you. Do not be intimidated by others, but keep your eyes upon Me. Keep your hand in My hand, and let us walk together, accomplishing that which I have purposed. Trust Me to handle others. Walk in My grace, and allow My grace to flow forth from you to those that are weak and to those that would try to intimidate you. Walk tall in the assurance of My presence within you and My hand and anointing upon you.

But my horn You have exalted like a wild ox;
I have been anointed with fresh oil.
Psalm 92:10

2 FEBRUARY

HERE AM I, LORD, SEND ME

Walk in obedience to Me, and hear the word of the Lord. Prepare your heart for revival, for revival is coming. It is coming first to My shepherds and My leaders. Then it is coming to My flock, and then it will reach out to the lost of the world. This revival will be unlike any that has been before. My fire will fall upon the people. There will be wonders that have not been seen before. My hand will be at work within the earth, and I will be separating the sheep from the goats. There will be greater distinction between good and evil. The world will look, and they will see holiness. My people will be filled with My holiness, and the world will be full of darkness. Prepare yourself to be a part of My revival. Prepare your heart. Prepare your time, and be prepared to say, "Yes, Lord, I will go. I will do what you are calling me to do." Say, "Yes, Lord, here am I, send me."

Also I heard the voice of the Lord, saying: "Whom shall I send, and who will go for Us?" Then I said, "Here am I! Send me."
Isaiah 6:8

3   FEBRUARY

GET READY TO RUN WITH ME!

Let Me share My heart with you. I am waiting for you to get ready to run with Me. I am ready for you to take off. Begin to move out. Take your stance at the beginning line of the race. Get ready to run with Me! I will take you on a journey that will bring great joy and fulfillment. You have never been on a run such as the one that is coming up. Get ready for exhilaration! Get ready for great joy! Get ready for that which you have not experienced. I am ready to use you in ways you have never thought or dreamed I could use you. Get ready, My beloved! Take My hand, and let us take off running!

Therefore we also, since we are surrounded by so great a cloud of witnesses, let us lay aside every weight, and the sin which so easily ensnares us, and let us run with endurance the race that is set before us, looking unto Jesus, the author and finisher of our faith, who for the joy that was set before Him endured the cross, despising the shame, and has sat down at the right hand of the throne of God.
Hebrews 12:1-2

4   FEBRUARY

GREAT EXPLOITS

Keep going, beloved; keep going by My Spirit, in My mercy and My grace. My hand is upon you. You are called for My purpose, and My anointing is upon you. Go forth in the name of the Lord, and do mighty exploits by My hand and with My authority. Move out in boldness and confidence in the calling that I have placed upon you. Go forth in obedience to Me and go through every door I open for you. Trust Me to guide and direct your path, for I am your God. I am a mighty God, a powerful God and a God filled with love, mercy and compassion. Walk in My grace. Express My Grace to others, and expect to see My miracles flow.

Those who do wickedly against the covenant he shall corrupt
with flattery; but the people who know their God shall be
strong, and carry out great exploits.
Daniel 11:32

5   FEBRUARY

STRONG ARM

Be still, My beloved, and listen, for I will tell you great and mighty things. The time is coming soon when I will use you to bring forth My truth to many. I am beginning to open up more doors to use you to further My gospel, and you will see doors open that will astound you. Do not hesitate – go forth in My strength and My power, for I am going to use you in ways that even you have not considered. You belong to Me, and you listen to Me and respond in obedience. You are learning more and more not to give in to what you consider to be your inabilities and weaknesses, but you are learning to respond to Me. You are learning to trust Me to work through you in My strength and My power. It is My arm that saves. Lean on My arm for it is strong, very strong! It is all that you need in the way of strength. Trust in My blood, in My name and in My Word, for I am with you. I am within you to fulfill all I call you to do.

Behold, the Lord God shall come with a strong hand, and His arm shall rule for Him; behold His reward is with Him and His work before Him.
Isaiah 40:10

6 FEBRUARY

LISTEN, HEAR AND OBEY

Dear ones, receive the love that I am holding out to you. Listen, hear and obey as I share with you the things of My heart – as I share with you the wonders of My plan for you. I choose to use My Church in the lives of many, so many that at this point, it is difficult for you to even begin to comprehend. Get ready for My move that is about to break forth. I am getting ready to move in such a way that My Church cannot even begin to imagine what is ahead, what is in store for those that will obey Me. Listen, hear and obey. Get ready to run with Me in these days of acceleration. Get ready to move in the wonder of Who I am. Signs, wonders and miracles are about to fall upon the earth by My strong hand. You, who are a part of My Church, rise up in the strength and the might of Who I am! Rise up and get ready to run with Me as My Spirit leads the way! Listen, hear and obey! Be Blessed as I choose to use you, My Church, in these last days.

But Jeremiah said, "They shall not deliver you. Please, obey the voice of the Lord, which I speak to you. So it shall be well with you and your soul shall live."
Jeremiah 38:20

7 FEBRUARY

THE GREAT I AM

Yes, My beloved, I have consecrated you, set you aside and called you, with My strong anointing, to speak My truth. I have called you to share the wonders of knowing Me intimately. I am calling My people to draw close and bask in the glory of My presence and knowing Me for Who I am. I have called you, and I am opening the doors. There are doors that are about to open that will astound you. Yes, I show you what you are to say "yes" to and "no" to. Do not feel guilty or condemned when you say "no" to those things others may be doing, but I have not called you to do. Seek Me, listen and only do those things I tell you to do. Be prepared and get ready, for I am about to thrust you forth. Seek Me, worship Me and listen, for it is imperative that you follow My directions. Do not be swayed by man, but follow the Living God, the Great I AM, and fulfill My purposes and My call upon your life.

And God said to Moses, "I AM WHO I AM." And He said, "Thus you shall say to the children of Israel, 'I AM has sent me to you.'"
Exodus 3:14

8   **FEBRUARY**

YOUR WORD, SWEETER THAN HONEY

As the honeycomb does drip with honey, so does My word drip from your lips. I have placed My word deep within you, and it will and does come forth with My anointing to bring strength, encouragement and power to My people. Walk close, Beloved. Let Me reveal the sweetness of My truth to you. Let Me reveal the depth of My strength and power to you. As I reveal these truths with you, I want you to share with those that I bring across your path.

I am opening doors for you to go through. Large double doors are about to open. Be not afraid, but walk through with Me at your side. Know and believe that everything I have called you to do, you can do because I am with you. I dwell within you in all My power. Walk in obedience to Me. Walk hand in hand with Me, and know the joy of fulfilling My purposes.

How sweet are Your words to my taste,
sweeter than honey to my mouth!
Psalm 119:103

My son, eat honey because it is good, and the honeycomb
which is sweet to your taste; so shall the knowledge of wisdom
be to your soul; if you have found it, there is a prospect, and
your hope will not be cut off.
Proverbs 24:13-14

9   FEBRUARY

MY PRESENCE IS WITH YOU

Come, come away, My beloved, and bask in My presence. Allow Me time with you that I may share great and wonderful things with you. Listen, for I have much to tell you. I have wisdom to impart to you. Go forth in the power of My strength and be the child of God that I have called you and empowered you to be. Bring forth the exploits that I call you to do. Listen, and be in tune with My Spirit as I show you the path to take. I am always with you. I will never leave or forsake you. You are My precious child, and I am your Daddy. Lean on Me. Let Me take your burdens from you, for I am able to take care of them. They are not too difficult for Me. My presence is with you. My presence encompasses you. My presence brings strength, encouragement and so much more. Seek My presence always!

And because He loved your fathers, therefore He chose their descendants after them; and He brought you out of Egypt with His presence, with His mighty power.
Deuteronomy 4:37

10 FEBRUARY

I HAVE CHOSEN YOU!

Beloved, lean on Me and allow My presence to build you up and to minister to you. As you seek Me, I will bring strength, wisdom and wholeness to you. I AM THAT I AM! I am able to take care of your every need. I am the God of the impossible, and I will do for you what seems impossible in your eyes. It is My will to bring forth strength, power and compassion within you and to come forth from you. It is My desire to bring forth wisdom, knowledge and discernment through you. It is My desire to teach you from My reserve. My reserve holds all the wisdom of the world and more – all the wisdom that exists throughout eternity. You have experienced greater anointing lately, and I say to you that there is more to come. I have chosen you!

You did not choose Me, but I chose you and appointed you that you should go and bear fruit, and that your fruit should remain, that whatever you ask the Father in My name He may give you.
John 15:16

11 FEBRUARY

LOVE, UNITY AND HUMILITY

Listen to Me! Listen to the words that I bring to you. I am doing a new thing in your area. I am bringing together those that have been apart – those that are divided. I am bringing My church together in unity. Go forth in battle as I give the battle plan to fight against warring spirits in your area. Go forth in love, unity and humility to break the strife and dissension that exists. I will shine My light, and I will give My wisdom. You will not have to wonder about what is to be done, for I will show you exactly what steps to take. Do not go forth on your own, but wait for My instruction. The time is near – the time is close! Get ready, for the trumpet is about to sound, and soon the battle cry will go forth. Be prepared for victory! Love, unity and humility always bring about victory!

I, therefore, the prisoner of the Lord, beseech you to walk worthy of the calling with which you were called, with all lowliness and gentleness, with longsuffering, bearing with one another in love, endeavoring to keep the unity of the Spirit in the bond of peace. There is one body and one Spirit, just as you were called in one hope of your calling; one Lord, one faith, one baptism; one God and Father of all, who is above all, and through all, and in you all.
Ephesians 4:1-6

12 FEBRUARY

SHINE MY LIGHT!

March forth, march forth in victory! Raise your banners high, shake your tambourines, clang your cymbals, sound the trumpets and move out in joy and in rejoicing! I am making the way for you to go forth in the highways and the byways to show the love, joy and peace of My kingdom to those who are in darkness. Shine My light, shine My light and continue to shine My light upon a world that is lost. Shine My light so that the darkness is dispelled. Go forth in victory, in joy and in rejoicing, for My way has come upon the earth.

You are the light of the world. A city that is set on a hill cannot be hidden. Nor do they light a lamp and put it under a basket, but on a lampstand, and it gives light to all who are in the house. Let your light so shine before men, that they may see your good works and glorify your Father in heaven.
Matthew 5:14-16

13 FEBRUARY

TEACH OF MY NATURE

Arise and go forth in the power of My name. Speak forth the truths of My word that have and will prevail down through the ages. Teach of My goodness. Show how My truth was and is, and will prevail forevermore. Teach of My eternal nature that never changes. My Spirit is being released upon the earth, and many hearts are being prepared to receive My truth. Go forth and teach, go forth and preach. Share with My people. Tell them to be prepared to receive great numbers of converts among themselves. Tell them to be disciples of My way, and nurture the flocks that are coming into My kingdom. Tell them to put aside selfish plans and get ready for revival. Revival means work for the family – My family must be prepared to take in and care for the many, for the multitudes, for the masses, that will soon be seeking Me.

And Jesus came and spoke to them, saying, "All authority has been given to Me in heaven and on earth. Go therefore and make disciples of all nations, baptizing them in the name of the Father and of the Son and of the Holy Spirit, teaching them to observe all things that I have commanded you; and lo, I am with you always, even to the end of the age."
Matthew 28:18-20

14 FEBRUARY

THE CALL THAT I HAVE PLACED UPON YOU!

My hand is upon you. My anointing is all over and within you. I have chosen you to take My truth to the multitudes. Be prepared! Get ready! Get ready for the new shoes that I am giving you. Get ready to open this present that I am presenting to you. As you slip on these shoes, you will KNOW – you will be aware of the call that I have placed upon you. You will desire to walk, to run, to move in the call that I have placed upon you. At times, you will feel as if you are flying. You will be flying as I take you to places that you have never been before. Get ready – the time is near! The time is now. Begin to prepare with all that I have placed within you. Begin to prepare as I show you the things to bring forth. I am pouring My creativity in and through you. Receive, walk, run, move and even fly with all that I am pouring out upon you!

For the gifts and the calling of God are irrevocable.
Romans 11:29 NKJ

God is not a man, that He should lie, nor a son of man, that
He should repent. Has He said, and will He not do? Or has He
spoken, and will He not make it good?
Numbers 23:19

15 FEBRUARY

IT IS SIMPLE

My beloved, listen to Me as I share My heart with you. I have called you to touch hearts with My heart. Therefore, I am going to, and I have been, sharing My heart with you. It is simple – some like to make it so hard, but it is simple. Draw close to Me. Draw into My presence. Spend time face-to-face with Me. Listen to Me and then do as I say. When you are obedient to Me after experiencing My presence – you become a reflection of Me to others, and they draw close. They are changed. It is simple.

The counsel of the Lord stands forever,
the plans of His heart to all generations.
Psalm 33:11

And when He had removed him, He raised up for them
David as king, to whom also He gave testimony and said,
"I have found David the son of Jesse, a man after My own
heart, who will do all My will."
Acts 13:22

For David says concerning Him: "You have made known to me the
ways of life; You will make me full of joy in your presence."
Acts 2:25a, 28

16 FEBRUARY

RECEIVE THE FULLNESS OF MY LOVE

Come to Me, My beloved, and spend time with Me. Cry out from the depths of your heart to Me. Open up to Me, and allow Me to minister to you from the depths of My being. Allow Me to wash over you with My presence. My Spirit longs to have time with you – quality time where we can commune together, and where we can grow in our knowledge of one another. I long to reveal Myself to you. I love you, and My love for you is forever. Reach out and receive the fullness of My love. Bask in My presence. Beloved, I am a great and powerful God. I am able to take care of every need in your life, in your family, in your church, in your nation and in the nations of the world. Call upon Me, and watch and see the mighty things that shall come forth from Me to you.

That Christ may dwell in your hearts through faith; that you, being rooted and grounded in love, may be able to comprehend with all the saints what is the width and length and depth and height – to know the love of Christ which passes knowledge; that you may be filled with all the fullness of God.
Ephesians 3:17-19

17 FEBRUARY

OPEN THE DOORS

Listen, listen to Me and know that I love you – My love surrounds and enfolds you. Lie back in My arms and rest in Me. I am all that you need. I AM that I AM! I am the all-sufficient One. It is I AM that will complete and bring forth all that I have purposed for your life. All I require of you is your obedience. Trust Me and obey Me, for I am your God. I hold all the keys, and I hold out the keys to you. Reach out and receive the keys, and unlock the doors that are shut. Yes, the time is ripe; the time is ready to go through doors that have been closed. I am opening doors for you to go forth, to go further in the calling that I have on your life. Stay close to Me. Stay in tune with Me. Listen, hear and obey. Walk in the anointing that I have placed upon your life. Do not doubt, but believe and go forth in My strength, by My power and by My Spirit, says the Lord of hosts.

And to the angel of the church in Philadelphia write, "These things says He Who is holy, He Who is true, 'He Who has the key of David, He Who opens and no one shuts and shuts and no one opens': 'I know your works. See, I have set before you an open door, and no one can shut it.'"
Revelation 3:7-8a

18 FEBRUARY

THE GREATNESS OF MY POWER

Step out, My beloved. Step out and walk in the path that I have laid out for you. Walk in the greatness of My power. Walk in the supernatural power that is Me. Walk in the path of signs, wonders and miracles. Expect to see Me work through you. Do not hold back, but move in the power of My resurrection that resides within you. Move out in boldness. Move out in courage and strength as I open doors before you. Expect to see the book of Acts come alive in your life. Expect to see Me move in My fullness through you. Allow My Spirit full reign in your life, and walk in constant submission to My will and direction for you. Listen! Listen! Listen! Hear and respond as I speak to you. Walk in obedience and love, and you will see My power at work in a mighty way upon this earth.

That you may know what is the hope of His calling, what are
the riches of the glory of His inheritance in the saints, and what
is the exceeding greatness of His power toward us who believe,
according to the working of His mighty power which He worked in
Christ when He raised Him from the dead and seated Him at His
right hand in the heavenly places.
Ephesians 1:18b-20

19 FEBRUARY

SHARE, TEACH AND PROCLAIM

My beloved, listen to My words. Let them minister peace and power to you. Soak up My words to you, and let them bring light and life to you. Wait upon Me. Wait upon Me with expectancy, for I will bring forth words of wisdom and words of revelation to you. As My words come forth, share them with others. Go forth in My strength and My power, and share and teach others My truth. Let My words flow through you to others. As you speak forth My words, others will be set free, healed, saved, encouraged and blessed! Do not hesitate to speak forth My words, for this is My call upon you.

Teach and share through My Spirit, and bring much fruit into My kingdom. Share with others. Do not hesitate to share the glories of My presence and My light with others. Be aware of the urgency of the day. Hear, teach and proclaim the good news. The world is waiting to hear My good news. The need is great, and there are so few that will go forth. Be an inspiration to others to go forth. Teach My people the urgency of the day. Share, teach and proclaim My good news.

Your word is a lamp to my feet and a light to my path.
Psalm 119:105

20 FEBRUARY

AN EXPLOSION OF MY ANOINTING

Rise up! Go forth in the strength of My Spirit and accomplish great exploits. Listen to Me, and hear My direction and plan for each of you. When you hear, you will know that it is the great I Am Who is instructing you. Go forth in obedience and reach out in the way that I have planned for you. Do not try to compare or copy one another, but go forth in the unique and individual way that I have purposed for you. Reach out with a sickle and reap the harvest. Yes, this is the harvest time, and the laborers are few. I am hiring laborers to bring in the fruit of the harvest.

Will you be one of My laborers? My anointing is ready to fall upon you as you respond to Me. The anointing that already resides within you will rise up and meet the anointing that I am getting ready to pour forth. There will be such an explosion of anointing that those of the world will look and say, "I want to be a part of that. I have never seen anything like this before. How can I become a part of this mighty move of God?" All you need to do is share the good news of Jesus Christ, and there will be multitudes coming into My kingdom.

But the anointing which you have received from Him abides in you, and you do not need that anyone teach you; but as the same anointing teaches you concerning all things, and is true, and is not a lie and just as it has taught you, you will abide in Him.
I John 2:27

21 FEBRUARY

NEVER LEAVE NOR FORSAKE

Trust Me, says the Lord. Trust Me in all things, and watch as I fulfill My purpose and My plan in your life. I am full of grace and mercy. I want My people to let My grace and mercy flow through them to those that are hurting, to those that are in despair and to those that feel there is no hope.

Reach out with My love and compassion. Share My truth and My life to those that are destitute of spirit. Tell them about the sacrifice of My Son, Jesus. Tell them that He died for them. If they were the only persons on earth, He would still have gone to the cross to pay the price for their sins. Tell them that there is victory in Jesus. The only way to experience peace, love and joy in their lives is to trust Jesus with all that they are and all that they have. Tell them to lean upon the One Who will never leave them nor forsake them. Tell them that He will always provide what is best for them. He will grant them a wonderful life on this earth filled with peace, joy, love and wonder at His goodness. Each will experience eternity in the presence of Almighty God.

Let your conduct be without covetousness; be content with such things as you have. For He Himself has said, "I will never leave you nor forsake you." So we may boldly say: "The Lord is my helper; I will not fear. What can man do to me?"
Hebrews 13:5-6

22 FEBRUARY

FACE-TO-FACE

Yes, My beloved, true reality is meeting with Me on top of the mountain. Meeting with Me face-to-face truly does bring such change in your life that you can and will face the difficulties of life with My strength. You will have My power rising up within you to be a shining light to the world. You will acknowledge and know that I am greater than anything that you face. As you look into My face, you will see and understand what truly is important. Your priorities will change as you catch a glimpse of eternity.

Hear, O Lord, when I cry with my voice! Have mercy also upon me, and answer me. When You said, "Seek My face," My heart said to You, "Your face, Lord, I will seek." Do not hide Your face from me; do not turn Your servant away in anger; You have been my help; do not leave me nor forsake me, O God of My salvation.
Psalm 27:7-9

23 FEBRUARY

PREPARE THE WAY OF THE LORD

Behold Me, watch for Me, says your Lord, for I am coming soon. The Prince of peace, King of kings is coming on a white horse. The eastern sky shall split open, and all will see. Every knee shall bow and every tongue confess that Jesus Christ is Lord.

Make way; prepare the way for the Living King is making Himself known in the midst of the world. Heads shall turn, and people will be in amazement as they see, hear and experience the Living King. Yes, He will manifest Himself in your midst as you prepare the way for the coming King. Prepare for the way of the Living Lord to come and restore, to reconcile and redeem. He is going the second mile and more to make Himself known in the midst of great darkness. He is calling His church to shine forth brightly. His light is being turned up within His church. There is a great shaking coming within the church that will separate the tares from the wheat. The goats will be separated from the sheep as He reveals Himself in mighty ways. Many will turn to Him, but many will also turn away. Pray, pray and continue praying without ceasing. Seek the Lord with all your heart, and trust Him to bring freedom and deliverance to His church. Let His light shine forth brightly from you as you seek Him, look into His face and reflect His image on this earth.

The voice of one crying in the wilderness: "Prepare the way of the Lord; make His paths straight."
Mark 1:3

24 FEBRUARY

MY LIVING WATERS

As you have watched the waves break upon the shore, I have shown you that the power and strength that are within the waters of the ocean are the same as the power and strength that reside within My people, through My living waters! The water of My Spirit is springing forth within each of you in such power as to bring about My purposes in this earth. I am using you to bring My life into the lives of many.

Yield yourselves to My Spirit, and allow Me to work through you. Those things that have seemed impossible to you, I will bring forth! Take hold of My promises, and believe that nothing is impossible with Me! I will bring forth all that I have spoken to you and all that you have received through My word.

Jesus answered and said to her, "If you knew the gift of God, and who it is who says to you, 'Give Me a drink,' you would have asked Him, and He would have given you living water. . .Whoever drinks of this water will thirst again, but whoever drinks of the water that I shall give him will never thirst. But the water that I shall give him will become in him a fountain of water springing up into everlasting life."
John 4:10, 13b-14

25 FEBRUARY

SEEK ME, AND YOU SHALL FIND ME

Call unto Me, My beloved. Call out with a force that will reveal the cry of your heart. Call out to Me as you seek Me with all that you are. Seek Me, and you shall find Me. Look up – look up into My face, and see the glory and light of My countenance. Look up and let Me shine My countenance upon you. Receive from Me. Receive all that I have for you. Allow Me to pour out My blessings from on high upon you. Reach out and receive from Me. I am your life. I am your holiness. I am your justice, and I will pour out My Spirit upon you with such abundance that you will go forth in My power and My anointing to set the captives free. Be a vessel that is filled to overflowing with My Spirit, and let My glory shine forth from you into the lives of others. Be an instrument of My grace and My goodness. Walk in obedience, and see the wonders of My glory.

Then you will call upon Me and go and pray to Me, and I will listen to you. And you will seek Me and find Me, when you search for Me with all your heart.
Jeremiah 29:12-13

26 FEBRUARY

IGNITED BY MY SPIRIT

Listen to Me, My beloved. Incline your ear to My sayings. Know and understand the wonders of My truth. Listen with an ear to receive the very depths of My wonders. Listen, hear and respond. I am speaking to you daily. I am speaking to you hourly. I am speaking to you moment by moment. Listen, hear and be obedient. I am drawing you close so that you can hear and share My truth with many. I have placed My words in your mouth, and I am opening up opportunities – yes, many doors – for you to share My word.

It is a time to be renewed. It is a time to receive so that you can go forth filled to overflowing with My Spirit. My Spirit will ignite others, and the fire of God will spread and grow. It is time for the harvest to be reaped. It is time for revival, and I want you to know that you have been called for such a time as this!

But as it is written: "Eye has not seen nor ear heard, nor have entered into the heart of man the things which God has prepared for those who love Him." Now we have received, not the spirit of the world, but the Spirit who is from God, that we might know the things that have been freely given to us by God.
I Corinthians 2:9,12

27 FEBRUARY

GO FORTH IN MY POWER AND MY STRENGTH

Beloved, listen to Me. Lift up your voice in praise and adoration of Me. Let your gratitude and worship be heard throughout. Lift up your voice in acclamation, and speak forth My truths. Let My attributes be known in the midst of those that I have brought before you. Lift up your voice and speak forth the oracles of God. Be used by Me to spread forth great and wondrous truths about My goodness and My grace. Open your mouth, and speak forth in every opportunity that I bring your way.

Be used by Me as I pour forth My anointing upon you. Go forth in My power and My strength, and fulfill the calling that I have upon you. Lead many into My truths that will further My kingdom. Express My heart to My people in such a way that their lives will be changed, and they will desire to fulfill My calling upon their lives.

Ascribe strength to God; His excellence is over Israel, and His strength is in the clouds. O God, You are more awesome than Your holy places. The God of Israel is He who gives strength and power to His people. Blessed be God!
Psalm 68:34-35

28 FEBRUARY

THE DAY OF THE LORD IS AT HAND

Walk in astuteness! Walk in clarity, observing what I am doing in your life and also in the life of your city, nation, Israel and the world. I have chosen you and set you apart to know truth, to share truth and to motivate others to walk in truth. I have chosen to share with you the wonders of the days ahead. Yes, these are the last days, and Jesus is coming back soon. The Day of the Lord is at hand, and there is much ahead.

There is a need for My people to respond to Me in great commitment. There is a need for My people to be aware of the seriousness of the day. They need to seek Me with all that is within them, so they will know Me better and be transformed by knowing Me in the fullness of Who I am.

Today is the day to draw close to Me as we begin to see the fulfillment of prophecy about the last days. The Alpha and Omega is about to appear. The bride and the Spirit say "Come!" It is time for the world to come unto Me, says the Lord!

Blow the trumpet in Zion, and sound an alarm in My holy mountain! Let all the inhabitants of the land tremble; for the day of the Lord is coming, for it is at hand.
Joel 2:1

29 FEBRUARY

CROWN OF GLORY

Go forth, My beloved, as a crown of glory in My hand and accomplish all that I have purposed for you. Walk in obedience to My direction for you as I show you open doors. There are doors opening that you would never have dreamed would be open to you. Go through each door with confidence that I am with you, and I will move and speak through you. As I pour forth My fire upon and within you, let it burn forth from you. Let My power and glory go forth in such a way that many will see and know that I am God. Only I could do the things through you that will be coming forth. Do not shrink back, but walk forward in the confidence of My Spirit that resides strongly within you. Every time a door is closed, many more will be opened.

Yes, I have chosen you, and I will use you to further My kingdom. Walk in the blessings and the power that I have poured forth and will continue to pour forth in your life. Be a vessel of honor for Me to use. Be a vessel that is empty of self and filled to overflowing with My Spirit.

She [wisdom] will place on your head an ornament of grace; a crown of glory she will deliver to you.
Proverbs 4:9

MARCH

1   MARCH

RESPOND IN OBEDIENCE

Rest assured, My beloved, that I have called you. You were called for such a time as this. Rest in Me as I prepare you for the days ahead. I have given you a time of rest and preparation, because the days ahead will be full. They will be full of My plans and purposes. I have chosen to use you mightily in these last days to lead My people into listening to Me. I have chosen you to lead them into entering into My presence, where they can know and hear My direction.

I am calling My people to walk in obedience to Me as I send forth the last great revival. They must hear and respond to be able to lead many (thousands upon thousands) into My kingdom. They must be closely tuned to Me so that they can disciple and teach the new converts.

Listen and respond. Be ready in and out of season. Speak My words to My people with My anointing upon and within you, so many will be set free to move in obedience to Me. These last days, months and years are vitally important for leading a great multitude into My kingdom. There has never been and never will be again a time such as this. Listen, hear, respond and enjoy My presence, as I pour out My Spirit upon all flesh!

But this is what I commanded them, saying, "Obey My voice and I will be your God, and you shall be My people. And walk in all the ways that I have commanded you, that it may be well with you."
Jeremiah 7:23

2   MARCH

SUCH A TIME AS THIS

Now you see and know something of why I cleared your calendar. You will need this time to prepare for the fulfillment of ALL that I have called you to do during this season! This is a mighty calling, and I chose to call you. Yes, you truly have been called for such a time as this!

Be prepared. Get ready to run with Me. You are learning what acceleration is all about. I told you this will be a time of exhilaration, and you are already beginning to experience it! Run with Me, move with Me and enjoy being My beloved during THIS TIME! There has never been a time like this before – a time ordained by Me, a time predestined by me, a time to prepare for the coming of the Lord!

For if you remain completely silent at this time, relief and deliverance will arise for the Jews from another place, but you and your father's house will perish. Yet who knows whether you have come to the kingdom for such a time as this?
Esther 4:14

3   MARCH

TWINKLING OF AN EYE

My beloved, you have heard the same word from Me over and over, as I have brought it forth through different people. You have had the words that I have spoken to you personally confirmed through others. I have reassured you over and over to My plan and calling upon your life. Get ready, for the door is now opening. Very soon the door will be wide open, and you can walk through. Listen to Me and follow My instructions and direction for you as we enter into an exciting time on this earth.

You are already sensing the birth pangs. You are seeing Bible prophecy fulfilled, and you will see much more. The day is very near when My Son will come forth and receive Our family unto Us. There will be a shout. And, yes, in a twinkling of an eye, My people will arise in the air to meet Jesus, the King of kings and the Lord of lords. Rejoice – rejoice for the time draws near!

Behold, I tell you a mystery: we shall not all sleep, but we shall all be changed – in a moment, in the twinkling of an eye, at the last trumpet. For the trumpet will sound, and the dead will be raised incorruptible, and we shall be changed.
I Corinthians 15:51-52

4   MARCH

WITHOUT SPOT OR WRINKLE

Come away, My beloved, and spend time with Me. Allow Me to share the wonders of My heart. Allow Me to share the glories of My being, and allow Me to share the things that are about to come forth. I have already told you that the church will not be the same. A change is coming.

It is truly the washing of the water of the word that will bring about change to My church. As My word goes forth in My power and with My life, there will be change. My church cannot stay the same as I sweep through with My word, My fire and My power. That which can be burned will burn. That which is pure and holy will stay and last. I am coming back for a church, a bride that is without spot and blemish. I will purify My bride through the washing of the water of the word. My word will stand forever, and My word will bring forth such power – such fire – that everything it touches will be purified or burn.

The Day of the Lord is at hand, and I want My bride to prepare for the great wedding feast. There will be a feast as never before, as My bride is prepared for the wedding. The day of preparation is here. Soon, very soon, the wedding ceremony will take place. Rejoice – rejoice forevermore – and join in the festivities.

Just as Christ also loved the church and gave Himself
for her, that He might sanctify and cleanse her with the
washing of water by the word.
Ephesians 5:25b-26

5   MARCH

GLORY AND MAJESTY

Come, My beloved, enter into My presence and let me share Myself with you. Soak up My presence and the very essence of Who I Am. Let My strength and My power wash over you. Let My wisdom and understanding indwell you. Let My grace and mercy permeate your entire being. Let My light shine so brightly upon and within you that you radiate My glory.

Walk in step with Me – step by step. When I take a step, you take a step. When I pause, you pause. When I leap, you leap. And always lean upon Me. Place the full weight of your being upon Me, and trust Me to take you into higher places. I am taking you into a realm of complete and total surrender to Myself. Bask in the glory and majesty of My presence as I lead you deeper and deeper into My presence.

Therefore David blessed the Lord before all the assembly; and David said: "Blessed are you, Lord God of Israel, our Father, forever and ever. Yours, O Lord, is the greatness, the power and the glory, the victory and the majesty; for all that is in heaven and in earth is Yours; Yours is the kingdom, O Lord, and you are exalted as head over all."
I Chronicles 29:10-11

6   MARCH

LET MY TRUTH SHOUT FORTH

Walk in truth, My beloved. Rejoice and get excited about My truth. Let My truth cover you and bathe (cleanse) you. Soak up My truth as it brings life and wholeness to you. As you walk and move more and more in My truth, you will find that it will begin to penetrate the lives of others. Others will hear, and their lives will be changed. Let My truth shout forth from you, even when your lips are closed. Live My truth in such a way that many will see, and their lives will be changed. Be a shining light that reflects My truth every day. Be an example of My truth to those around you.

Then the Lord heard the voice of Elijah; and the soul of the child came back to him, and he revived. And Elijah took the child and brought him down from the upper room into the house, and gave him to his mother. And Elijah said, "See, your son lives!" Then the woman said to Elijah, "Now by this I know that you are a man of God, and that the word of the Lord in your mouth is the truth."
I Kings 17:22-24

7   MARCH

DOUBLE DOORS TO OPEN

Walk in obedience to Me, says your Lord. Walk in accordance to all that I show you. My call upon your life will bring great fruit to My kingdom. You wonder at times about the doors being opened to you, but I say to you, "Do not be impatient. I will open the right doors at the right time!" I am preparing you for the double doors to open. The day is coming very soon when those doors will spring open.

You will wonder how you can fulfill all that is opened to you, but you will because I will strengthen you. I will encourage you as you stay close to Me. I will open doors that will bring great joy and fulfillment into your life, as you walk in perfect obedience to Me.

Thus says the Lord to His anointed, to Cyrus, whose right hand I have held – to subdue nations before him and loose the armor of kings, to open before him the double doors, so that the gates will not be shut: "I will go before you and make the crooked places straight; I will break in pieces the gates of bronze and cut the bars of iron. I will give you the treasures of darkness and hidden riches of secret places, that you may know that I, the Lord, who call you by your name, am the God of Israel."
Isaiah 45:1-3

8   MARCH

WHOLE HEART

My beloved, do not doubt My presence and My love for you. I am here, waiting to respond to you. As you seek Me, I will answer. It is My desire to pour out My presence and My glory upon you. I am simply waiting for you to come to Me with your whole heart. Yes, I am filling you afresh with a hungering and thirsting for more of Me. And, yes, you know that as you hunger and thirst for more of Me, I will respond. I will answer, and I will fill you with more of Me. I long to pour out greater and greater understanding of Who I am. I long to fulfill all the desires of your heart to KNOW Me better and better. I am continuously revealing Myself to you so that you will grow in your likeness of Who I am. Reach out, reach out and touch Me. Touch, feel and know that I am your Father. I am God Almighty, Creator of the universe. I choose, and I desire to spend time revealing Myself to you, precious one. Look into My eyes and see the reflection of My grace and goodness. Let My reflection permeate your soul, and then let My light shine forth from you in such a way that others' lives will be changed.

Oh, yes, it is the day of revival. It is the day of the great harvest. Get ready, and be prepared by staying in My presence. Then, you can fulfill My calling on your life to be a part of the ushering in of the great and glorious day when Jesus will return.

Jesus said to him, "You shall love the Lord your God with all your heart, with all your soul, and with all your mind."
Matthew 22:37

9   MARCH

ASSURANCE

Be assured, Beloved, that I am coming soon. I am about to reveal Myself in the world in such a way that those that doubt will doubt no more. Only those whose hearts are hardened will turn from Me. This age is about to come to a close, and the thousand-year reign of Jesus upon the earth is about to begin. I am reaching out for all those that will come into My kingdom. There will be thousands upon thousands, and even millions upon millions, that will respond to My glory. They will respond to My call, and the church will need to be ready to take them in.

I am moving in many ways through My people in these last days. Those that are discouraged will have an opportunity to know the assurance of My plan. They will need to listen, walk in obedience and enjoy the pleasure of responding to My grace. I am moving in the earth today in ways that have not been seen and understood before. But, I am ready to reveal Myself. I am ready for the harvest. I am ready for My people to arise and shine.

Truly, these times of ignorance God overlooked, but now commands all men everywhere to repent, because He has appointed a day on which He will judge the world in righteousness by the Man whom He has ordained. He has given assurance of this to all by raising Him from the dead.
Acts 17:30-31

10 MARCH

GOD REVEALS

Beloved, I want you to get ready. Be prepared, for the Day of the Lord is at hand. I am getting ready to reveal Myself to the masses. I am getting ready to pour forth My light and My grace and My power in such great measure that millions will turn to Me. It is truly the time and the season of harvest. Be prepared, because I will use you in these days!

The doors will literally open before your eyes in the days ahead. You must be ready to go through those doors! Be of good courage, My beloved, for I will be with you. You will never have to go forth alone. I will always be with you, guiding and directing you, showing you step by step what to do. I will not leave you out on a limb. Those things that you think you are to do but do not know how, do not do. Only do those things that I show you how to do. I do not try to make things difficult. I will reveal to you all and everything that I want you to do at the right time. Always seek Me. Always listen. Always be yielded to Me, and you will walk in accordance to My perfect will.

Daniel answered in the presence of the king, and said, "The secret which the king has demanded, the wise men, the astrologers, magicians, and the soothsayers cannot declare to the king. But there is a God in heaven who reveals secrets, and He has made known to King Nebuchadnezzar what will be in the latter days."
Daniel 2:27-28a

13 MARCH

BE SET APART

I am coming for a bride who is spotless and blameless. I am transforming My church. The time is coming when those who truly love Me will grow stronger and stronger. They will be set apart like a light on a hill. Those who are playing games will see that I am truly God. Many will come running back to Me. Some will fall away.

I am reaching out in great compassion, but the day is soon coming when the strength of righteousness will truly rule and reign. I will reveal My power and My holiness in such a way that there will no longer be any question about what it means to serve Me. There will be a dividing line, and those that are on a fence will have to jump off. There will no longer be a fence. They will either be all for Me or they will not. I am coming like a consuming fire to present My holiness and My splendor to the church.

But know that the Lord has set apart for Himself him who is godly; the Lord will hear when I call to Him.
Psalm 4:3

14 MARCH

GOD'S CONSUMING FIRE

Come! Come to Me, says your Father. Come and rest in My presence. Let My presence bring life and hope to you. Bask in the glory of My presence as I wash over you with My holiness. Reach out and receive all that I hold out to you. Reach out and receive My grace. Reach out and receive My mercy. Yes, and reach out and receive My fire. Let My consuming fire come and burn away all the dross. Let My consuming fire come and burn within you, as you are filled with zeal for My way. Let My fire bring forth My power within you as you walk in obedience to Me.

See and wonder at the glory of My presence as I choose to work through you. Watch as the power of My life comes forth in great strength, as you speak forth My word. Watch, as those to whom I send you are set free. And, begin to move forth in My life. Be used of Me as you yield yourself to Me. Watch and see as lives of many – yes, many – are transformed through My fire and My power, that is alive within you.

For the Lord your God is a consuming fire, a jealous God.
Deuteronomy 4:24

15 MARCH

THE ALPHA AND THE OMEGA

Reach out and touch those that are hungry. Reach out and touch those that are hurting. Reach out with My truth, and see the shackles fall away. I am getting ready to send a spirit of deliverance across the land that will set multitudes free. This is the day of revival. This is the day of harvest, and many will reach out and receive their freedom as they call upon Me, their Redeemer.

I am the Alpha and the Omega. I am the Beginning and the End. It is the day to look up and know that I am coming soon. As My people receive freedom and then share My freedom with others, there will be such revival as the world has never known before. I am revealing Myself in My greatness and My power. It is the time to say, "Yes!" It is the time to get ready to be used by Me in a powerful way, as I move mightily across this land!

Behold, He is coming with clouds, and every eye will see Him, even they who pierced Him. And all the tribes of the earth will mourn because of Him. Even so, amen. "I am the Alpha and the Omega, the Beginning and the End," says the Lord, "Who is and who was and who is to come, the Almighty."
Revelation 1:7-8

16 MARCH

LIGHT OF THE KNOWLEDGE
OF THE GLORY OF GOD

Call to Me, My beloved. Draw close to Me, and let Me reveal Myself to you. Let Me reveal My goodness and My glory. Bask in the wonder of My presence as I surround you with My magnificence. Look to Me, and see the wonders of My glory. Look into My face, and see My reflection upon and within you. Let Me change you from glory to glory into My image.

As you draw close to Me, the things of darkness will fade away. My light is so brilliant that darkness has to flee in My presence. Do not doubt. Do not dwell on the things of darkness, but dwell upon Me, and you will see and experience great joy. My joy dwells within you. Let it rise up and overcome you. My joy will wash away all condemnation and sorrow. Seek Me with all that is within you. Seek Me, and let My light and life consume you.

For it is the God who commanded light to shine out of darkness, who has shone in our hearts to give the light of the knowledge of the glory of God in the face of Jesus Christ.
II Corinthians 4:6

17 MARCH

DISASTERS AND DESOLATIONS

Listen to Me as I tell you of things to come. There will continue to be disasters upon the earth. There will be desolations that will be a catalyst to draw many to Me. I desire for My creation to come to Me without disasters, but so many go their own way and do their own things. There will be disasters that will bring the attention of many to Me. They will begin to seek Me, but many will fall back as their lives begin to move back in place.

There will be, however, a remnant that will come alive in Me and begin to walk in obedience to Me. I will place a strong anointing on My people that are following Me in obedience. This is the day that I am prepared to move, in great supernatural power, throughout the earth. I have placed My hand upon those that I have purposed to be a part of this end time movement that will bring the masses into knowledge of Me. Yes, My beloved, you are one that I have placed My hand upon. Listen carefully, and I will reveal to you My plan and purpose for you.

For many will come in My name, saying, "I am the Christ," and will deceive many. And you will hear of wars and rumors of wars. See that you are not troubled; for all these things must come to pass, but the end is not yet. For nation will rise against nation, and kingdom against kingdom. And there will be famines, pestilences, and earthquakes in various places. All these are the beginning of sorrows.
Matthew 24:5-8

18 MARCH

EAT MY WORD

Take; eat My Word. My Word brings life to you. It brings the very essence of life and everything that you need into your life. I am able to do all things well, and it is My desire to work in and through you. It is My desire to accomplish much through you. As you surrender yourself to Me over and over again, day-by-day, I will be free to move and work My perfect will through you. It is My desire to teach, preach and work miracles through you. As you eat of My Word and bask in My presence, you will grow in your likeness of Me. I will do signs and wonders as you are filled to overflowing in My Word. Reach out to those around you. Reach out to those I bring across your path, and see the mighty works that I will do.

Your words were found, and I ate them, and Your word was to me the joy and rejoicing of my heart; for I am called by Your name, O Lord God of hosts.
Jeremiah 15:16

19 MARCH

MY GRACE AND PRESENCE

Listen, My beloved, and I will tell you of the mercies of My grace. I pour out My grace, and, yet, there are so many that do not understand. They think they have good luck, or they think in some way they have brought about good things in their own lives. They fail to recognize and acknowledge My work and My presence in their lives. The day is coming, however, when I will reveal Myself in all My glory, righteousness and power. I will rain down the fullness of Who I am, and those that know Me will receive Me with great joy. Those that have been going their own way will be dismayed as they suddenly realize that they have turned away from My grace all these years.

Share the goodness of My grace to those I bring your way. Share the love that I have for each one that I have created. Share My plan of salvation and redemption, so that those that continue on in their own way will hear and know that I am holding out to them the only way that will bring eternal joy. Speak forth My truth. When some turn away, know that they are rejecting My way and Me. Pray for them to have ears to hear and hearts to respond. Listen, hear, share, pray, and many will hear and respond!

If I have found grace in Your sight, show me now Your way, that I may know You and that I may find grace in Your sight. . .And He said, "My presence will go with you, and I will give you rest."
Exodus 33:13b-14

20 MARCH

BY MY SPIRIT

Awake, My church; awake and rise! Rise up, and receive My life in your midst! As you receive My life, you will spread My life to many. Walk in the wonders of My life. Walk in the wonders of My power. Let Me be Myself through you. Do not try to figure out how to do and what to say, but simply let Me be Myself through you.

Walk in the joy and peace of trusting Me. Walk in the holiness that comes from Me. Let My word that says, "Christ in you, the hope of glory," come alive in your spirit. It is not you. It will never be you, but always Me. It is My Spirit bringing My power and My strength through you.

So he answered and said to me: "This is the word of the Lord to Zerubbabel: 'Not by might nor by power, but by My Spirit,' says the Lord of hosts."
Zechariah 4:6

To them God willed to make known what are the riches of the glory of this mystery among the Gentiles: which is Christ in you, the hope of glory.
Colossians 1:27

21 MARCH

DO NOT TAKE MY CALL LIGHTLY

Fasten your seat belts, for I am getting ready to take you into the heavenlies. You will see and understand the fullness of My call upon you. Do not take My call lightly. This is the time! This is your time to shine and reflect My nature to the church, to the lost, to those who are in bondage and to those who are in deep need. Take My love, My compassion, My grace, My mercy and My wisdom to pour out upon those that I bring your way. I am empowering you to be a reflection of Who I am to the world.

You have already begun to step out, but I am accelerating My call upon you. I will strengthen you, and I will guide you. I will show you each step as you move into this new season – a season of preparing the church for My harvest, which will be My last great outpouring. I am taking you into a deeper place of rest in Me, for what is ahead will require My strength – My supernatural strength!

Again, he sent out other servants, saying, "Tell those who are invited, 'See, I have prepared my dinner; my oxen and fatted cattle are killed, and all things are ready. Come to the wedding.'" But they made light of it and went their ways, one to his own farm, another to his business."
Matthew 22:4-5

22 MARCH

REFINED VESSEL

My anointing is burning within you. Yield to My anointing and My power that is rising up strong within you. I have placed My fire within you to burn and burn, and burn some more. My fire will come forth from your lips when you open your mouth to speak. My fire will come forth from your hands when you reach out to pray for those that I bring across your path. My fire is a consuming fire. It burns away all dross and leaves a refined vessel to be used by Me. When My fire is spoken, the very force of power that comes forth changes lives. When the laying on of hands spreads My fire, the physical response to My power is so evident that the person that is touched will not forget. Each life will be changed. My fire and My power are coming upon the earth so strongly at this time, that some people will not be able to stand in My presence.

I am ready! The time is ripe for a mighty move of My presence and My Spirit upon the earth! This is a time when I will be revealing Myself in great strength and power! It is time for righteousness to come forth. It is time for holiness to rule and reign. "It is My time," says the Lord, "and the whole world will know that I am the great I AM – Jehovah God!"

But now, O Lord, You are our Father; we are the clay, and You our
potter; and all we are the work of Your hand.
Isaiah 64:8

23 MARCH

THE BEAUTIFUL TEMPLE

Make way! Make way for the King! I am coming soon, and I want My bride to be prepared to receive her bridegroom. Church, rise up and become the beautiful temple that I created you to be. Rise up and be a blazing lampstand reflecting My glory to the whole earth. Prepare! Prepare for My coming with joy and expectancy! Prepare for the wedding feast. Put on garments of white.

Be aglow with My Spirit as you make your preparations for My coming. Share My light, truth and glory with all those around you. Join hands, and draw others into the circle as you prepare for the great Day of the Lord.

Or do you not know that your body is the temple of the Holy Spirit
who is in you, whom you have from God, and you are not your
own? For you were bought at a price; therefore glorify God in
your body and in your spirit, which are God's.
I Corinthians 6:19-20

Never lag in zeal and in earnest endeavor; be aglow and burning
with the Spirit, serving the Lord.
Romans 12:11 AMP

24 MARCH

THE EVERLASTING ARMS OF GOD

Come, My beloved, and listen to Me. It is time to hear My word for you! It is time to listen with ears that hear. I am here for you. I am with you continuously. I surround you with My presence. I enfold you in My everlasting arms. I pour out My glory upon you. My living waters cascade over and through you. The wind of My Spirit blows upon you. My fire is burning within you.

Reach out and receive the full measure of My love, My presence and the very essence of Who I am, that is washing over you in waves. Receive all that I hold out to you. Do not be afraid to take what I give to you. Bask in the wonder of My generosity to you. Receive, bask, reflect and live Who I am in you – Christ in you, the hope of Glory!

The eternal God is your refuge, and underneath are the
everlasting arms. He will thrust out your enemies before you,
saying, "Destroy them!"
Deuteronomy 33:27

25 MARCH

WAVES OF MY SPIRIT

I'm getting ready to turn this world upside down. Great revival is ready to break forth. I am coming with waves of My Spirit – one wave after another – that will blow across the earth mightily. There will be countless numbers of people that will see and know that I am Who I say I am. I will bring such holiness forward within My church that even those with hard hearts will turn and accept Jesus. There will be many, many that will flow into My kingdom.

There needs to be a preparation of My people to receive the masses. My people need to be prepared to teach and serve these that will be born again into My kingdom. Yes, they will come as children, but many will mature quickly. I am calling you to refuel the fighter planes. I am calling you to teach and encourage the warriors. There will be such great warfare going on that the refueling will need to be done quickly. You will need to stay close and in tune with Me, so that you can provide what is needed for those to whom I am sending you. There is a great movement of My Spirit coming forth, and you feel this in the depths of your being. I have placed My fire within you. Release My fire, and let it do its work through you. Let My consuming fire come forth from your mouth. Let My fire come forth from your actions as long as you are on this earth!

But you will receive power when the Holy Spirit comes on you; and you will be my witnesses in Jerusalem, and in all Judea and Samaria, and to the ends of the earth.
Acts 1:8

26 MARCH

THE FAITH OF ABRAHAM, MOSES AND ENOCH

I have a calling on your life, and it will require strict obedience to Me as you learn to listen very closely to My instruction for you. Stay close, and keep your eyes upon Me. Do not look at the circumstances, but put your total trust in Me. Walk in accordance to My ways. Yes, walk in the faith of Abraham, Moses and Enoch. Walk in a way that is pleasing to Me. Be not upset or dismayed if there are those that do not understand. Continue to walk in My ways. Keep on trusting, and keep on keeping on. Set your face like flint toward that which you know is of Me, and do not be swayed.

For by it [faith] the elders obtained a good testimony. . .By faith Enoch was taken away so that he did not see death, and was not found, because God had taken him; for before he was taken he had this testimony, that he pleased God. But without faith it is impossible to please Him, for he who comes to God must believe that He is, and that He is a rewarder of those who diligently seek Him.
Hebrews 11:2,5-6

27 MARCH

BE STILL, AND KNOW THAT I AM GOD

Rest in Me. Be still, and know that I am God! Just as you have so often approached Me, saying, "I wait upon You," I now say to you, "I wait upon you." I am waiting for you to let go. You need to rest in Me, and release those things that have you bound. Be still, and know that I am God. I am waiting for you to awaken to Who I Am! I long to share with you the glory of My presence. I long for you to sit at My feet, and look up into My face – into My eyes – as I share My agape love with you.

I knew you before creation. I have looked forward to this day when you would come to Me and seek Me in stillness and in wonder. You are Mine, and I am yours. Hold on to Me, cling to Me and stay in My presence as I continue to reveal Who I Am to you, My precious Beloved.

Be still, and know that I am God; I will be exalted among the
nations, I will be exalted in the earth!
Psalm 46:10

28 MARCH

HOLD FAST TO MY WORD

Come! Come to Me, My beloved, and let Me share My wonders with you. I am raising you up in these last days to go forth with My message of salvation and truth. It is I Who am at work within the world to bring about a mighty move of My Spirit. There is soon coming a mighty wave of My Spirit that will sweep across the land. It will sweep across with such power and such force that those who flow with the wind of My Spirit will be swept into My plan and purpose for them. Those who resist will find that My wind will disrupt the things around them. Those things that they thought to be so important to them will be disrupted, and they will see that it was not important after all.

That which is of Me will remain strong and secure. That which is not of Me will be moved, destroyed and disengaged. Hold fast to My Word and My truth, for they are truly life to you. "Hold fast to My words and live life abundantly through My Spirit," says the Lord.

I rise before the dawning of the morning, and cry for help;
I hope in Your word. My eyes are awake through the night
watches, that I may meditate on Your word.
Psalm 119:147-148

29 MARCH

THE FULLNESS OF GOD IN US

Look up, look up and listen. Listen with ears to hear, "Thus says the Lord!" I am waiting to share truth with you. I am waiting to share Myself with you. Get ready to run with Me. Get ready to fly with Me. Get ready to be overcome and undone by the wonder of Who I am.

Yes, My desire is to reveal to you the fullness of Who I am in your life. Reach out and receive all of Me. I hold out Myself to you. I do not hold back anything from you. Reach out and receive My goodness, My grace, My love and compassion. Receive My mercy, wisdom, comfort, strength and encouragement. Yes, and reach out and receive the healing that I hold out to you. Walk in wholeness as you walk, run and fly with Me.

John bore witness of Him and cried out, saying, "This was He of whom I said, 'He who comes after me is preferred before me, for He was before me.' And of His fullness we have all received, and grace for grace."
John 1:15-16

30 MARCH

I CAN DO ALL THINGS THROUGH CHRIST

My Beloved, I am moving in your life, bringing My truth and My purpose to completion. Listen carefully as I reveal Myself to you afresh and anew. Yes, I am doing a new thing in your life. I am bringing about fulfillment of My purposes in your life. I know you are amazed, but I will provide all that you need to complete and fulfill My plan.

Do not stand in amazement, for I am able to do all things well through My precious ones who are willing to be obedient to Me. I will provide the time. Be sensitive to My leading, and I will show you when, where, how and what to do. I will move and work through you as you yield yourself to Me.

I know how to be abased, and I know how to abound. Everywhere and in all things I have learned both to be full and to be hungry, both to abound and to suffer need. I can do all things through Christ who strengthens me.
Philippians 4:12-13

31 MARCH

THE BEAUTY OF HOLINESS

My beloved, I love to talk to you. I love to tell you of My love for you. I love to tell you of My love for all My people. I love to open up revelation to you to share with My children. Listen as I tell you and teach you about My holiness. Holiness is an essential to seeing My face. Holiness is an essential to seeing My house built and for Me to dwell within. My house is not brick or mortar; My house is made up of My people. Holiness is a part of these last days that cannot be overlooked or sidestepped.

Holiness is essential to seeing the culmination of the Church Age, which will usher in My kingdom on earth. I am coming for a bride without spot or blemish – a church filled with My holiness. Learn about My holiness, and share My holiness with others. Worship in the beauty of holiness!

Give to the Lord the glory due His name; bring an offering, and come before Him. Oh, worship the Lord in the beauty of holiness! Tremble before Him, all the earth. The world also is firmly established, it shall not be moved. Let the heavens rejoice and let the earth be glad; and let them say among the nations, "The Lord reigns."
I Chronicles 16:29-31

APRIL

1 **APRIL**

STRENGTH OF COMMITMENT

I am getting ready to use you in a powerful way. Be prepared, and stay before Me. Pray and intercede much, for I am getting ready to move in a powerful way through My body. There will be a move of repentance, which will bring cleansing and anointing, that will sweep through My church. There will be many that will come to know Me in a deeper realm. Their commitment will be greatly strengthened as they begin to recognize Who I am.

Some will fall by the wayside. This will be a time that some will turn away from you. Do not be discouraged, because they are really turning away from Me. Pray much, keep your eyes upon Me and walk in obedience. You will be greatly blessed as you walk in obedience to Me, even as there are some turning away. Be blessed, and let My joy rise up strong as I use you to fulfill my plan and purpose.

*For you are my rock and my fortress; therefore, for Your name's
sake, lead me and guide me. Pull me out of the net which they
have secretly laid for me, for You are my strength. Into Your hand I
commit my spirit; You have redeemed me, O Lord God of truth.*
Psalm 31:3-5

2   APRIL

SOUND OF THE HARVEST

Just as the waves come roaring in on the beach, the last great wave of God's Spirit is getting ready – and already is beginning – to sweep across this nation and the world. The sound of the waves reverberates strongly on the beach, and the sound of the wave of God will be greatly evident. His Spirit will sweep strongly across the nations of the world, bringing the sound of revival, renewal and harvest.

Waves come onto the shore with great force and power. God's move will come with great force and power. Be prepared to move in the power of God's plan in these last days. Listen, listen and hear the sound reverberating across the nations. Rejoice, and join in the sound of the harvest.

And another angel came out of the temple, crying with a loud voice to Him who sat on the cloud, "Thrust in Your sickle and reap, for the time has come for You to reap, for the harvest of the earth is ripe." So He who sat on the cloud thrust in His sickle on the earth, and the earth was reaped.
Revelation 14:15-16

3   APRIL

DEEP CALLS UNTO DEEP

My beloved, listen as I share My light with you. Draw close and hear what I am telling you to do. I have a plan for your life, and it requires strict obedience. I do not mind your checking and confirming My direction. I want you to be sure in your spirit. I want you to walk in discernment. Do not allow doubt any place in your life. As soon as you recognize doubt, immediately replace it with My word. Let faith rise up strong within you so that you can go forth and become the one that I have called you to be.

Step out and move forward as I launch you out into the deep. Trust Me, and walk hand in hand with Me. I will take you up on heights that you never dreamed. Let Me place My dreams within you. Do not quench them by thinking that I could not use you in such a way. Yes, I can! I am able to do all things well through whom I choose. And I choose you! Yes, I choose you! Walk in obedience as I reveal step by step My plan for you. There will be a suddenly for you – a knowing that I am at work. You will have a door opened, and you will know that this is the launching. This is the baby bird being pushed out of the nest. Get ready to fly!

Deep calls unto deep at the noise of Your waterfalls; all Your waves and billows have gone over me. The Lord will command His lovingkindness in the daytime, and in the night His song shall be with me – a prayer to the God of my life.
Psalm 42:7-8

4   APRIL

CHOOSE WHOM YOU WILL SERVE

This is a time of trusting Me, leaning on Me, listening, hearing and being obedient to Me! Make choices to take time with Me. I wait on you! I want to experience your presence with Me. I want to have your undivided attention and presence. Look at your priorities. What do you think about the most? What do you spend more time doing? Check your priorities out carefully, and then choose Me. Choose time with Me. I have such glory to share with you. I have mysteries to reveal to you. I have wisdom to pour out upon you. Come up on the mountain with Me. Come up to a higher realm with Me. Come to a place of deeper commitment with Me. Come and wait upon Me as I pour Myself – all that the Great I Am is – upon you!

Now therefore, fear the Lord, serve Him in sincerity and in truth. . . . serve the Lord! And if it seems evil to you to serve the Lord, choose for yourselves this day whom you will serve, whether the gods which your fathers served that were on the other side of the river, or the gods of the Amorites, in whose land you dwell. But as for me and my house, we will serve the Lord.
Joshua 24:14a, 15

5   APRIL

SEEK HIS FACE

You will begin to see differences in the church, because there are major changes coming soon and have already begun. Watch for moves. There will be people moving about. There will be pastors moving about. There will be moves of My Spirit that sweep across whole congregations. There will be pastors that fall on their faces before My Spirit. There will be some that will fall back, but there will be thousands that draw closer to Me and seek Me as they see and experience My manifested presence. Some will fear, but as they repent and seek Me, the fear will leave and will be replaced by the wonder of drawing into that glorious place of being in My presence.

This is a time of holiness. I am pouring forth a desire for holiness as never before. Those that respond will glow with the joy of walking side by side and face to face with Me.

Sing to Him, sing psalms to Him; talk of all His wondrous works!
Glory in His holy name; let the hearts of those rejoice who seek the
Lord! Seek the Lord and His strength; Seek His face evermore!
I Chronicles 16:9-11

6   APRIL

THE HEART OF GOD

My beloved one, listen to Me as I share My truth and Light with you. Listen, seek and draw close to Me, and I will reveal My heart to you. My heart is filled with love and compassion for My people. My heart is filled with holiness. Holiness is My heart! Holiness and purity are mine. Walk in holiness, and let My purity rise up within you. Be an example of My light, My holiness, My purity, love and compassion. Walk in the footsteps that are Mine. Walk according to My truths and precepts. Do not walk according to some, but walk according to all. Do not leave out that which is uncomfortable. Do not leave out that which you do not understand, but walk in all My ways.

My word is filled with the truth about My heart. Seek My heart through My word and through close communion with Me. My word reveals truth about My heart, and entering into My presence brings that truth alive in your heart. In other words, My heart becomes your heart. Reach out and receive.

And when He had removed him, He raised up for them
David as king, to whom also He gave testimony and said,
"I have found David the son of Jesse, a man after My own
heart, who will do all My will."
Acts 13:22

7   APRIL

WALK, RUN AND FLY WITH ME!

I am in you, and you are in Me. Walk the path that I place before you. Walk in love with Me. Walk in obedience to Me, and watch and see the wonders that I will do. Trust Me, love Me, seek Me, cling to Me and depend on Me. Then, I will bring My glory upon you and upon those around you. You will see Me at work through you as you yield to Me.

I have only good for you. I have only glory for you. I hold out My presence to you. Be still, and know that I am God. Rest in Me. Take My hand and walk with Me, run with Me and fly with Me to heights that you have never seen before, but now will. It is time. It is My time, and it is the season to soar with Me!

For You are my lamp, O Lord; the Lord shall enlighten my darkness. For by You I can run against a troop; by my God I can leap over a wall. As for God, His way is perfect; the word of the Lord is proven; He is a shield to all who trust in Him.
II Samuel 22:29-31

8   APRIL

PEACE THAT SURPASSES
ALL UNDERSTANDING

Come close, precious one, and I will show you My direction for you. I will guide you into all truth – truth for today and truth for the days ahead! Leave it all at My altar. Leave all fear, all doubt and all that is not of Me at My altar, and walk in the peace and freedom that can only come from Me.

Let Me pour forth My peace and rest upon you as you reach out and receive the comfort of complete surrender and trust. Place all anxieties in My hand, and let Me sweep over you with the peace that surpasses all understanding.

*Rejoice in the Lord always. Again I will say, rejoice! Let your
gentleness be known to all men. The Lord is at hand. Be anxious
for nothing, but in everything by prayer and supplication, with
thanksgiving, let your requests be made known to God; and the
peace of God, which surpasses all understanding, will guard your
hearts and minds through Christ Jesus.*
Philippians 4:4-7

9   APRIL

MIND OF CHRIST

I am calling you to walk in obedience and submission to Me, and as you do, I will show you amazing and awesome things. As you seek Me and keep your eyes on Me, you will see the wonder of My glory and the greatness of My grace. As you seek Me more and more, you will begin to be changed from glory to glory into My image. I have told you in My word that you have the mind of Christ, and you do have the mind of Christ available to you. You will begin to see the mind of Christ manifested in you in greater measure as you seek Me, submit to Me and know Me more and more.

Time with Me brings about great change and wondrous results in your life – and in each life that will take hold of My truth and walk in My presence. Seek Me moment by moment, day after day, and see the changes that will occur in your life and in the lives of others. Enjoy the peace and contentedness that comes with a close relationship with Me.

For who has known the mind of the Lord that he may instruct Him?
But we have the mind of Christ.
I Corinthians 2:16

10 APRIL

WALK IN OBEDIENCE

Come into My presence. Let Me share the wonders of My truth with you. As I bring My truth alive within you, I want you to share with others. Walk in obedience to Me as I show you, step by step, how My truth applies to your life. As you walk in obedience to Me, the anointing I have placed within you will grow. You will find greater and greater measure of My power and presence flowing through you as you minister in My name.

Do not be discouraged, but continue to walk in obedience to Me. When you fail to some degree, draw closer to Me and continue to move ahead with freshness and in obedience to Me. In the days ahead, you will see great and mighty moves of My Spirit as you walk in obedience to Me. Do not try to plan and do as you have done in the past, but listen carefully as I show you My plan for each time I use you.

Now to Him who is able to establish you according to my gospel and the preaching of Jesus Christ, according to the revelation of the mystery kept secret since the world began but now made manifest, and by the prophetic Scriptures made known to all nations, according to the commandment of the everlasting God, for obedience to the faith—
Romans 16:25-26

11 APRIL

IMPART TO OTHERS

My beloved, listen to what I have to share with you. I have given you revelation, and I want you to share with others. I have opened up opportunities lately, but there will be many opportunities in the future. Be prepared and trust Me. I will place the words in your mouth. Rivers of living water will flow from your mouth and from your hands to impart to others.

I have chosen you for such a time as this. This past year has been a time of preparation. Go forth and share what I have placed within you. Remember, you do not go alone, for I am always with you!

For God is my witness, whom I serve with my spirit in the gospel of His Son, that without ceasing I make mention of you always in my prayers, making request if, by some means, now at last I may find a way in the will of God to come to you. For I long to see you, that I may impart to you some spiritual gift, so that you may be established.
Romans 1:9-11

12 APRIL

THE HOUSE OF GOD

I have taught you about My power coming into your life through entering into My presence and knowing My heart. My anointing arises upon and within My people to be an instrument of My power on the earth, today, in order to build My house. My church will rise up and become a beautiful dwelling place for Me, and a massive dwelling place for My family to dwell with Me. As that is beginning to come about, it is time for Me to teach about the culmination of this earth, as you know it.

The time of the great Day of the Lord is at hand. It is a day when evil and darkness will be cast away, and eternity will stretch forth with light, holiness and goodness. There will be a rejoicing unlike anything the world has ever seen before. Be prepared to rejoice for the day is at hand – the great Day of the Lord!

It is imperative that My people KNOW My presence and My power in the season in which they are living! This is the time for My people to reflect Who I am upon this earth! This is the time for My house (not built with bricks and stone) to be built with the lives of people that have come to know the wonder of Who I am! Be that reflection wherever I send you!

(You) having been built on the foundation of the apostles and prophets, Jesus Christ Himself being the chief corner stone, in whom the whole building, being fitted together, grows into a holy temple in the Lord.
Ephesians 2:20-21

13 APRIL

WALK IN BOLDNESS

Walk in boldness, My beloved. Walk in My boldness, speaking My word under My anointing. Let My anointing rise up within you and go forth in power. Yes, be desperate for Me. Long for Me with such hungering and thirsting that nothing else will satisfy. Seek Me, long for Me, and I will reveal Myself to you in such power that you will stand in amazement.

The time is coming and is even now here when there will be such a move of My Spirit and My power through you. Yes, I will use you and many others – who are living with Me, loving Me and seeking after Me – to walk in greater boldness than you have ever known before. None of you will be able to stand in My presence. You will be on your face before Me in total amazement.

Now when they saw the boldness of Peter and John, and perceived that they were uneducated and untrained men, they marveled. And they realized that they had been with Jesus. And seeing the man who had been healed standing with them, they could say nothing against it.
Acts 4:13-14

14 APRIL

JOURNEY WITH JOY, EXCITEMENT AND EXPECTATION

Be still and listen to My voice, and hear what I am saying to you. Walk in obedience to My word to you, and hold fast to Me in ALL that you do. Long for Me – stir up a longing for Me. Run after Me, hold on to Me and spend time of sweet communion with Me. Receive My love that I am pouring out upon you and through you. Be watchful, and be prepared for all the opportunities that I bring to you to express My love, My compassion and My grace to those around you. See with My eyes, hear with My ears, reach out with My hands and walk with My feet down the path I place before you.

Take your Journey down that path with joy, excitement and expectation. Shine forth My light and My glory that covers and consumes you. Let My brightness shine forth through you, so many will see Me and turn to Me!

Then the Lord said to me, "Arise, begin your journey
before the people, that they may go in and possess the land
which I swore to their fathers to give them."
Deuteronomy 10:11

15 APRIL

CAPTAIN OF THE HOST

Awake and arise, soldier of the cross. Rise up and prepare to march. March into Zion. March into My land – the promised land. Be prepared to take back that which has been stolen. March in unison. March in obedience, and see the mighty works of your Lord, who is the Captain of the Host. Follow your Captain. Follow Him wherever He may go. Watch and see what He does, and you do as He does. Watch and see what He says, and you say what He says. Follow your Captain in strict obedience. Watch Him and adore Him. Know that He is your salvation. He is all that you need. He will provide all that you require. Let Him be to you all that you need.

Follow Him, love Him, adore Him and worship Him. Watch as the enemy crumbles before Him. Watch as victory rises up. Walk in the fullness of His victory. He holds it out to you!

So He said, "No, but as Commander of the army of the Lord I have now come." And Joshua fell on his face to the earth and worshiped, and said to Him, "What does my Lord say to His servant?" Then the Commander of the Lord's army said to Joshua, "Take your sandal off your foot, for the place where you stand is holy." And Joshua did so.
Joshua 5:14-15

16 APRIL

THE BRIDE OF CHRIST

I am getting My bride ready! The time is short, and it is time for My bride to have only eyes for her bridegroom. The bridegroom is waiting for the word from His Father to come to meet His bride. It is time for My bride to put on her robe of righteousness, and it is time for My bride to have her oil lamps filled.

It is time! The preparation has been going on for a long time. The preparation time is coming to a close. Get ready! Be dressed in your white array, for I am coming! Listen, hear and follow My ways. Give up your ways. Follow My ways, for I am coming for a bride without spot or blemish.

Now I saw a new heaven and a new earth, for the first heaven and the first earth had passed away. Also there was no more sea. Then I, John, saw the holy city, New Jerusalem, coming down out of heaven from God, prepared as a bride adorned for her husband. And I heard a loud voice from heaven saying, "Behold, the tabernacle of God is with men, and HE will dwell with them, and they shall be His people. God Himself will be with them and be their God."
Revelation 21:1-3

17 APRIL

JUMP IN FULL FORCE

Come to the waters and bask in My presence as I pour forth My waters upon you. Melt before Me as My living waters pour over you. Do not be satisfied with a little, but jump in full force. As I pour forth My waters in greater force, jump in with all your might. My power is about to explode within My people who are not afraid to jump in full force. My living waters are available at whatever level you will receive, but those who jump in with all their might will experience the thundering waters – waters that rush forth with such a force that there is nothing that can stand before them.

My power is about to and has begun to erupt upon the earth through My people. I am preparing My church to receive Me in ALL My fullness, in ALL My strength and in ALL My power. There has never been a day like the day that is at hand. The people of the earth have never experienced Me as they are about to experience Me. Prepare, prepare, prepare, for the day is at hand.

The water was flowing from the right side of the temple, south of the altar. . .the water came up to my ankles. . .the water came up to my knees. . .the water came up to my waist. Again he measured one thousand and it was a river that I could not cross; for the water was too deep, water in which one must swim. . .And it shall be that every living thing that moves, wherever the rivers go, will live.
Ezekiel 47:1b,3b,4b,5,9

18 APRIL

WALK BY THE SPIRIT

Walk with Me, My beloved. Take each step, knowing that I am guiding you to walk the walk of righteousness. Walk by the Spirit – by My Spirit – and be filled to overflowing with My fullness, My light and My life. Walk My path that I have placed before you. Walk in strength, in courage, in boldness and in endurance. Do not let up. Do not give up – but walk forward, knowing that I am with you every step of the way.

Walking by My Spirit is the only way that you can know and experience true peace, joy and contentment. As you walk by My Spirit, you will know the peace that passes all understanding and the rest that can only come from Me. You have experienced physical rest, and you have experienced My rest that comes within. You have learned that the rest that comes from Me brings you such a deep peace and contentment that you cannot explain it to someone else. They can see it, but you cannot explain it to them. Only I can do that! As you walk by My Spirit more and more, you will experience My rest more and more. You will also be a greater reflection of Who I am. Walk by My Spirit!

*And those who are Christ's have crucified the flesh with
its passions and desires. If we live in the Spirit, let us also
walk in the Spirit.
Galatians 5:24-25*

19 APRIL

INCREASE, EXPAND AND GROW

I am getting ready to expand the ministry to which I have called you. You will spread out to the left and to the right. I am preparing to move in your life in a mighty way. You have longed to see signs and wonders and miracles. You will begin to see them increase and grow. You are getting ready to experience a mighty move of My Spirit.

Stay in tune, listen to Me and be obedient to Me. I will show you, step by step, what to do and what to say. I have a plan for your life. Follow My plan as I lay it out before you. Walk in total obedience, and you will surely see great and mighty things. The time is now. Be prepared and ready to move out as I lay it all out before you!

Enlarge the place of your tent, and let them stretch out the curtains of your dwellings; do not spare; lengthen your cords, and strengthen your stakes. For you shall expand to the right and to the left, and your descendants will inherit the nations, and make the desolate cities inhabited.
Isaiah 54:2-3

20 APRIL

REALM OF MY GLORY

The river is flowing, and it is time to jump in and flow with Me. I am taking you to a place you have never been before. I am taking you to a realm of My glory that will lift you, sustain you and catapult you to the heights with Me.

Get ready to move in My realm. Get ready to grab hold of others and take them with you to My realm. My realm is filled with all goodness, holiness, truth, grace, forgiveness and all that I am. I am enough for you. I am all that you need. Reach out and receive all that I have for you. Ride with Me to My realm of Glory!

I was watching in the night visions, and behold, One like the Son of Man, coming with the clouds of heaven! He came to the Ancient of Days, and they brought Him near before Him. Then to Him was given dominion and glory and a kingdom that all peoples, nations, and languages should serve Him. His dominion is an everlasting dominion, which shall not pass away, and His kingdom the one which shall not be destroyed.
Daniel 7:13-14

21 APRIL

WALK IN THE STRENGTH AND POWER OF ALMIGHTY GOD

Rise up, rise up, men and women of God! Rise up to the calling, the high calling of Christ Jesus in your life. Do not be satisfied with mediocre, because you walk in the strength and power of Almighty God. Walk in the strength and power of almighty God, instead of being caught up in the ways of the world.

Do you not know? Have you not heard? Have you not seen that the power of Almighty God is available to you? Yes, His power even resides in you. Rise up, and become the people of God He has created you to be. Walk in obedience to His truth. Walk in the holiness and righteousness that He has provided for you. Ignore the distractions of the things of the world, as you walk in the power and strength of Almighty God!

For who is God, except the Lord? And who is a rock, except our God? God is my strength and power, and He makes my way perfect. He makes my feet like the feet of deer, and sets me on my high places.
II Samuel 22:32-34

22 APRIL

REFUGE AND RESTORATION

There is a fire burning. There are flames that are shooting up. Look up, look up and place your eyes upon Me. Make Me your focus, and as you do, My fire will rise up in you, and you will see Me working mightily through you. My power and My presence will move among you to reach out to those who are seeking more of Me.

I have made you a place of refuge and restoration. My name for you is "refuge and restoration." Many will see and experience My power and presence as My fire rises up within you and spreads throughout your area. Hold out your arms, for the prodigals will be coming home. Hold out your arms to the wounded, for they will run to you. Hold out your arms for the lost, tired, weary and hurting to come to a place that is inhabited by Me – a place of refuge and restoration.

In God is my salvation and my glory; the rock of my strength, and my refuge is in God. Trust in Him at all times, you people; pour out your heart before Him; God is a refuge for us.
Psalm 62:7-8

23 APRIL

FEAR GOD, NOT MAN

Come to Me, My beloved. Come before Me boldly. Come before Me openly. Come expecting to hear from Me. Come expecting to see Me. Come expecting to receive from Me, for I am your God. I will bring you to a place of knowing Me as you have never known Me before. I hold out to you all that I am. The great I AM is calling to you, holding out My arms to you, saying, "Come to Me." Walk in obedience and trust. Let Me reveal to you just how much I can and will do for you. Let Me show you the greatness of My power and strength that is available to you. My desire is to move and work through you, as you yield more and more of yourself to Me. Do not hold back, but trust Me in every area of your life.

Do not fear man, but fear Me. Revere Me, and see what I will do for you and through you. You are getting ready to experience such an explosion of My presence and My power that you will truly be amazed. The days ahead will be mighty days. They will be powerful days. Get ready to be used by Me as a holy vessel. Be prepared, and keep close. Seek the excitement and urgency that I hold out to you. As you allow this urgency, this unction, to rise up within you, you will see what I will accomplish for My kingdom through you.

Let us hear the conclusion of the whole matter: fear God and keep
His commandments, for this is man's all.
Ecclesiastes 12:13

24 APRIL

BRING PLEASURE TO THE HEART OF GOD

Hear Me, My beloved. You are mine! You are mine, forevermore! There is such joy that awaits you as you come to Me. There is such peace and contentment as you come to Me. There is life everlasting – an abundance of life that awaits you. Come running into My light as you come running into My arms, and I will hold you, forevermore.

My love for you is eternal. My love is everlasting. Walk hand in hand with Me, and learn more about My ways. Let My ways become your ways. You bring pleasure to My heart as we walk hand in hand together.

I know also, my God, that You test the heart and have pleasure in uprightness. As for me, in the uprightness of my heart I have willingly offered all these things; and now with joy I have seen Your people, who are present here to offer willingly to You. O Lord God of Abraham, Isaac, and Israel, our fathers, keep this forever in the intent of the thoughts of the heart of Your people, and fix their heart toward You.
I Chronicles 29:17-18

25 APRIL

WATCH AND WAIT

Make no mistake, for the time is near. Watch and wait with perseverance. Be a watchman on the wall, and look and see what is about to occur. Do not speculate, but watch with expectancy. Expect to hear from Me as I show what is ahead, and how to pray and intercede.

There are some that I have chosen to use to bring forth My truth to the church. You are one of those that I have chosen. It will require of you your devotion and commitment to spend time with Me – knowing Me better, hearing from Me and worshiping Me. As you draw closer and closer, I will use you to teach and motivate others to draw close to Me. It is imperative in these last days that My people draw close to Me. I need them to allow My light to shine forth from them greatly. I need those of the world to see Me in the lives of My children. I am getting ready to pour out My Spirit upon all flesh. It is the day of revival and the great harvest, and I need My church to shine!

I wait for the Lord, my soul waits, and in His word I do hope. My soul waits for the Lord more than those who watch for the morning – yes, more than those who watch for the morning.
Psalm 130:5-6

26 APRIL

VICTORY IS YOURS

Victory is yours, My beloved. I created you for victory. Victory will rule and reign in your life. Even as the enemy is trying to destroy, I am bringing physical sight, and also brilliant spiritual sight and discernment to you. Even as you face this giant, I am opening the door to your destiny.

Spiritual sight, spiritual insight and discernment are increasing, increasing and increasing, until there will be those that will say, "Look at the brilliance!" Oh yes, My beloved, My brilliance will shine forth in you in such a way that you will be astounded at how I will use you in the lives of multitudes! Go forth in victory, keeping your eyes focused on Me, and I will bring about the wonders of My glory through you.

But thanks be to God, who gives us the victory through our Lord Jesus Christ. Therefore, my beloved brethren, be steadfast, immovable, always abounding in the work of the Lord, knowing that your labor is not in vain in the Lord.
I Corinthians 15:57-58

27 APRIL

SURRENDER AND YIELD

The day is coming very soon when you will know the depth of Who I am in your life. You will know the depth of My calling upon your life, and you will experience My presence, My power and My Spirit so strongly in your life that you will completely yield yourself. No longer will it be you, but it will be the great I Am at work in and through you, flowing forth with My power and anointing so that all present will know it is Me, and not you.

Surrender more and more of yourself, and know the pure joy of reflecting My Spirit everywhere you go.

Do not continue offering or yielding your bodily members [and faculties] to sin as instruments [tools] of wickedness. But offer and yield yourselves to God as though you have been raised from the dead to [perpetual] life, and your bodily members [and faculties] to God, presenting them as implements of righteousness.
Romans 6:13 AMP

28 APRIL

TRUST ME

Watch and wait, says the Lord. Watch and wait for the coming of the Lord. Yes, the Messiah has come and is coming again. Just as John the Baptist was called to prepare the way of the first coming, there are many that are called to prepare the way for His second coming. Yes, you are one of the ones chosen to prepare the way.

Keep your eyes upon Me. Trust Me with every area of your life, and you will see miracles. Trust Me with every pain, and you will see them disappear. Trust Me with every care, and you will see Me at work to bring about peace and contentment. Trust Me with every fear, and you will experience freedom, as My faith rises up within you. I have come that you might have life more abundantly – life free of pain, worry and fear. Watch and wait, for the time is near.

I wait for the Lord, my soul waits, and in His word I do hope. My soul waits for the Lord more than those who watch for the morning – yes, more than those who watch for the morning.
Psalm 130:5-6

29 APRIL

LIVE AND MOVE AND HAVE
OUR BEING IN HIM

My hand is upon you. I have called you for such a time as this. This is not the end; this is a new beginning, where I will take you places that have not even occurred to you. I am opening doors for you to go through, and I will move mightily through you. You will see Me accomplishing much through you!

My hand is upon you now to bring strength – My supernatural strength to flow through you. I am healing you even now from the top of your head down to your toes. Receive all that I have for you. I speak release to your body to move, live and have your being through Me. Receive and proclaim My truth to your body. Rise up and shine, for the glory of the Lord is upon you. I made you for this time – the time to arise and shine!

For in Him we live and move and have our being, as also some of your own poets have said, "For we are also His offspring."
Acts 17:28

30 APRIL

CALL FORTH MY KINGDOM

I have placed a watch around you. Rest in the knowledge that there is nothing that can touch you with My protection around you. Walk in trust that I am able to keep you.

Look up. Look up, for I want you to make Me your focus. Look up, and know that I am in control. Look up, and know that My kingdom has come. Call forth My kingdom in your life and in the lives of those in your state, nation and nations of the world. I am a BIG GOD! Wait, watch and see what I will do.

I make a decree that in every dominion of my kingdom men must tremble and fear before the God of Daniel. For He is the living God, and steadfast forever; His kingdom is the one, which shall not be destroyed, and His dominion shall endure to the end.
Daniel 6:26

But seek first the kingdom of God and His righteousness, and all these things shall be added to you.
Matthew 6:33

MAY

1 MAY

DO ALL THINGS THROUGH ME

Yes, My beloved, as I am in the Father, you are in Me, and I am in you. You do nothing on your own, but you do all things in and through Me. You are saying, "But I know there are times I do things on my own." Yes, but My desire, My perfect will, is for you to do all things in and through Me.

Draw closer, and let Me rise up big and strong within you. I have much to do and to accomplish through you. Draw close, and seek Me with all that is within you. Stay close, and become closer as I reveal more and more of Myself to you.

Move into that place by My Spirit that you trust Me in all things. Seek to know Me in such a way that you are aware of what I am saying, and how I am reaching out to those that I bring across your path. As you do, you will find yourself doing as I do and saying what I say. You will see many come into the kingdom of God. As you reflect Me wherever you are, you will see many within My body growing in their knowledge of Me.

I am the vine, you are the branches. He who abides in Me, and I in
him, bears much fruit; for without Me you can do nothing.
John 15:5

2 MAY

MAGNITUDE, MAJESTY AND SPLENDOR

Come and enter into that place with Me. Enter into a place with Me that will bring you great joy, peace and comfort. Seek Me with your whole being. Desire this time with Me that will bring everlasting love, joy, peace, patience, kindness, goodness and all things that are of Me! As you seek Me and as you enter into the Holy of Holies, you will begin to see the magnitude, majesty and splendor that I am! As you come to KNOW Me better and better, you will find yourself being changed as you are transformed into My image. I have placed you on this earth to reflect Who I am!

You bring Me great joy as you seek Me, hunger for more of Me, and thirst for more and more of My presence and glory! I am pouring out Myself upon and through you. My power resides within you, and I am releasing you to the multitudes. Go in My name, and shine forth with My glory!

Who being the brightness of His glory and the express image
of His person, and upholding all things by the word of His
power, when He had by Himself purged our sins, sat down at
the right hand of the Majesty on high.
Hebrews 1:3

3 MAY

COMPLETING THAT WHICH
I HAVE BEGUN IN YOU

Listen as I speak to you, My beloved. Yes, I am speaking, and I have much to share with you. I have placed My words in your mouth. I want you to share them with those that I bring across your path. I want to minister to My people through you. I can trust you. Yes, you sometimes make mistakes and sometimes your motive is wrong; but as soon as you realize it, you correct it through Me. Your heart is to serve Me, and I am completing and perfecting that which I have begun in you.

Move out and move in the direction that I give to you. Continue to seek Me with all that is within you, and fulfill My call and My will in your life.

Being confident of this very thing, that He who has begun a good work in you will complete it until the day of Jesus Christ.
Philippians 1:6

4   MAY

CHRIST IN YOU

I have called you to walk the path that I have placed before you. I have things for you to do that you have not even imagined. Look up, look up and seek My face. Seek Me with your whole heart, and I will show you great and mighty things. I will show you each step to take as I direct your path. I have called you on this journey to walk with Me, step by step, growing in your knowledge of Me.

Yield yourself to the One Who loves you with an everlasting love. Yield yourself to the One Who calls you beloved! Take hold of My hand, and walk hand in hand with Me as I reveal Myself to you and I reveal your true identity in Me. Hold on to My word that tells you that I live in you. I live in you to enable you to reflect Who I am! Take hold of Me, cling to Me and commune with Me. Watch and see Who I am! As you do, you will see yourself being transformed, from glory to glory, into My image. Walk with Me, My beloved. Bask in My presence and My glory. Let My light shine forth from you in such a way that others will not see you, they will see Me – Christ in you, the hope of glory!

But if the Spirit of Him who raised Jesus from the dead dwells in you, He who raised Christ from the dead will also give life to your mortal bodies through His Spirit who dwells in you.
Romans 8:11

5 MAY

HUNGER AND THIRST FOR RIGHTEOUSNESS

I have called you for such a time as this. This is a time that I am moving greatly upon the earth. I have begun a movement that will increase and enlarge upon this earth. Many are drawn to Me, but there will be multitudes upon multitudes that will come unto Me as My church yields unto Me. The time is past of playing games, of being complacent and lethargic. The time is now to be zealous for Me – zealous with wisdom. It is a time to be full of passion for My ways and My kingdom.

The day of thinking "I can do it myself" is over. This is the time to take up your cross and follow Me. This is the time to say, "Your way and Your will only, O God!" Take the messages that I have placed within you everywhere you have the opportunity. Take the revelation I give you and share it with others. It is a time of hungering and thirsting for Me, says the Lord, and those that hunger and thirst will be filled. Move ahead. Follow My direction and My lead. I will open doors for you. Do not be distracted by what I am doing in and with others, but follow My plan and purpose for you.

Blessed are those who hunger and thirst for
righteousness, for they shall be filled.
Matthew 5:6

6 MAY

LEAN BACK IN MY ARMS AND REST IN ME

Listen, listen and listen some more! I am always sharing truth with you. I may take you upon a mountain, or I may whisper to you while you are in the valley. I am always with you, guiding and directing you. I am always showing you which step to take, where to go and how to make the next move.

All you have to do is listen. Learn how to hear Me. You may hear a small, still voice within, or you may have a nudge in your spirit. You may hear a sermon or a teaching, and all of a sudden, something that is said comes alive within your spirit. You know, that you know, that you know! You may be having a conversation with someone and the same thing happens. You know that it is the answer that you have been seeking. I speak to you in many ways, and all it takes is for you to be sensitive to the Holy Spirit at work in you. The more you seek Me, the more that you will be aware of My Spirit working within you. I am with you from everlasting to everlasting. Lean back in My arms, and rest in Me.

I have set the Lord always before me; because He is at my right hand I shall not be moved. Therefore my heart is glad, and my glory rejoices; my flesh also will rest in hope.
Psalm 16:8-9

7   **MAY**

IN THE PRESENCE OF HIS GLORY

I have called you for such a time as this. It is My desire to bring My glory upon the earth. This is the time of the last great outpouring upon the earth before the coming of My Son. Do not get sidetracked. Do not get distracted, but follow My directions for you. You will not be disappointed, for you see the fulfillment of My plan and purpose for your life fall into place with My plan and purpose for My kingdom upon this earth.

You will, I say you will, experience My glory and My presence in such a way that you will cry out in absolute wonder at what I am doing. You will think you cannot survive the wonder of My presence and yet, you will not want My presence to stop. You will walk in absolute amazement and delight as I prepare you for the coming of the Lord. Get ready, for I am preparing to pour forth My glory in great measure.

Now to Him who is able to keep you from stumbling, and to present you faultless before the presence of His glory with exceeding joy.
Jude 24

8   MAY

THE KNOWLEDGE OF THE GLORY OF GOD

Walk in submission to My will for you! Walk in the truth that I have placed before you. Walk, holding My hand, and walk in cadence with My step. Let your heart beat with My heartbeat. Let your desires be the same as mine. Draw close, and spend time in My presence. Receive My glory upon and within you.

Be a part of the whole earth being filled with the knowledge of My glory. Speak, teach, pray, according to My Spirit, and live your life in Me! Always know that I am in you! My dwelling within you is the hope of glory! Receive My glory, and walk in My glory. Live and move, and have your being in My glory! Arise and shine, for My glory has risen upon you!

Behold, is it not of the Lord of hosts that the peoples labor to feed the fire, and nations weary themselves in vain? For the earth will be filled with the knowledge of the glory of the Lord, as the waters cover the sea.
Habakkuk 2:13-14

9   MAY

CLOAKED IN HIS GLORY

Wait upon Me. Wait upon Me, and hear the joys of My truth. Let Me share with you the wonders of the things that are to come. Let Me tell you about the great and mighty things that will occur upon the earth. There is a time that is coming that will be unlike any previous time. This will be a time when My church will be cloaked in My glory. This will be a time when My church will seek after Me, love Me and reflect My nature as never before. This will be a time when I will exhibit Myself through My church in such power and such glory that multitudes of unsaved will become saved. They will see Me working and moving through My church, and they will know that I am real! They will know that there is no other way. They will fall on their faces before Me, and the Kingdom of God will come upon this earth. Great revival will break forth as My church lets Me live big through them!

In the year that King Uzziah died, I saw the Lord sitting on a throne, high and lifted up, and the train of His robe filled the temple. Above it stood seraphim; each one had six wings: with two he covered his face, with two he covered his feet, and with two he flew. And one cried to another and said: "Holy, holy, holy is the Lord of hosts; the whole earth is full of His glory!"
Isaiah 6:1-3

10 MAY

THAT YOU MAY KNOW ME!

This is My time for My people to arise and shine. Your light has certainly come, and My glory is all over and within you. Do not let My light fade! Reach out, and receive all that I have for you during this season – this NOW season. Reach out, and receive My light. Receive My glory and walk, live and have your being in the glory of Who I am in YOUR life!

I am awakening you to this time – this season when I am revealing more and more of Myself to you. I created you to KNOW Me. Receive Me into your life in such a way that you reflect My image to the world around you. Bask in My glory, and go forth in the beauty of Who I am!

Then Moses said to the Lord, "See, You say to me, 'Bring up this people.' But You have not let me know whom You will send with me. Yet You have said, 'I know you by name, and you have also found grace in My sight.' Now therefore, I pray, if I have found grace in Your sight, show me now Your way, that I may know You and that I may find grace in Your sight. And consider that this nation is Your people."
Exodus 33:12-13

11 MAY

THE SOUND OF GOD – A SYMPHONY!

My beloved, listen to Me. Incline your ear to My sayings. Listen, hear and be set free. Be set free to be all that I have created you to be. Walk in obedience to Me. Trust Me to bring forth all that I purpose through you. Do not look to your own abilities, and do not look to your inadequacies. Look to Me, for I am able to complete and work through you all that I choose. I choose to do great and mighty things through you, but you must submit to Me and allow Me full place.

Walk in tune with Me. Listen and hear the symphony that I have written for you. It is a symphony that brings together many instruments to bring forth a beautiful sound. As you allow these instruments to play through you (as you allow My ways to come forth), the result will be a beautiful symphony. Do not be distracted by "what ifs," but trust Me with every detail and every note. You will see and hear the beautiful sound that will come forth from you!

So then faith comes by hearing and hearing by the word of God.
But I say, have they not heard? Yes indeed: Their sound has gone
out to all the earth, and their words to the ends of the world.
Romans 10:17-18

12 MAY

FAITH, COURAGE, BOLDNESS AND WISDOM

Rise up within My presence, and move out. Move forward without fear, without doubt, without pride and without anything that is not of Me. Move forward with faith, courage, boldness and wisdom. Walk tall, knowing that I live within you and want to move through you. Walk in fear of Me – in reverence of Me. Walk in My steps and carry My heartbeat, for I am ready. I am ready to reveal Myself even more through you. Are you ready for all that I want to do in your life?

This is the time to move ahead in total obedience to Me, with great joy and excitement. This is the time to recognize that faith, courage, boldness and wisdom are gifts from Me. I have and will supply all that you need to fulfill My plan and My purpose for your life. Be astounded as you move out in faith, with great courage and boldness in My wisdom!

Have I not commanded you? Be strong and of good
courage; do not be afraid, nor be dismayed, for the Lord
your God is with you wherever you go.
Joshua 1:9

Now when they saw the boldness of Peter and John, and perceived
that they were uneducated and untrained men, they marveled. And
they realized that they had been with Jesus.
Acts 4:13

13 MAY

I AM A LIFE-CHANGING GOD!

Come, My beloved, and worship at My footstool. Come and sit before Me, and lift up your face to Mine. Let Me gaze into your eyes for as I gaze into your eyes, I will impart to you the glory of Who I am. My light will shine forth from Me to you. You will see Me in all My glory, and you will know the depth of My integrity. You will know and experience the glory of My presence. Time in My presence brings change in your life. You cannot see Me and experience My glory without change occurring in your life. I am a life-changing God, and the more that you allow My presence to enter your life, the more change will occur in you. Let My light enter into you in greater and greater measure, and then let My light shine forth from you to others.

Then Jesus spoke to them again, saying, "I am the light of the world. He who follows Me shall not walk in darkness, but have the light of life."
John 8:12

You are the light of the world. A city that is set on a hill cannot be hidden. Nor do they light a lamp and put it under a basket, but on a lampstand, and it gives light to all who are in the house.
Matthew 5:14-15

14 MAY

WALK IN MY FULLNESS

My beloved, you have seen Me at work in your life. I want you to walk in My fullness. Do not look to the right or to the left, but look full ahead at Me. Do that which you see Me doing. Say that which you hear Me saying. My Spirit resides with you, and I say to you, "Arise and walk in My fullness that dwells within you."

Serve those around you, as I give the words and the deeds. Go through the doors that I open for you. I choose to use you in these last days to bring forth My light into the lives of many. Do not hold back, but go forth as I move in and through you. Know what it means to move and live and have your being in Me, says the Lord.

And He Himself gave some to be apostles, some prophets, some evangelists, and some pastors and teachers, for the equipping of the saints for the work of ministry, for the edifying of the body of Christ, till we all come to the unity of the faith and of the knowledge of the Son of God to a perfect man, to the measure of the stature of the fullness of Christ.
Ephesians 4:11-13

15 MAY

REJOICE IN THE LORD, ALWAYS WITH EXPECTATION

Skip, dance and shout before Me. Rejoice with all that is within you, for the time has come to enter into My gates with thanksgiving, and into My courts with praise. Enter into My Holy of Holies with reverent silence, waiting upon Me to reveal Myself to you afresh and anew!

I am waiting to bring revelation to you. I am waiting for you to come. Come, even now, into My presence, expecting to meet with Me; expecting to hear from Me, expecting to be overcome with the joy of My majesty and My holiness! Reach out; reach out to receive all that I have to give you. Reach out to receive more and more of Me. I am waiting!

Rejoice in the Lord always. Again I will say, rejoice!
Philippians 4:4

For I know that this will turn out for my deliverance through your prayer and the supply of the Spirit of Jesus Christ, according to my earnest expectation and hope that in nothing I shall be ashamed.
Philippians 1:19-20 a

16 MAY

ABUNDANCE OF LIFE AND VICTORY

Listen to Me, My beloved. I am all that you need. Hold onto Me with every ounce of your being, and you will know the abundance of life and victory that only I can give. Hold on to Me, and praise Me. Worship Me and know the glory of My presence. Seek Me, and bask in My presence as I reveal Myself in ways that you have not experienced yet. Seek Me and know Me in all My fullness. Walk in the joy and peace that come from that close intimate communion with Me. Walk with Me, talk with Me, rest in Me and enjoy My presence.

Let Me share the joy of Who I am with you. Rejoice in Me, and lean on Me. Let Me lift you up higher and higher. Reach up into the height of Who I am. Know Me, love Me, seek Me and adore Me. Receive from Me all that I have for you now at this time.

For if by the one man's offense death reigned through the one, much more those who receive abundance of grace and of the gift of righteousness will reign in life through the One, Jesus Christ.
Romans 5:17

But thanks be to God, who gives us
the victory through our Lord Jesus Christ.
I Corinthians 15:57

17 MAY

THE VEIL IS TORN

Look up. Look up into My face. Reach up. Reach up to Me, and I will lift you up higher and higher. Come sit at My feet; sit upon My lap, and bask in the love that I pour out upon you. Listen to Me, know Me and enter into that place of the Holy of Holies. The veil is torn – come into My presence and experience My glory. I am pouring My glory out upon you, and I am pouring My glory out upon many others through you.

Dance with Me, My beloved, and enjoy the wonder of Who I am! Rejoice, for I am right here, waiting for you to look up and reach up to Me. I am waiting to pour out the fullness of Who I am upon you and upon those that I bring across your path. Remember – the veil is torn! Come into My Holy of Holies, and experience My glory!

Therefore, brethren, having boldness to enter the Holiest
by the blood of Jesus, by a new and living way which He
consecrated for us, through the veil, that is, His flesh, and
having a High Priest over the house of God, let us draw near
with a true heart in full assurance of faith.
Hebrews 10:19-22a

18 MAY

SEEK HIM WITH YOUR WHOLE HEART!

I beckon to you, My beloved. I beckon to you and ask you to listen closely. This is the time to seek Me. Seek Me and Me alone. Do not seek ministry. Seek Me. Seek Me with your whole heart. Stay before Me by setting aside an hour each day to simply seek Me. Seek Me while I may be found. Be still, and know that I am God.

Let Me reveal Myself to you through dreams and visions, through My voice and through My word. Hear and receive from Me. My dear one, I want your attention, your presence and your whole self. Listen attentively, and I will share that which I am doing with you. My precious one, let Me hold you closely. I am your strength, and I am your salvation. I am all that you need. Receive of Me.

Blessed are the undefiled in the way, who walk in the law of the Lord! Blessed are those who keep His testimonies, who seek Him with the whole heart!
Psalm 119:1-2

19 MAY

PORTALS OF HEAVEN OPENED

Enjoy! Enjoy! Rest in Me, as you see and experience the move of My Spirit all across this land and all across the nations of the world. Jump in, splash, swim and float in the current of My living waters. Enjoy My presence that I am pouring out upon you and upon the earth! Move in delight as I open doors and as My path unfolds before you! Walk, run and dance with Me as I open the portals of heaven over the earth at this time. Seek Me! Seek all that I am. Seek to know Me better. Seek to live and move and have your being in Me.

My beloved, I created you for such a time as this. There has never been a time like this time, this season. I am at work all over the earth, and soon the whole earth will be filled with the knowledge of My glory!!!

Jesus answered and said to him, "Because I said to you, 'I saw
you under the fig tree,' do you believe? You will see greater
things than these." And He said to him, "Most assuredly, I say to
you, hereafter you shall see heaven open, and the angels of God
ascending and descending upon the Son of Man."
John 1:50-51

20 MAY

ABUNDANCE OF YOUR WORD

Get ready, My Beloved. Get ready to move out, for now is the time. I pulled you aside for a time, and I showed you things about yourself that you had not been ready to face before. But now you have faced them, and you have repented. I am ready to move you and thrust you forth to fulfill My calling upon your life.

Expect to move out. Be prepared to go forth in the abundance of My word, as I use you to share My good news with My people. There will be salvations. There will also be an equipping of My people to go forth in the gifting's and callings I have placed within them. Yes, it is time for revival and renewal. It is the time of harvest. I need My people to draw near to Me so they will be prepared to go forth with My anointing to bring in the harvest!

The law of Your mouth is better to me
than thousands of coins of gold and silver.
Psalm 119:72

The entirety of Your word is truth, and every one of Your righteous judgments endures forever. Princes persecute me without a cause, but my heart stands in awe of Your word. I rejoice at Your word as one who finds great treasure.
Psalm 119:160-162

21 MAY

FULLNESS OF RIGHTEOUSNESS AND HOLINESS!

The fire of God is rising up! It is raging with the cleansing power of Jesus. I Am is sweeping across this nation and the nations of the world to bring forth a harvest for the bridegroom. His bride is being prepared. The spots and the blemishes are beginning to disappear, as His living waters flow over and within His bride. He is coming for a bride of fullness – fullness of righteousness and holiness! He is coming for a bride of fullness of grace and goodness! He is coming for a bride of fullness of the wonder of the Great I Am!

Are you ready? Are you prepared, and are you ready to go forth through the doors that I am opening for you to work in the harvest field? Stay so close to Me that you know and are aware of each opportunity that I bring your way to share My fire, as I send you out.

To grant us that we, being delivered from the hand of our enemies, might serve Him without fear, in holiness and righteousness before Him all the days of our life.
Luke 1:74-75

22 MAY

CONFIDENCE IN ME

Make straight the path. Go not to the left or to the right, but go straight ahead in the path that I have placed before you. Yes, run, for the time is short, and I have much for you to do. I will show you each step of the way what My will is for you. I am opening doors – doors that you cannot imagine. Doors you never dreamed are about to open for you. Go through these doors, for I am with you every step of the way.

You do not have to rely upon yourself, for it is I Who dwells within you. As you trust Me, I will move and speak through you. Walk humbly, and walk firmly with confidence in Me. You will see great and mighty things as I move mightily through you.

Blessed is the man You choose, and cause to approach You,
that he may dwell in Your courts. We shall be satisfied with
the goodness of Your house, of Your holy temple. By awesome
deeds in righteousness You will answer us, O God of our
salvation, You who are the confidence of all the ends of the
earth, and of the far-off seas; who established the mountains
by His strength, being clothed with power.
Psalm 65:4-6

23 MAY

SPEAK FORTH MY TRUTH

See what I am about to do. There is a great breakthrough coming, even as I pour out Myself in greater measure upon and within My beloved. This is your time to move out in such a way that barriers will begin to fall as you open your mouth, and speak forth My truth.

This is a time for multitudes to come into My kingdom, and I am sending forth My kingdom builders with My construction plans. This is the time for world changers to come forth, and you are one of My world changers. Put on your construction clothes. Pull out all your construction tools, and draw together in unity to put My plans together. Listen, hear, and I will reveal My plans to you!

"As for Me," says the Lord, "this is My covenant with them: My Spirit who is upon you, and My words which I have put in your mouth, shall not depart from your mouth, nor from the mouth of your descendants, nor from the mouth of your descendants' descendants," says the Lord, "from this time and forevermore."
Isaiah 59:21

24 MAY

MY DWELLING PLACE

I am with you always. I am with you in the good times, and I am with you in the bad times. I am always holding out My arms to you, waiting for you to take the time to run into My arms. My beloved, run into My arms, and know the safety and security of being with Me in My dwelling place. Do not look to the left or to the right. Stay focused on Me, and run to Me with all your strength! There is nothing that can overtake you as you focus on Me and run into My dwelling place. Stay in My presence, and seek My presence. Know and understand that My presence is where you belong.

I am your high tower, your fortress, and your strength and protection. Look to Me, love Me, stay close to Me and let Me express My everlasting love to you.

Lord, You have been our dwelling place in all generations. Before the mountains were brought forth, or ever You had formed the earth and the world, even from everlasting to everlasting, You are God. . .And let the beauty of the Lord our God be upon us.
Psalm 90:1-2, 17a

25 MAY

I AM YOUR FORTRESS AND STRONG TOWER

My precious one, lift your eyes upward. Look into My face. My face expresses Who I am. I am your fortress and your strength. I am a strong tower for you. I hold out the wonder of holiness, goodness and righteousness. I hold out humility, mercy and grace. I hold out to you peace, joy and love. I am forever and forever, and My love is everlasting and enduring.

Hold My hand, and walk with Me. Walk into the water that is brimming with My life. Walk into the fire that cleanses, refines and empowers. Walk into the wind that blows in the direction that I am taking you. Hold My hand, wait upon Me and listen as I direct your path – the path of holiness, humility and grace!

*From the end of the earth I will cry to You, when my heart
is overwhelmed; lead me to the rock that is higher than I.
For you have been a shelter for me, a strong tower from the
enemy. I will abide in Your tabernacle forever; I will trust
in the shelter of Your wings. Selah.*
Psalm 61:2-4

26 MAY

THE GLORY OF GOD'S PRESENCE

It is time to seek Me as never before. It is a time to draw close and let Me reveal Myself to you. Draw close, so close that My presence and My countenance cover you. Look into My face, and let me shine My light upon you. Let My radiance overcome you. Bask in the glory of My Presence, and receive Who I am into your life. Be changed as I reveal Myself to you. Be changed, from glory to glory, into My image. Let My holiness cascade over you and rise up within you. Walk in the purity of Who I am in you.

Yes, it is a time to seek Me, and it is a time to know My heart. It is a time to live and move upon the earth as I would, if I were physically on the earth today. I am calling you to reflect My nature and My ways in your everyday life. To do that, you MUST KNOW Me better! You need to draw closer. You need to receive the very essence of Who I am into your life today. You need to be prepared to bring in the harvest, for the time is short. Walk intimately with Me day by day, and see the wonders that I will accomplish through you. This is a time when the world will see that I am Who I say I am!

Declare His glory among the nations, His wonders among all peoples. For the Lord is great and greatly to be praised.
I Chronicles 16:24-25a

27 MAY

REFLECTING MY TRUTH BRINGS GLORY

It is time for My church to burn with the fire of My power. It is time for you who are called by My name to rise up strong, blazing with the wonder of My light and My glory, at work within and through you. Go into the cities, go into the schools, go into the workplaces and go into the rural farm areas. Go wherever I send you, and open your mouth to speak. As you speak, the fire of My truth will come forth, bringing freedom and liberty. And My deliverance will blow across this land.

Be prepared to let Me be Me in you. Do not hold back. Allow Me to be Me through you as I sweep over the church, bringing a melting away of those things that are not of Me. As My church is melted and molded into My image, reflecting the truth of Who I am, My glory will fill the earth as the waters cover the sea.

But we are bound to give thanks to God always for you, brethren beloved by the Lord, because God from the beginning chose you for salvation through sanctification by the Spirit and belief in the truth, to which He called you by our gospel, for the obtaining of the glory of our Lord Jesus Christ.
II Thessalonians 2:13-14

28 MAY

YOU ARE STRONG – A MIGHTY WARRIOR!

I made you strong – a mighty warrior! I placed within you the depth of My love, the height of My love, the length and width of My love. I placed within you a strength that can withstand all that comes against you. I placed within you a strength that can turn every challenge into a possibility. I placed within you a compassion that can feel any and everything that others are going through. I placed within you a discernment that will reach out and reveal truth to those that are walking in deception.

You are mine, and I am yours! Never – I say never – doubt My love and provision for you! I made you to be much, much more than you can even imagine. Walk in the strength and courage that I have placed within you! Walk in the glory of Christ in you!

Have I not commanded you? Be strong and of good
courage; do not be afraid, nor be dismayed, for the Lord
your God is with you wherever you go.
Joshua 1:9

29 MAY

SEEK ME UNTIL YOU FIND ME

Come away, My beloved, and seek Me with every ounce of your being. Seek Me until you find Me. Run after Me, and do not give up! Wait upon Me! Let Me show you the wonders of Who I am! I long to show you and disclose to you what I am doing in your life and in the life of the church. I am preparing you for that great and glorious day that is ahead!

Yes, I am coming soon to gather My family to Myself. I am coming to reveal Myself to a church that has forgotten what it means to truly worship Me – a church that no longer knows Who I am! I long to reveal Myself in all My glory, and all My majesty and splendor. I long for My church to see, know and understand My holiness, purity, wisdom, strength, compassion, mercy and grace. I hold out My hands, My heart and all My being for My children to receive the wonder and the glory of Who I am! Reach out, receive, live and move, and have your being in Me!

But from there you will seek the Lord your God, and you will find Him if you seek Him with all your heart and with all your soul.
Deuteronomy 4:29

30 MAY

CAN YOU HEAR ME SINGING?

Wait upon Me! Sacrifice your time to Me. Give up things that seem important to you to spend time with Me. Listen, hear and commune with Me! I am your Father, your Papa and your Daddy. Come sit on My lap, and lay your head on My shoulder. I love to hold you in My arms and sing to you. Can you hear Me singing to you?

I sing songs of love, encouragement, comfort, strength and healing! I whisper in your ear the mysteries of the ages. I whisper to you about the span of My love! I whisper to you about what is on My heart! I whisper to you about things that are ahead, and what I have been preparing you to do by My Spirit in being a part of furthering My Kingdom on earth. Come, beloved child. Release the things of the world, and listen, hear and commune with Me! I am waiting on you!

The Lord your God in your midst, the Mighty One, will save; He will rejoice over you with gladness, He will quiet you with His love, He will rejoice over you with singing.
Zephaniah 3:17

31 MAY

OVERCOMING ALL THINGS

Stand strong in the might of My power. Having done all, stand! Trust Me with My truth of My power. Having done all, stand! Trust Me with My truth of what I have promised you. Do not sway from My truth that I have spoken to you. Live, day-by-day, believing that I am and I will do that which I have promised. Keep your focus on My word, and stay in My presence! As you stay focused on Me, you will find that fear, doubt, worry and unbelief will fade away. You will find joy and peace rising up strong within you. You will find that those difficulties surrounding you will not be suffocating you any longer.

You will walk and live, knowing that I am more than enough to overcome all things. You will bask in the wonder of My everlasting love as I reveal more and more of Myself to you. Wait on Me, speak to Me, and know the joy and contentment of a deeper and deeper knowledge of Me that comes with experiencing My manifest presence.

These things I have spoken to you, that in Me you may have
peace. In the world you will have tribulation; but be of
good cheer, I have overcome the world.
John 16:33

JUNE

1   JUNE

HEAVEN TO EARTH

Speak and continue to speak of My goodness, My glory and My grace. Share with the people that I will bring across your path that I AM is waiting for them to come – to come closer and closer – for I want to reveal Myself, in the fullness of Who I am, to them. I am holding out the knowledge of the mystery of Almighty God, Who chooses to come and dwell within them.

My love is so massive that I can and I will provide all that they need for every area of life. I hold out My *Zoë* life to them. I hold out life more abundant, so that they can experience Who I am. I choose to live within each of My children. I choose to live through each of My children. Take hold of My gift of Myself, and experience heaven on earth! Share heaven on earth with all!

So He said to them, "When you pray, say: our Father in heaven, hallowed be Your name. Your kingdom come, Your will be done on earth as it is in heaven."
Luke 11:2

2 JUNE

KNOWING THE LOVE AND PRESENCE OF GOD

You are My beloved, and I love you! You bring Me pleasure, and I want you to know that strength is coming. Purpose is also coming. I am pouring out Myself upon you with freshness and newness. It is time for strength, and it is time for majesty – experiencing and knowing My majesty! It is time for the fulfillment of destiny. You, My beloved, are fulfilling the destiny that I have placed before you. This is your time, for all in the past was to prepare you for this time. I am placing My hand upon your head. My anointing is on you! I am taking you in My arms and hugging you, as you sit on My lap.

Take hold of the picture that I am painting for you with My words. I am cheering you on, and I am letting you know that I am with you every step of the way. Remember, Christ in you is truly the hope of Glory! Get ready! It has only just begun!

Serve the Lord with gladness; come before His presence with singing. Know that the Lord, He is God; it is He who has made us and not we ourselves.
Psalm 100:2-3

3 JUNE

REST AND REJOICE

Rest! Let rest flow through you! Let My rest abide within you, and trust Me in all things. Trust Me with your family, your loved ones, your friends and with everything for which you have concern. I am working and moving in each of their lives as you pray for them and trust Me with them! I am well able to take them to the place that will lead to their destiny.

Now is the time of preparation, and now is the time to watch and see what I will do, and what I will accomplish through them. Get ready to rejoice, and begin to rejoice even now. Praise Me before you know and see what I am doing. Rejoice with great fervor, for this is the time for My purpose and My will to come forth with great power! And rejoice again when you see the answers to your prayers in the lives of your loved ones and those that mean so much to you. Remember to rejoice before you see the answer, and then rejoice again when the answer comes!

Be glad in the Lord and rejoice, you righteous;
and shout for joy, all you upright in heart!
Psalm 32:11

4 JUNE

PREPARE THE WAY

My beloved, I am coming soon! Your portion is to prepare the way of My coming. The portion of the Church is to prepare the way of My coming. Just as I used a young Jewish woman for My first coming, I am using My precious ones, those who are a part of the Body of Christ, to prepare the way of My second coming!

Listen, hear and obey! Be prepared to move when I say move, be prepared to speak when I say speak, be prepared to listen when I say listen. Be prepared to be silent when I say be silent! I trust you! You please Me and yes, you make me smile. I hold out all that I am to you, precious one, My beloved. Walk in cadence with My sound and with My beat. Walk, and prepare the way! My hand is upon you, and My words are in your mouth. Go forth in the power of My Spirit – leaning on Me – and you will see Me in all My splendor!

The voice of one crying in the wilderness; "Prepare the way of the Lord; make straight in the desert a highway for our God. Every valley shall be exalted and every mountain and hill brought low; the crooked places shall be made straight and the rough places smooth; the glory of the Lord shall be revealed, and all flesh shall see it together; for the mouth of the Lord has spoken."
Isaiah 40:3-5

5   JUNE

HEAVENLY SOUND

Expect to hear a heavenly sound. Expect to hear a heavenly sound come forth from My church, in unison with the sound coming from heaven. As the church begins to reverberate with this heavenly sound, you will begin to see the flow of revival. My glory will come upon My church in such a way that the world will begin to "hear." Revival will sweep across this land and the nations of the world. The light – My light – will shine so brightly in the midst of darkness that darkness will not have any choice but to flee. My glory, the knowledge of My glory, will cover the earth.

Difficulty will come in a major way, but difficulty will make way for the presence of the Lord to be sought and to be received. My presence will bring joy unspeakable, peace, love, kindness, patience and all of the fruit of the Spirit in a far greater way than the world has ever seen. Be prepared to see and experience such a move of My Spirit that all will see and know that truly the Spirit of the Lord is alive in the world today! The knowledge of the glory of the Lord will cover the earth!

And suddenly there came a sound from heaven, as of a rushing mighty wind, and it filled the whole house where they were sitting.
Acts 2:2

6   JUNE

RUNNING THE RACE

Come and sit on My lap, and I will share with you. Listen, hear, and then share with others. I choose to share with you the magnitude of My calling upon the Church at this time. I am calling My people to a place of listening, a place of hearing and a place of spreading My truth to the masses! I am sending laborers into the fields of harvest! This is a time to be prepared to bring in the harvest and to disciple the harvest.

This is a time of great acceleration! This is a time when My babes in Christ will grow and learn with great acceleration! My babes will go out and begin to bring in more harvest! There will be a great ripple effect, and it will happen so quickly that many will wonder, "How could this have happened?" It will happen, because My hand is upon the Church. I am preparing My Church for such a time as this! Get ready. I say, "Get ready!" This is a time to run! Run into the fields, and see the great harvest come in!

Therefore we also, since we are surrounded by so great a cloud of witnesses, let us lay aside every weight, and the sin which so easily ensnares us, and let us run with endurance the race that is set before us, looking unto Jesus, the author and finisher of our faith.
Hebrews 12:1-2a

7   JUNE

NEW SEASON

This is a new season in so many respects! Be prepared to move with Me! Be prepared to move in new ways. Set aside the old, for this is a new day, a new season. Take hold of Me! Listen, hear and only do those things you see Me doing. Only say the things you hear Me saying!

This is My time to live and move through you! This is your time to live and move, and have your being in Me! This time in the natural is difficult. But this time living, moving and having your being in Me is glorious! You will see and experience My glory in amazing and awesome ways! Be prepared! Be prepared to move in this new season – a time when My glory will cover you and will cover the earth with My fullness!

Behold, the former things have come to pass, and new things I declare; before they spring forth I tell you of them.
Isaiah 42:9

Then He who sat on the throne said, "Behold, I make all things new." And He said to me, "Write for these words are true and faithful."
Revelation 21:5

8   JUNE

WALK INTO MY LIGHT

Take My hand, and walk with Me. Walk into the light. Walk into My light. As you enter deeper and deeper into My light, you will see with a vision that cannot be explained, except by Me. You will see as I see! You will express as I express! Walk into My light, and I will reveal more and more of Myself to you. You need more of Me! Ask Me for more, and bask in the glory and light of My presence! As more of Me is revealed to you, and as you receive more and more of Myself, you will shine forth so brilliantly that many lives will be changed.

My light will illumine your understanding. You will grow and increase in My wisdom. Reach out for Me! Cry out to Me for more and more of Me, and I will answer! Wait upon Me, listen to Me and expect Me to respond to your cry!

But if we walk in the light as He is in the light, we have
fellowship with one another, and the blood of Jesus Christ
His Son cleanses us from all sin.
I John 1:7

9   JUNE

WAIT WITH AN EXPECTANCY

During those times when you do not know what to do, what direction to take or what choice to make, wait upon Me! Wait with an expectancy that I will show you, reveal to you, and guide and direct you. Think on this: I am your heavenly Father, and I live in a realm that is beyond your comprehension. My love for you is so massive, My grace that I hold out to you is so immense, and My peace is so huge that there are no words on earth to describe it. I will always be with you, holding you in My arms, whispering in your ear and telling you to go in the direction that I have placed before you.

Hold on to Me, cling to Me and expect My guidance and direction in your life, and you shall receive. I have much more to show you, and there is so much to reveal to you. All you need to do is wait upon Me, with listening ears, and then respond as I pour out My truth upon you!

My soul, wait silently for God alone, for my expectation is from Him. He only is my rock and my salvation; He is my defense; I shall not be moved.
Psalm 62:5-6

10 JUNE

I STAND AT THE DOOR AND KNOCK

Knock, knock, knock. Do you hear Me knocking on the door of your heart? I knock on the door of the hearts of those that have never committed their lives to Me, but I also knock on the door of My people's hearts to awaken them to My presence. I am seeking to make Myself, My ways, and My plan and purpose for each of their lives known to them. I am knocking, desiring to come and fellowship in every area of their lives.

Listen and hear the knocking on the door of your heart, for I have much to share with you. This is the time to open your heart to the fullness of Who I am and who I desire to be in your life!

Behold, I stand at the door and knock. If anyone hears My voice and opens the door, I will come in to him and dine with him, and he with Me. To him who overcomes I will grant to sit with Me on My throne, as I also overcame and sat down with My Father on His throne.
Revelation 3:20-21

11 JUNE

YOUR LATTER SHALL BE GREATER THAN YOUR FORMER

You think that you have been around for a while and what I have for you to do is diminishing, but you are not seeing as I see. Your latter shall be better than your former. The time is now for you to burst forth with My glory. Arise and shine, for this is your time to reach out in ways you have never dreamed. There is goodness, grace and glory ahead for you.

You have only just begun. There is an acceleration of all that I have placed within you. Be prepared to move with fervor and zeal. Be prepared to move with passion for My plan and My purpose. Seek My will in all that you do, and enter into a greater rest in Me than you have ever known, as you move ahead in great acceleration. Much will be accomplished for My kingdom, and it will seem as if there has been no effort at all, because My Spirit will accomplish it through you.

"The glory of this latter temple shall be greater than the former," says the Lord of hosts. "And in this place I will give peace," says the Lord of hosts.
Haggai 2:9

12 JUNE

MY COUNTENANCE FILLED WITH MY GLORY

As My presence fills and covers you, receive the fullness of My grace. Let My love wash over you and wash away every hurt, every wound and all grief and sorrow. Look up! Look up into My face, and let My countenance that is filled with My glory transform you. I am here to be everything that you need. I am here to love you into My image.

I love you so much, and I long for you to receive all that I hold out to you. Receive My grace and My goodness; receive the very essence of Who I am. Receive My holiness, My strength, My might and My power. Receive My everlasting compassion, mercy and peace. Receive the fullness of My joy as you come to know Me in all that I am!

The Lord bless you and keep you; the Lord make His face shine upon you, and be gracious to you; the Lord lift up His countenance upon you, and give you peace.
Numbers 6:24-26

But we all with unveiled face, beholding as in a mirror the glory of the Lord, are being transformed into the same image from glory to glory, just as by the Spirit of the Lord.
II Corinthians 3:18

13 JUNE

MY PLACE IN YOU AND YOUR PLACE IN ME!

Come before Me with thanksgiving and praise! Enter into My Holy of Holies, and meet with Me face-to-face. Know Me in all My righteousness, My holiness, My justice, and My grace, glory and goodness. Know My mercy and compassion as you seek Me with greater intentionality than ever before. You know you need Me and only that which is of Me.

Do not let the things of the world distract you from placing Me first place in every area of your life. Know Me in all My fullness, and bask in the wonder and glory of My presence, which will sweep over you and within you as you accept your place in Me, and receive My place in you.

I do not pray for these alone, but also for those who will believe in Me through their word; that they all may be one, as You, Father, are in Me, and I in You; that the world may believe that You sent Me. And the glory which You gave Me I have given them, that they may be one just as We are one: I in them, and You in Me; that they may be made perfect in one, and that the world may know that You have sent Me, and have loved them as You have loved Me.
John 17:20-23

14 JUNE

BY MY SPIRIT!

I have come that you might have life more abundant! What is life more abundant? It is My *Zoë* life – the very life of God pulsating through you! It is living life by My Spirit so that there are no dull moments or times – only life brimming over with the power, love, compassion, mercy, grace, holiness and strength of God. I could go on and on, but you get the picture.

Abundant life is Me living My life through you. It is Me transforming you as you draw into that "holy place" with Me. It is you seeing everything around you and everyone around you through My eyes! It is you finding what it means to let My Spirit have full reign in your life. You will begin to see yourself responding in difficult situations as I would. You will begin to see yourself loving others (even the unlovely) through My eyes. You will see and understand what it means to reflect Who I am on the planet earth, as you draw closer and closer to Me by My Spirit!

If we live in the Spirit, let us also walk in the Spirit.
Galatians 5:25

Now the Lord is the Spirit; and where the Spirit of the Lord is,
there is liberty. But we all, with unveiled face, beholding as in a
mirror the glory of the Lord, are being transformed into the same
image from glory to glory just as by the Spirit of the Lord.
II Corinthians 3:17-18

15 JUNE

IT IS GOOD!

I am here to listen to you, and I want you to have the freedom to share your heart with Me. I am your creator. I made you and formed you. I breathed life into you, and then I looked at My creation and said, "It is good!" You are good, because I made you to be good! I am continuing to mold and shape you as you release yourself to Me. Just as I am here to listen to your heart, I want you to listen to My heart. As I share My heart with you, the process of molding and shaping continues. It is hearing and knowing My heart that transforms and changes you.

Yield yourself to Me, and watch with expectation to see what beautiful creation is coming forth. It is My joy to create a tiny baby, but it is also My joy to see the baby grow up, becoming a beautiful creation that has been shaped and molded by Me until finally complete. I want you to get a glimpse of the beauty that is ahead for you as you yield yourself to Me, and allow Me the joy of shaping and molding you into My beautiful creation!

So God created man in His own image; in the image of God He created him; male and female He created them. . .Then God saw everything that He had made, and indeed it was very good. So the evening and the morning were the sixth day.
Genesis 1:27, 31

16 JUNE

ENTER THE HOLY OF HOLIES

Take hold of My hand, and let Me guide you into a walk, a place of holiness. Do not settle for coming into My outer court, or even My inner court. Choose to come all the way into My Holy of Holies. Come into the place that I have planned for you. Yes, I have planned before you were ever born a place for you in My Holy of Holies – a place that only the high priest could come. But now that the veil is torn, that place is open for you, My beloved, and for all My believers who will come.

This is a place where you will hear My heartbeat. This is a place where you will see the glory of My countenance. And as you see the radiance of My light shining upon you, you will begin to see, to understand and to grow into the place that you are in awe of who I am! You will see and understand a greater depth of Who I am, and your life will be transformed. Each time you come into My presence, into the Holy of Holies, you will continue to be transformed! My glory and My radiance will shine forth from you to those around you. That is My plan and My purpose for My precious ones, for all that believe on the name of Jesus! Share the wonder of My Holy of Holies with others, so they will know the fullness of Who I am.

Therefore, brethren, having boldness to enter
the Holiest by the blood of Jesus.
Hebrews 10:19

17 JUNE

THE TRUTH OF LIFE ABUNDANT!

I am Life! All life comes from Me. There are those that believe they are living. Yes, they are breathing, but they have no concept of life! Breathing, going to work, school, whatever fills your day is not living. Knowing Me is living life abundantly! I am revealing Myself with freshness to My body of believers so they can see the truth of Life – Life more abundant!

I am pouring out My *Zoë* life upon My precious ones so they can reflect Me – truly Who I am – to the world! It is time for My life to spring forth with great fervor within My believers. I am calling My church to be flooded with My life and go forth!

Blessed be the God and Father of our Lord Jesus Christ, who according to His abundant mercy has begotten us again to a living hope through the resurrection of Jesus Christ from the dead, to an inheritance incorruptible and undefiled and that does not fade away, reserved in heaven for you.
I Peter 1:3-4

The thief does not come except to steal, and to kill, and to destroy. I have come that they may have life, and that they may have it more abundantly.
John 10:10

18 JUNE

I AM THE RESTORER

Do you feel as if everything has passed you by? Are you feeling lonely, desperate, discouraged and in despair? I am telling you now to take heart, for I am the Restorer! I have come to set you free, and I have come to restore to you all that has been taken from you.

Listen! You are My beloved, and I bring hope and joy to you. Right now, you feel as if there is nothing that can help. Oh, you know that I am able, but you think I will not help you. Do you not know that I love you with an everlasting love, and I will never let you down?

Take hold of My hand, and walk with Me. Listen with your spiritual ears, and hear My small, still voice within you. I have words of truth if you will only listen! I have been speaking to you in many ways, but you must take time to be still before Me and listen. I have words of life, peace, comfort and guidance. This is your time to make time for Me! Listen, hear and rejoice!

He restores my soul; He leads me in the paths
of righteousness for His name's sake.
Psalm 23:3

Restore us, O God; cause Your face
to shine, and we shall be saved!
Psalm 80:3

19 JUNE

THE GREATEST STRENGTH
OF ALL – MEEKNESS!

You have heard it said, "The meek shall inherit the earth," and you have wondered, who are the meek? What does it mean to be meek? I thought it would take strength to inherit the earth. Meekness is strength! Meekness is My kind of strength – a strength that is not afraid to show love, compassion, caring and grace. Meekness is winning the heart of someone with kindness, goodness, truth, and expressing the integrity of your God in all that you say and do!

Look at the life of Jesus, and you will see true strength, true meekness – being willing to turn the other cheek and being willing to lay down His life for all. Look at how He lovingly and graciously helped the woman at the well face her iniquity in such a way that her life was transformed. I say to you today, "If you, My beloved, would reach out to others with the heart of meekness, you would see multitudes running into the arms of Jesus!" Seek Me with your whole heart, and discover the greatest strength of all –Meekness!

Come to Me, all you who labor and are heavy laden, and I will give you rest. Take My yoke upon you and learn from Me, for I am gentle and lowly in heart, and you will find rest for your souls. For My yoke is easy and My burden is light.
Matthew 11:28-30

20 JUNE

SACRIFICE OF JOY

You might ask, "How can I have joy in the midst of difficulties and in the direst of circumstances?" And I would say to you, "It takes an act of sacrifice." When you make a sacrifice of lifting your voice and beginning to praise Me when you do not feel like praising, when you are in the midst of despair, you will find that joy will begin to bubble up within you. As you turn your eyes upon Me and offer a sacrifice of praise, your whole perspective will begin to change.

Trust Me, even as the disciples trusted Me when they were being persecuted for spreading the truth. They shook the dust off their feet and were filled with joy. I ask you to praise Me in these difficult times and times of despair, because I know what will happen to your heart. As you focus on Me, you will find your heart being renewed by the glory of My presence. In My presence, there is fullness of joy because you are being transformed to have My heart. You begin to think as I think, act as I act and speak as I speak. I am calling you to know the fullness of joy that comes from My presence in whatever circumstance you find yourself.

And now my head shall be lifted up above my enemies all around me; therefore I will offer sacrifices of joy in His tabernacle; I will sing, yes, I will sing praises to the Lord.
Psalm 27:6

21 JUNE

KNOW MY TRUTH

Seek after My truth, for My truth brings freedom and light into your life. My truth is a treasure, and you need to choose truth. Each day, you are faced with many choices. You can choose My truth, or you can choose the way of the world, which is to accept a lie and be deceived. Ah, I hear you asking, "How do I know truth?"

Look to Jesus, for grace and truth come through Jesus. Study the life of Jesus. Study the words of Jesus, and you will find light and truth rising up within you. You will begin to know and understand what choices to make in your daily walk. Jesus came to earth to reflect My nature and My truth. My word is truth, and Jesus came in the flesh as the Word of God to reveal to the world My truth. My truth will set you free. My truth will bring light and illumination into your life. Abide in My word, and you will know My truth!

If you abide in My word, you are My disciples indeed. And you shall know the truth, and the truth shall make you free.
John 8:31-32

22 JUNE

THE TESTING OF YOUR FAITH
PRODUCES PATIENCE

My beloved, listen to Me as I share something with you that will bring great joy and rest to you. Many laughingly say, "I will not pray for patience." If they do, they know that they will have opportunities in their lives to develop patience. Most do not like to go through what it takes to develop patience. But, if you and My people could understand the immense benefits of growing in patience, all of you would welcome every opportunity with total trust in Me!

When the difficulties come, the testing of your faith produces patience. Trusting Me in all things, even the most difficult, helps faith to grow in your life. Patience comes forth with greater measure. The result of a greater measure of patience is joy and rest! You will find that you experience less stress, and you will become aware of greater peace as you determine not to struggle with issues, but to place your trust in Me. Do not fight and struggle; place your hands in My hands, your heart and your mind in Me, and trust Me!

My brethren, count if all joy when you fall into various trials,
knowing that the testing of your faith produces patience. But
let patience have its perfect work, that you may be perfect and
complete, lacking nothing.
James 1:2-4

23 JUNE

HOPE COMES FROM ME!

When you look at the world around you today, you see a lot of hopelessness. For those who do not know Me and for those that continue to live according to the world's standards, it is impossible to have hope. Hope comes from Me! When you are going through the hardest thing you have ever been through, when you are in the depths of despair, and when there seems to be nowhere to turn or no one who can help you, look again! I Am the One that you need, the One that is always ready and willing to take you in My arms and pour out My grace and My love upon you, and showing you the way!

Seek Me and seek My believers – those that know Me, trust Me and walk with Me. You will find the comfort and hope for which you are desperate. Sometimes it takes desperation to bring you to your knees, but when you turn to Me, you will find strength and hope. Your hope is in Jesus! Your hope is in the promise that the Holy Spirit is alive at work in the world today and in you, as you yield yourself to Him!

Now may the God of hope fill you with all joy and
peace in believing, that you may abound in hope by
the power of the Holy Spirit.
Romans 15:13

24 JUNE

STRENGTH OF MY MAJESTY!

Sing of My majesty. Shout from the rooftops of the glorious things that I have done. Do not hold back – afraid of what people will think. They are hungry and thirsty to know of My might, My power and the strength of My Majesty! Tell them to listen for My sound, to listen as I thunder from Heaven, for I will shout to them the wonders of Who I am and Who I want to be in their lives. Tell them of the wonder of Who I am in your life. Share My word with them, for they are eager to hear.

They need to know there is an answer for all that is going on in their lives, and they need to know there is an answer for the problems in the world today. They need to know of My grace and love, but they also need to know of My strength, power and might. Tell them about ALMIGHTY God! Share testimonies of what I have done in your life, and in the lives of your family and friends. Tell them of My majestic acts that I have been doing down through the ages and even today – especially today!

Give unto the Lord, O you mighty ones, give unto the Lord glory and strength. . . . The voice of the Lord is over the waters; the God of glory thunders; the Lord is over many waters. The voice of the Lord is powerful; the voice of the Lord is full of majesty.
Psalm 29:1,3-4

25 JUNE

LIGHT OF LIFE!

What a blessing My light is to those that will receive! There is an answer for the darkness that permeates the world, and that answer is the light of God! Why is light the answer? Because light comes from Me, and I am called the Word. In Me is life, and My life brings light into those that will reach out and receive. People can say they are alive because they are breathing, but it is My life that brings light into My precious ones, making them truly alive.

There are many walking through life without any concept of My light that comes from My life. These are the ones that I am sending you forth to reach, with My light shining so brightly in you that they will see, and long for the One Who brings the light of life! Do not hold back, but go wherever I send you! Take My life and My light that are within you, and share My word with them. You will be amazed at their response because you are going in obedience to Me, with My anointing that comes with walking in My life and light!

In the beginning was the Word. . . In Him was life,
and the life was the light of men.
John 1:1a,4

The entrance of Your words gives light; it gives
understanding to the simple. . . Make Your face shine upon
Your servant, and teach me Your statutes.
Psalm 119:130,135

26 JUNE

I AM YOUR WARRIOR!

Do you not know that the battle is Mine? When you are facing fierce trials and tribulations, I am your Warrior! I will fight your battles; all that you have to do is to trust Me! Those sound like simple words: "trust Me." Living in the world as you do, trusting is not always easy. You constantly see things around you that try to steal trust away.

This is a time to intentionally decide to renew your mind. You may say, "But how do I renew my mind?" This is accomplished by staying focused on Me and My word. Remember, the battle is mine, but you must focus on My ability, My will and My desire to fight your battles for you. You will find evidence all through the scriptures, telling you I can, I will and I want to set you free. I am your Warrior. What better warrior could you have? Trust Me, and let Me fight your battles for you.

Then all this assembly shall know that the Lord does not
save with sword and spear; for the battle is the Lord's, and
He will give you into our hands.
I Samuel 17:47

Who is this King of glory? The Lord strong
and mighty, the Lord mighty in battle.
Psalm 24:8

27 JUNE

HONOR COMES TO THE HUMBLE

It is the way of the world to walk in pride and selfishness – to place yourself first. I say to you today that the way of the world is not My way. As you humble yourself before Me and before others, you will see your life changing. It is My desire to bring honor to you, but honor can only come to the humble. The more that you seek My face and come to know Me and My ways, you will find yourself growing in humility and in all of My attributes. You cannot make this happen. It only happens through Me as you come to know Me better.

Come and let Me shine the light of My glory upon you. You will see My grace, goodness, kindness, meekness, love and humility – as well as My might, strength, majesty and power. Knowing Me – experiencing Me – is life changing! Come before Me, seeking to know My humility, and see what glorious changes begin to happen in your life.

"Because your heart was tender, and you humbled yourself
before God when you heard His words against this place
and against its inhabitants, and you humbled yourself
before Me, and you tore your clothes and wept before Me, I
also have heard you," says the Lord.
II Chronicles 34:27

The fear of the Lord is the instruction of wisdom,
and before honor is humility.
Proverbs 15:33

28 JUNE

THE JOY OF A LIFE FILLED WITH PEACE

Seek after peace! Sow peace! Do not let the cares of the world slip in and choke out the joy of a life filled with peace. Peace brings joy, contentment and righteousness. I say to you to pursue peace with all that is within you. As peace rises up in you, you will be able to be an example to others of the joy-filled life that comes from being a peaceful person. You will be sowing peace wherever you go.

What does the world need? The world needs My peace being lived out in the lives of My people. When the world sees My peace through you, they will begin to understand that peace cannot come through governments, but only from Me! I am the author of peace, and only those who love Me and live for Me will be able to show the world what the world wants to see – how to live with the kind of peace that surpasses all understanding! Be one of My own that chooses to grow in a daily walk of peace, so that you will shine forth the glory of Who I am wherever you go.

Deceit is in the heart of those who devise evil,
but counselors of peace have joy.
Proverbs 12:20

Now the fruit of righteousness is sown in peace
by those who make peace.
James 3:18

29 JUNE

MY WISDOM POURED OUT WITHIN YOU!

I am pouring out My wisdom upon you – upon My church. I am bringing forth knowledge and understanding that has been hidden down though the ages. Get ready to receive, to share and to rejoice, as perception and revelation break forth as waters when the flood-gates are opened. It is time for My people to take hold of My truth and take My truth to the masses. There is a hunger within the world to know truth, and there is only one truth – Jesus Christ!

My wisdom poured out upon you and upon My believers will release My truth across this land and the nations of the world with new fervor, with a greater urgency and in demonstration of My power at work within My people. Get ready to move out as I give the word. Watch and listen for the sound of rushing waters, for once My flood of living waters begins to strongly flow, you will see the change. You will experience joy unspeakable, and you will know that I Am has spoken!

To the intent that now the manifold wisdom of God might be made known by the church to the principalities and powers in the heavenly places.
Ephesians 3:10

For the Lord gives wisdom; from his mouth come knowledge and understanding.
Proverbs 2:6

30 JUNE

HEAVENLY CALLING!

Do you understand your heavenly calling? I have come to dwell within you! You are mine, and I am yours! I created this world, and I created you to live in this world. I did not create you to succumb and give in to the ways of the world. I created you to know Me, to grow in your understanding of Me, and to see your daily circumstances through My eyes – My perspective. As you draw closer and closer to Me, you begin to understand My perspective. You begin to not only see the circumstances around you through My eyes, but you begin to see yourself through My eyes – My heavenly perspective!

You see that I made you beautiful in My eyes. You see that I created you, and placed gifting within you to enable you to fulfill the destiny that I chose for you. You begin to realize that you truly can do all things through Me, and you begin to see others through My eyes. This, My beloved, is your heavenly calling: to walk, live and be on earth who I created you to be, reflecting My image as you grow in your understanding of My heavenly calling upon you!

Therefore, holy brethren, partakers of the heavenly calling, consider the Apostle and High Priest of our confession, Christ Jesus.
Hebrews 3:1

And as we have borne the image of the man of dust, we shall also bear the image of the heavenly Man.
I Corinthians 15:49

JULY

1   JULY

THE SPLENDOR OF MY MAJESTY

Come before Me in the splendor of My Majesty. As I sit upon My throne and look out at the multitude that is called by My name, I long for more. It is My desire that My family would grow to be an immense family so that it is as numerous as the stars in the sky. I promised Abraham that his descendants would be as numerous as the stars. My family is made up of Abraham's descendants, both Jew and Gentile, who choose to believe that I am Who I say I am, and I will do what I say I will do!

Many, even multitudes, have come into My family over the ages, but there are so many more yet to come! Tell of the majesty of My splendor that awaits them as they choose to give their hearts to Me. One day, when you are standing before My throne, you will be amazed to see the glory, the majesty and the splendor of My eternal dwelling place that I also created for you, and for all who have chosen to be called by My name.

I will meditate on the glorious splendor of Your majesty,
and on Your wondrous works.
Psalm 145:5

Even now men cannot look at the light when it is bright in the skies, when the wind has passed and cleared them. He comes from the north as golden splendor; with God is awesome majesty.
Job 37:21-22

2   JULY

LIVE BY THE POWER OF GOD

My power exists for you! Power is within Me, and power surrounds Me. I am Power, and I choose to use My power to bring about good in and through you and all My believers. I hold out My power to you, for I want you to live with My power coming forth in a way that will bring the hearts filled with darkness into My light.

There are those that will only be swayed by strength and power, and I want them to see and understand My power. But I also want them to understand submission, being yielded, gentleness and meekness. As you and all of My believers walk and live by My power, the world will see and know that power was never meant for darkness and destruction. My power is meant to draw those that will come into the arms of Jesus! My power is meant to turn hearts to the light and life that comes from following Me!

Since you seek a proof of Christ speaking in me, who is not weak toward you, but mighty in you. For though He was crucified in weakness, yet He lives by the power of God.
II Corinthians 13:3-4

And my speech and my preaching were not with persuasive words of human wisdom, but in demonstration of the Spirit and of power, that your faith should not be in the wisdom of men but in the power of God.
I Corinthians 2:4-5

3   JULY

THE GLORIOUS MAJESTY OF MY KINGDOM

Take hold of the glorious wonder of Who I am! I am here for you, and I am drawing you into a deeper walk with Me. As you let go of the things of the world, you will find the glorious truth of living a life that is filled with the joy of a deep, intimate walk with Me. I love to walk and talk with you – sharing Myself with you. As you know Me better, as you hear My truth and as you open up and share with Me from your heart, you will find that you are desiring more and more of Me. You will lose the desire to follow after the things of the world. Move into that glorious place with Me, where you experience My presence and power in such a way that you wonder why you have not spent more time with Me in the past. You have heard it said that My kingdom is glorious and full of majesty. Move into that place where you experience the glorious Majesty of My Kingdom!

To make known to the sons of men His mighty acts, and the
glorious majesty of His Kingdom.
Psalm 145:12

Strengthened with all might, according to His glorious power, for
all patience and longsuffering with joy.
Colossians 1:11

4   JULY

BEAUTY OF HOLINESS

Look through My eyes, and you will see true beauty. Beauty comes from the heart of someone who seeks righteousness and holiness. If you want to see magnificence of beauty, look at My Son, Jesus.

While Jesus walked this earth, He loved with a love that cannot be equaled by anyone else. He saw each person He was with through the eyes of agape love. He did not criticize or complain. He was continually seeing those around Him, through eyes that understood who that person was created to be, and He knew how to encourage and admonish, in order to draw that person into a place of beginning to understand he was created for a purpose. He helped those around Him to begin to see themselves through My eyes – the eyes of love. Each life He touched went on to become a life surrendered to the King of kings and Lord of lords!

Give unto the Lord, O you mighty ones, give unto the Lord glory
and strength. Give unto the Lord the glory due to His name;
worship the Lord in the beauty of holiness.
Psalm 29:1-2

5 **JULY**

FAITHFUL AND TRUE

There is One Who is faithful, and I am called Faithful and True! I, the faithful One, came to give you life – the kind of life that is continually growing in faith, that is a gift from Me! Jesus is your example, teacher and mentor of what it is like to live a life filled with faith. You were given a measure of faith when you were born again into the Kingdom of God. The more you read My word and then apply the truths within My word to your everyday life, the more faith will grow within you. Every time that you believe My word – My promise to you – your faith will grow to another level.

As a human being, it is natural for you to believe what everyone around you is saying. It is much easier to believe the world's ways, but it is immensely rewarding to not walk by sight, but to walk in faith! I reward those who follow Me, believe Me and walk in faith! Listen to Me, for I am faithful and true, and I am everlasting!

Now I saw heaven opened, and behold, a white horse. And
He who sat on him was called Faithful and True, and in
righteousness He judges and makes war.
Revelation 19:11

For we walk by faith, not by sight.
II Corinthians 5:7

6 JULY

THE TREASURE OF KNOWLEDGE

It is My desire that you abound in the treasure of My knowledge. I want you to grow in the knowledge of Who I am and what My purpose is for you. Seek after knowledge. Be enriched by knowledge, for wisdom comes alongside of knowledge. Knowledge is the fact – the truth. Wisdom is the understanding of what to do with knowledge. Make knowledge a priority in your life, and then seek after wisdom so you can put knowledge to work in your everyday life. I love to pour out My knowledge upon you, but you must read and study My word. You must listen to Me. Listen for My direction, and listen to hear, so you can understand and receive the knowledge you need to move out and live in My wisdom.

I created you to learn. Learning is an ongoing process in your walk with Me. Seek after the treasure of knowledge, and share My knowledge with those around you. Be a supplier of My knowledge to those that are hungry to know more of Me!

That their hearts may be encouraged, being knit together
in love, and attaining to all riches of the full assurance of
understanding, to the knowledge of the mystery of God,
both of the Father and of Christ, in whom are hidden all the
treasures of wisdom and knowledge.
Colossians 2:2-3

7   JULY

STRONG WITH A STEADFAST SPIRIT

I created you to be steadfast. You may wonder why I want you to be steadfast. Many of My believers and multitudes of unbelievers think that being steadfast is boring and dull, but I want to tell you that being steadfast in My truth brings faith alive within you. When faith is alive within you, you see My power at work, and that is the exact opposite of boring! If you want to live an exciting and dynamic life, you must begin with the discipline of steadfastness.

When you are steadfast about My truth, you will not be moved, but will stand firm with what you know to be true. The church today needs believers that are so abounding in My truth that they will stand immovable with confidence in My truth! I am calling My people to stand in confidence with a steadfast heart. This is not a time to give in, or be double-minded, but this is the time to be strong with a steadfast spirit and see what mighty things come forth by My hand – the hand of Almighty God!

Therefore, my beloved brethren, be steadfast, immovable,
always abounding in the work of the Lord, knowing that
your labor is not in vain in the Lord.
I Corinthians 15:58

Create in me a clean heart, O God, and renew
a steadfast spirit within me.
Psalm 51:10

8   JULY

MY FORTRESS AND MY DELIVERER

Place your trust in Me, for I am your fortress. I am a strong tower for you. No matter what the enemy brings against you, I will prevail for you. I am your strength when you feel you cannot go on. I am your deliverer when there seems to be no way. I am the One Who fights your battles.

Place your trust in Me. Take Me at My word, and believe that I will do as I say. My word is full of promises of protection for My people who trust in Me. Why would you not believe that I would do as I say? I am filled with lovingkindness, and that will never change. Reach out, take My hand and place your trust in the One Who loves you, Who will fight for you and Who will deliver you from the snare of the enemy. Rejoice, for your deliverer is ready and willing to fight for you!

The Lord is my rock and my fortress and my deliverer: my God, my strength, in whom I will trust; my shield and the horn of my salvation, my stronghold.
Psalm 18:2

My lovingkindness and my fortress, my high tower and my deliverer, my shield and the One in whom I take refuge, who subdues my people under me.
Psalm 144:2

9 JULY

BE STRONG AND COURAGEOUS

Be of good courage because I am with you, and I will never leave you. When everything else fails, I am that I am! I am your God! I will strengthen you and enable you to do all that I send you forth to do. I will enable you to be a strength and help to others around you, and to stand strong in hope filled with faith, to believe that I Am Who I say I Am. I will do all that I promise you.

Listen carefully for My truth, which is your help and your strength in difficult times. As you listen to My truth, faith rises up within you to believe that I am able to help you overcome. I say to you to be strong and courageous. Do not fear! I made My people to be courageous, and you must rely on Me to be courageous and strong in the worst of times! I am your strength, your fortress and your high tower – all that you need!

Be of good courage, and He shall strengthen your
heart, all you who hope in the Lord.
Psalm 31:24

Be strong and of good courage, do not fear nor be afraid of them;
for the Lord you God, He is the One who goes with you.
Deuteronomy 31:6

10 JULY

ENTER MY REST!

Do not struggle and strive. Do not work yourself into a frenzy, but come and enter into My rest! I want you to know the peace and rest that can only come from Me – from being in My presence and seeing the wonder of My glory! I have come to bring you into that place of total trust in Me, relinquishing your way and your plan, and letting Me bring forth My will and My plan through you.

Yes, I hear you. You are saying that it is hard to do that. It is only hard at first until you learn to let go of your way, to let go of trying to control and simply let Me be Who I choose to be in and through you. When you cease from your "works" and seek to know My way, you will find that it is not hard. It is easy as you trust Me and as you trust My Holy Spirit within you to lead, guide and bring you into a place of surrender. Remember it is not your strength or might, but it is all accomplished by My Spirit! Enjoy resting in Me and in the joy that comes from allowing Me first place in all things!

There remains therefore a rest for the people of God. For
he who has entered His rest has himself also ceased from
his works as God did from His.
Hebrews 4:9-10

11 JULY

SPEAK WITH GREAT BOLDNESS!

My people are bold! I have placed My boldness in them so that they can know it is the great I Am at work in them. Be bold as a lion when you are going through adversity. Rise up in My strength and go forth in My power, and speak My truth with boldness. Remember, you are My beloved, and you have access to My throne. Come before Me with boldness, and I will send you out in boldness to share the glory of being with Me in My throne room.

You do not need to apologize for your credentials, or lack of credentials. The people were amazed that heard Peter and John speak My truth with boldness, because they were uneducated men. It was not Peter and John, and it will not be you. It is all by My Holy Spirit, Who spoke through them and will speak through you with great boldness!

Now when they saw the boldness of Peter and John, and perceived that they were uneducated and untrained men, they marveled. And they realized that they had been with Jesus. . . And when they had prayed, the place where they were assembled together was shaken; and they were all filled with the Holy Spirit.
Acts 4:13,31

The wicked flee when no one pursues,
but the righteous are bold as a lion.
Proverbs 28:1

12 JULY

THE ZEAL OF THE LORD

Gather together, and encourage one another to stir up the same kind of zeal that comes from Me and is within you. I am zealous for you and for My people. There is a fire that comes forth from Me, and that fire is meant to stir you up and to burn within so that you will not give up when things are hard.

Come, My beloved, and learn from Me. It is My nature to be zealous, to have great passion for My plan and purpose to be fulfilled. I have great desire and fervor to see you and My family moving, living and having your being filled with My fire and passion. It is good to be zealous, and I say to you that I am calling you to let the fire of My Spirit burn within you. Do not quench My Spirit, but allow Him to draw you into a place of passion and zeal, to see all My will and plan fulfilled in your life and in the life of multitudes that are hungry for more of Me!

Of the increase of His government and peace there will be no end,
upon the throne of David and over His kingdom, to order it and
establish it with judgment and justice from that time forward, even
forever. The zeal of the Lord of hosts will perform this.
Isaiah 9:7

Then His disciples remembered that it was written,
"Zeal for Your house has eaten Me up."
John 2:17

13 JULY

I AM GOD ALMIGHTY!

I am the Lord God Almighty! There is none other. Look to Me, trust Me and abide in the shadow of My wing. When you begin to comprehend more and more the magnitude of Who I am, when you begin to understand the massive goodness, kindness and grace as well as My strength, power and magnificence, you will realize there is no need to doubt Me, for I can do all things.

I am God Almighty – was, am and always will be! Cast all your care on Me, for I am well able to take care of everything that concerns you. I hold out peace unlike anything you can imagine. There is tremendous peace in knowing that your Father in heaven can care for you and all those around you – even every care that exists in this world – and that allows you to rest in Me. Place your head upon My shoulder, and lean on Me. I have enough strength for every person on the face of the earth to lean on Me! I am Almighty! I am all might!

He who dwells in the secret place of the Most High shall abide under the shadow of the Almighty.
Psalm 91:1

They sing the song of Moses, the servant of God, and the song of the lamb, saying: 'Great and marvelous are Your works, Lord God Almighty! Just and true are Your ways, O King of the saints!
Revelation 15:3

14 JULY

THE COMFORT OF GOD

I am a God of comfort! I bring comfort to you, through My Holy Spirit, every time that you are in need. My heart is to express comfort to My people because I know when you are comforted, you will let My comfort flow forth from you to others. Seek My comfort, rest in My comfort and let the peace of My comfort surround you and dwell within you. When I bring others across your path, be ready to express My comfort to them.

It is My desire to express love, compassion, comfort and so much more to My people. You can express Who I am to those who do not know Me. The world is hungry for the comfort that I bring! Use My word to build yourself up and then to share My comfort with others, for the time draws near for the sound of the trumpet, for the dead in Christ to rise, and then for you who are alive to be caught up to meet your Lord Jesus!

For the Lord Himself will descend from heaven with a shout, with the voice of an archangel, and with the trumpet of God. And the dead in Christ will rise first. Then we who are alive and remain shall be caught up together with them in the clouds to meet the Lord in the air. And thus we shall always be with the Lord. Therefore comfort one another with these words.
I Thessalonians 4:16-18

15 JULY

SANCTIFY THEM BY YOUR TRUTH

When My Son, Jesus Christ, shed His blood for you on the cross of Calvary, the way was made for you to be sanctified. You might say, "But I am not holy!" And I would say to you that holiness begins with the cross. When you say "yes" to Jesus, you are sanctified. You then begin the process of sanctification (living in holiness) through learning My truth, through My word. As you soak in My word and begin to put My word into practice, you will see changes happening in your life. Old ways will begin to fall away. They will not have the same hold upon you they used to have.

Consume My word, and draw near to the Author of My word. Draw near to Me, and My word will begin to come alive in your heart. Seek to know Me better, even as Moses sought more and more of Me, and you will know the delight of being called aside, sanctified and truly living your life day by day, exhibiting My holiness!

Sanctify them by Your truth. Your word is truth.
John 17:17

By that will we have been sanctified through the offering of the
body of Jesus Christ once for all.
Hebrews 10:10

16 JULY

THE ROCK OF YOUR SALVATION

Come before Me with thanksgiving, and sing praises to Me. Sing to the rock of your salvation, for truly I am your Rock! No matter what comes your way, I am greater and stronger – your solid Rock!

I will never let you down, but I will always lift you up. I will encourage, strengthen, comfort and teach you. I will bring you victory as I draw you close to Me, as I reveal more and more of Myself to you, and as I show you the wonder and glory of Who I am in your life. You may think that I will do that for others, but waiver in your belief that I will do it for you. Do not waiver! Believe every word and promise that I have given you. Hold on to Me, for there is nothing that can shatter the Rock of your salvation!

"The Lord lives! Blessed be my Rock!
Let God be exalted, the Rock of my salvation!"
II Samuel 22:47

He only is my rock and salvation; He is my defense; I shall not be moved. In God is my salvation and my glory; the rock of my strength, and my refuge, is in God
Psalm 62:6-7

17 JULY

JESUS CHRIST THE MESSIAH

I came to earth the first time as a baby born in a manger. I came in a way that none expected the Messiah to come, but I came to reveal the nature of God to the world. I came to reveal humility, goodness, kindness, love, mercy, grace and so much more. I came to a world that did not want to receive Me, but some heard the truth and believed. I walked the earth as a servant to the people, and I reflected the character of God to all. Many persecuted Me, and eventually crucified Me, but I rose again and left an empty tomb!

I am coming back again, and, this time, I will be coming back as King of kings and Lord of lords. I am coming back to be recognized as Messiah, and to rule and reign in righteousness. When that day comes, be ready! Be ready to receive your Messiah, for every knee shall bow and every tongue shall confess that I am Lord!

The woman said to Him, "I know that Messiah is coming" (who is called Christ). "When He comes, He will tell us all things." Jesus said to her, "I who speak to you am He."
John 4:25-26

That at the name of Jesus every knee should bow, of those in heaven, and of those on earth, and of those under the earth, and that every tongue should confess that Jesus Christ is Lord, to the glory of God the Father.
Philippians 2:10-11

18 JULY

EVERLASTING KINGDOM

Can you grasp the idea of everlasting? Can you begin to see and understand the concept of eternal? I know that it is difficult for you to understand everlasting and eternity, but I want to give you a taste of what is ahead for you. It is beyond what you can think or imagine with your finite mind. Let Me speak to your spirit, so you can begin to get an idea of the vastness of what I hold out to you. My kingdom is from everlasting to everlasting. My kingdom is not of this world, but it is of My spiritual realm. When you begin to live in close communion with Me on a day-by-day basis, you begin to taste of My spiritual realm.

My Holy Spirit came to dwell within you when you were born again, and since then I have been drawing you closer and closer in sweet communion with Me. As you yield to My Spirit, you begin to understand My everlasting kingdom that is forever. You begin to experience those things that I reveal to you from My word. My presence becomes alive within you, and you get a taste, a glimpse of what My everlasting kingdom is all about! Now you see in a mirror dimly, but in the day that you stand face-to-face with Me, you will see and understand clearly the wonder and glory of My everlasting kingdom.

Your kingdom is an everlasting kingdom, and Your dominion
endures throughout all generations.
Psalm 145:13

19 JULY

LIFT YOUR VOICES AND SING MIGHTILY TO ME!

Have you ever wondered why My word is full of verses, telling you to sing praises to Me? It is because as you sing praises to Me, you are releasing the cares and the worries of the world. You begin to place your focus on Me, and the things of the world begin to fade. You begin to see Me for Who I am. You see Me as your strength, defender, comforter and much more.

Remember reading about Paul and Silas being in prison. That was a difficult time for them, and yet they lifted their voices in prison and sang praises to Me. The result of their singing praises to Me brought a prison guard to his knees, wanting to receive salvation. You never know what will happen as you sing praises to Me. Lift your voices and sing mightily to Me, your Lord and Savior! Then listen, for you may hear Me singing back to you, for I love to sing over My beloved ones! Listen, do you hear Me singing of My love for you?

But at midnight Paul and Silas were praying and singing hymns to God, and the prisoners were listening to them.
Acts 16:25

The Lord your God in your midst, the Mighty One, will save; He will rejoice over you with gladness, He will quiet you with His love, He will rejoice over you with singing.
Zephaniah 3:17

20 JULY

THE ALPHA AND OMEGA

I am the one true God! I am the Alpha and Omega, the Beginning and the End. I have always been, and I will always be. I am the One Who was, Who is and Who is to come! When I walked on this earth, there were many who experienced a face-to-face encounter with the one true living God. Since My resurrection, My believers are those that have truly walked in faith and not by sight.

There is a day coming when I will return! There is a day coming when many will see Me face-to-face again. Be watchful and wait for My appearing! While I was on the cross, I said that it is finished. The veil was torn in the temple, and the way was made for My believers to approach Me in the Holy of Holies. The day is coming when I will say that it is done! It will be time to live throughout eternity in My presence, rejoicing forevermore. There will be no more tears and no more sorrow! All darkness will be gone, and My glorious light will shine throughout eternity!

"I am the Alpha and the Omega, the Beginning and the End," says the Lord, "who is and who was and who is to come, the Almighty."
Revelation 1:8

And He said to me, "It is done! I am the Alpha and the Omega, the Beginning and the End. I will give of the fountain of the water of life freely to him who thirsts."
Revelation 21:6

21 JULY

ASSURANCE OF MY SPIRIT

Receive the assurance that I hold out to you. It is so easy to doubt, but I have made assurance so available to you to allow your faith to grow. As I share the knowledge of the mystery of Who I am with you, assurance should rise up strong within you that the power of the Holy Spirit dwells within you. With My Spirit dwelling with you, you can accomplish anything and all that I call you to do! I have made you to hunger for more of Me. As you hunger and seek more of Me, you are being transformed into My image! The more you know Me, assurance and steadfastness will grow stronger and stronger, and shine forth from you brilliantly.

Every time you begin to doubt yourself, remember that you are My beloved! I have placed My Spirit within you, and you can do all things through Me. You do not have to depend on yourself, for I am more than enough to accomplish My will through you. Stand tall in the assurance that the Spirit of Almighty God dwells within you!

That their hearts may be encouraged, being knit together in love, and attaining to all riches of the full assurance of understanding, to the knowledge of the mystery of God, both of the Father and of Christ.
Colossians 2:2

For our gospel did not come to you in word only, but also in power, and in the Holy Spirit and in much assurance.
I Thessalonians 1:5

22 JULY

BE KIND TO ONE ANOTHER

I am the epitome of kindness. I created kindness, and My nature is to express and shower kindness upon My people and upon My creation. If you are looking and are aware of what is around you, you will see examples of My kindness. My people learn from Me. As you enter into a place of intimacy with Me – knowing Me better, listening to what I have to say to you and spending time in My presence – you cannot help but be aware of My kindness. I show you My marvelous kindness as I hear your prayers and respond to you! I show you My kindness as I pour out My love, compassion, mercy and grace upon you. Draw into that place of intimacy, and spend time in My presence so that you will experience the wonder of My kindness in such a way that you find it growing within you, and you find yourself responding to those around you in My kindness. It is My desire for My beloved people to respond to each other, and also to unbelievers, with My kindness! Let us draw the multitudes into My kingdom, through expressing My kindness and love!

And be kind to one another, tenderhearted, forgiving one another,
even as God in Christ forgave you.
Ephesians 4:32

Blessed be the Lord, for He has shown me
His marvelous kindness in a strong city!
Psalm 31:21

23 JULY

PURE IN HEART

Pureness of heart brings you into My presence. Being in My presence causes your heart to be pure. Seek after purity of motives and thought, seek after Me. Then you will find purity becoming stronger and stronger in your life. You will begin to find your thoughts turning away from the things of the world to focusing on Me and My ways. You will notice your attitude changing towards those with whom you have had difficulty getting along.

You will begin to rejoice as you find yourself wanting to help others, and seeking for ways to express kindness and goodness to even the unlovely and difficult to like. As you move, by My Spirit, deeper and deeper into My presence – knowing Me better and loving Me more – you will begin to understand what it means to be pure in heart!

Blessed are the pure in heart, for they shall see God.
Matthew 5:8

Since you have purified your souls in obeying the truth through the Spirit in sincere love of the brethren, love one another fervently with a pure heart, having been born again, not of corruptible seed but incorruptible, through the word of God which lives and abides forever.
I Peter 1:22-23

24 JULY

TRUE SATISFACTION COMES FROM ME!

Have you ever asked, "What is true satisfaction?" Does satisfaction come from things or people? No, true satisfaction comes from above – from Me! Do not look to the things of the world to bring you satisfaction, but look to Me, for I am your Father. I will bring satisfaction in your life as you seek Me and My ways. Come into My presence, and let me pour out My glory and My goodness upon you.

Look to Me for all with which you are struggling. Look to Me for strength, wisdom, comfort, grace and mercy. Look to Me for love, compassion, patience and forgiveness. There is nothing too big for Me. I can bring refining, restoration, and make all things new and fresh for you. Seek Me, seek My face and shine forth the glory of My light wherever you go. True satisfaction is being a reflection of Who I Am to a destitute world that needs to know Me and My grace.

The backslider in heart will be filled with his own ways, but a good man will be satisfied from above.
Proverbs 14:14

As for me, I will see Your face in righteousness; I shall be satisfied when I awake in Your likeness.
Psalm 17:15

25 JULY

I AM YOUR SHIELD

I am your strength and your salvation. When you feel as if you can go no further, when you feel as if everything is coming against you, and when you feel as if you are drowning, look up, for I am your shield! I will protect you from all that comes against you. I am your fortress and your refuge. There is nothing too difficult for Me.

Reach up and take My hand, and place your trust in Me. My word is pure. Take My word, and hold on to My promise to you. Put on My shield of faith, for it will quench everything that the enemy is bringing against you. Hold on to Me, and do not let go. Stay in My presence, and receive the peace and joy that radiates from Me. Let the words of your mouth speak forth My words in each situation, and you will experience the greatness of My powerful shield surrounding you!

Every word of God is pure; He is a shield to those
who put their trust in Him.
Proverbs 30:5

Above all, taking the shield of faith with which you will be able to
quench all the fiery darts of the wicked one.
Ephesians 6:16

26 JULY

LIFTER OF YOUR HEAD

I am the One Who is the lifter of Your head. Do not look down and do not look all around you, but look up, for I am the One who will reveal My glory to you. I will lift up your head so that you can see Me. You will look into My eyes, and you will know that there is not one thing on this earth that I cannot conquer for you!

Look up! Look up, for I am your redemption. I came to earth to reveal the depth of My love for you – to go to the cross for you! I sent My Holy Spirit to dwell within you, to draw you closer and closer to Me, and one day you will look up and you will see Me appear in the sky. I say to you look up, for I am your God!

But You, O Lord, are a shield for me, My glory and the One who lifts up my head. I cried to the Lord with my voice, and He heard me from His holy hill. Selah.
Psalm 3:3-4

Then they will see the Son of Man coming in a cloud with power and great glory. Now when these things begin to happen, look up and lift up your heads, because your redemption draws near.
Luke 21:27-28

27 JULY

MY HOLY SPIRIT WILL TEACH YOU

My Holy Spirit is your teacher, and there is none other who can teach as He teaches. He can, however, teach you to teach others, for I have called all My people to teach in some form or fashion. Seek after My Spirit, for He will teach you in every area of your life. He will draw you into a place that you will know that the Holy Spirit is moving within you. He will bring opportunities in your life to teach you about the fruit of the Spirit. He will teach you to be kind and gentle. He will instruct you about being humble and filled with compassion. He will teach you all about forgiveness and grace.

As He is teaching you, He is preparing you to teach others through both actions and words. Do not be afraid when an opportunity comes up in your everyday life to share with a family member, friend, co-worker or stranger, for He will give you the words to say. He knows the need of that person, and He will guide and direct you to be a witness through teaching about Me, the triune God, Who is all knowing, all present and all powerful. Trust Me, as I teach you through My Spirit!

Now when they bring you to the synagogues and magistrates and authorities, do not worry about how or what you should answer, or what you should say. For the Holy Spirit will teach you in that very hour what you ought to say.
Luke 12:11-12

28 JULY

GIFTINGS OF CREATIVITY

I created the heavens and the earth, and I created mankind! I am the Creator! I have chosen to create through My creation of mankind. I have gifted you with a desire to create. Your place on earth is to grow to where you reflect Who I am, which includes reflecting My creativity. I have gifted each of My beloved ones with diverse desires to create.

Some of you are gifted in music – singing, playing instruments and even bringing forth new songs. I love to create music through My people. Some of you love to express yourself through art – painting and drawing. Others love to write. I have made My beloved ones with many diverse giftings of creativity. Do not say that you are not creative, because I choose to create through you. Seek Me to find out what area of creativity I have placed within you, and then begin to move out, trusting Me to show you each step of the way. Be prepared to be amazed and in awe at what I will create through you!

*For we are His workmanship, created in Christ
Jesus for good works, which God prepared
beforehand that we should walk in them.
Ephesians 2:10*

29 JULY

THE GIFT OF GRACE

I have poured out My grace upon My people – those who have turned to Me and believe in My Son, Jesus Christ! My grace is a gift, for there is no way that you can earn My grace. It is a gift to you that comes from the depth of My heart. I have poured out My grace and truth upon you abundantly so you can walk in My fullness! My grace has sought you and drawn you into the place of receiving salvation. My grace continues to be poured out upon you as I give you favor in the different areas of your life. Your life is covered with grace.

Think back about those upon whom I poured My favor and grace. There was Noah, a righteous man in an ungodly world. He chose to believe Me, and I poured out My grace upon him. There also was Moses, who led My people out of Egypt. Receive My grace and the favor that accompanies it! Receive an abundance of My grace that I hold out to you. Reach out and receive, for My grace is a gift to you.

And God is able to make all grace abound toward you, that
you, always having all sufficiency in all things, may have
an abundance for every good work.
II Corinthians 9:8

And of His fullness we have all received, and grace for
grace. For the law was given through Moses, but grace and
truth came through Jesus Christ.
John 1:16-17

30 JULY

THE REFINER'S FIRE

You have heard it said that a silversmith keeps the silver in the fire until the silver is so pure, he can see his reflection. I want you to know that I am the Refiner who knows what will bring purity to My people. Those who yield themselves to the Refiner's fire will find themselves coming out of the fire as pure as shining silver. They will be so pure and so shining that I can see My reflection in them. Is that not what you want? Do you desire to be so pure that I can see My reflection in you?

Count it all joy to be shaped and cleansed by the Refiner's fire, for the end result is pure joy, pure wonder and pure glory! Think of what it means to know that you are reflecting Who I am wherever you may go! What joy awaits those of My people who have been through My purifying fire. When your faith has been tested by My fire, the result is a blessed beloved of God who brings praise, honor and glory to My name!

For You, O God, have tested us;
You have refined us as silver is refined.
Psalm 66:10

In this you greatly rejoice, though now for a little while, if need be, you have been grieved by various trials, that the genuineness of your faith, being much more precious than gold that perishes, though it is tested by fire, may be found to praise, honor, and glory at the revelation of Jesus Christ
I Peter 1:6-7

31 JULY

MY SPIRIT BRINGS REVELATION

I want you to know that you can read, study and hear messages, but it is My Spirit that brings revelation to you that changes you. When you seek Me and My truth, revelation will come that will enlighten you and bring life to you. As you receive revelation from Me, go forth and share that revelation with others, so they can experience the life of God even as you have. There is an anointing upon the revelation that I give to you, and it is that anointing that continues to bring life to others as My revelation is shared.

Remember when Peter told Jesus that He is the Christ, the son of the living God? Jesus told Peter that flesh and blood had not revealed this, but it had come from God the Father. I am giving you, and all My people who will receive, revelation that brings My *Zoë* life.

That the God of our Lord Jesus Christ, the Father of glory,
may give to you the spirit of wisdom and revelation in the
knowledge of Him.
Ephesians 1:17

Jesus answered and said to him, "Blessed are you, Simon Bar-
Jonah, for flesh and blood has not revealed this to you, but My
Father who is in heaven."
Matthew 16:17

AUGUST

1   AUGUST

PROCESS OF TRANSFORMATION

I love to see My people transformed. I love to see My people being changed to the place of reflecting Me. Being transformed is both a decision to accept Jesus, and then a process of seeking Me more and drawing closer to Me until you begin to take on My qualities and My ways. You begin to say the things I say, and you begin to see others the way I see them. You also begin to reach out to others to help them as you see their needs.

Being transformed is a beautiful process that takes you into My presence on a regular basis where I share with you, and you open up your heart to Me. It is an ongoing process where your mind is being renewed as you communicate with Me more, and spend more time giving Me first place in your life. It is an awesome process of maturing in the arms of your loving triune God – Father, Son and Holy Spirit! Come fellowship with Me, and continue your process of being transformed!

But we all, with unveiled face, beholding as in a mirror the glory of the Lord, are being transformed into the same image from glory to glory, just as by the Spirit of the Lord.
II Corinthians 3:18

And do not be conformed to this world, but be transformed by the renewing of you mind, that you may prove what is that good and acceptable and perfect will of God.
Romans 12:2

2 AUGUST

COME TOGETHER IN ONENESS

Come together in oneness! Walk in unity with one another, for unity brings a bond of peace. Come by My Spirit, and walk in unity as you grow in your knowledge of the Son of God. Let your minds be of one accord as you come together in My presence, lifting up your voices in worship of Me. As you draw closer to Me and together, you will begin to see each other through My eyes. As your understanding and knowledge of Me grows, your understanding and acceptance of one another grows also. Each of you begins to be transformed as you draw into My presence. Then, you find that you are becoming of one mind, because you begin to think as I think. It is good for you to dwell in unity with one another as you reflect Who I am on this earth.

Come before Me with thanksgiving, and offer up your praises to Me. I inhabit the praises of My people, and I pour out the goodness and wonder of Who I am so that you enter into a place of oneness with Me, and with each other!

Till we all come to the unity of the faith and of the knowledge of the Son of God, to a perfect man, to the measure of the stature of the fullness of Christ.
Ephesians 4:13

Fulfill my joy by being like-minded, having the same love, being of one accord, of one mind.
Philippians 2:2

3 AUGUST

NO OTHER FOUNDATION THAN JESUS CHRIST

There is only one foundation, and the name of that one foundation is Jesus Christ! Yes, I am the foundation, and everything built upon another foundation will crumble. Seek out the One Who laid the foundation of the earth and heavens. Seek out the One Who is filled with righteousness and justice. I am waiting for you to come to Me with all that you are. I am waiting for you to lay down those things that are hidden within you. I am waiting for you to come to Me openly and honestly, with a deep desire to be rid of that which has been buried deep within you. Even though you believe it hurts too much to even go there, please know that I can take the deepest hurt, the buried wound and bring healing!

I can bring joy unspeakable to you and such freedom and victory that once you let go and let Me take over, you will be overcome with the wonder of Who I am. You will take hold of Me in fresh and new ways as you live your life in the freedom that I have always held out to you.

For no other foundation can anyone lay than that which is
laid, which is Jesus Christ.
I Corinthians 3:11

Righteousness and justice are the foundation of Your throne; mercy
and truth go before Your face.
Psalm 89:14

4   AUGUST

THE GENTLE ONE

I am the gentle One! I am gentle as a dove, but My strength and power are beyond what the human mind can comprehend! If I, Who am filled with strength and power above your comprehension, can be as gentle as a dove, be assured that My gentleness can rule and reign within you. Be open to having a gentle spirit that will do more to tame a raging lion than the display of strength. Remember that a gentle answer turns away wrath!

I am your example of gentleness, for I created gentleness. It is much harder in the natural to answer someone who is furious with a gentle word than it is to lose your temper. But, the results are astounding when you do. Decide today to learn gentleness from Me, the author of gentleness, and you will begin the adventure of your life. Trust Me and seek Me to discover the treasure of gentleness, and the effect that it has on those around you.

But the wisdom that is from above is first pure, then peaceable,
gentle, willing to yield, full of mercy and good fruits, without
partiality and without hypocrisy.
James 3:17

Take My yoke upon you and learn from Me, for I am gentle and
lowly in heart, and you will find rest for your souls.
Matthew 11:29

5   **AUGUST**

TABERNACLE WITH ME!

Do you not know that you are My temple? My Holy Spirit dwells within you to guide you, to teach you, to comfort you and to strengthen you. I abide in you, and you abide in Me. I am your everything, and I am always with you. As you deepen your walk with Me by spending time with Me, listening to Me, sharing your heart with Me and receiving My heart, you are becoming more aware of My presence dwelling within you.

The prophets of old knew they needed to be in My presence to hear from Me. They went to the tent of tabernacle in the earliest days, and in later years to the temple, because they knew they could encounter Me there. They expected to meet Me in My dwelling place. Since My Son, Jesus, died on the cross and was resurrected, My Holy Spirit is sent to dwell within each believer. Do not quench My Spirit, but receive the fullness of My Spirit by entering into My presence – the place where I dwell – and tabernacle with Me!

Or do you not know that your body is the temple of the
Holy Spirit who is in you, whom you have from God, and
you are not your own?
I Corinthians 6:19

And what agreement has the temple of God with idols? For
you are the temple of the living God. As God has said: "I
will dwell in them and walk among them. I will be their
God, and they shall be My people."
II Corinthians 6:16

6   AUGUST

THE LORD, STRONG AND MIGHTY

Because I am strong and mighty, you can be strong and mighty as you walk in My Spirit. Trust Me and lean upon Me when you are going through difficult times, when you are at a place of desperation, and also when you are experiencing a normal day. Always trust Me, and lean upon Me. I can and will bring you through difficult times by reminding you of My strength. There is nothing too difficult for Me.

As you take your focus off your circumstance and begin to focus on Me, you will find fear, worry and doubt fading away. Think upon the mighty works that I did through Moses, Daniel, Elijah and all the prophets. Think upon the mighty works that I did through Peter, John, Paul and the other followers of Jesus. Know that I am waiting to do mighty works through you, as you trust Me.

Finally, my brethren, be strong in the Lord and in the power of His might. Put on the whole armor of God, that you may be able to stand against the wiles of the devil. For we do not wrestle against flesh and blood, but against principalities, against powers, against the rulers of the darkness of this age, against spiritual hosts of wickedness in the heavenly places.
Ephesians 6:10-12

Who is this King of glory? The Lord strong and mighty, the Lord mighty in battle.
Psalm 24:8

7   AUGUST

REFLECT MY RIGHTEOUSNESS

My way is a righteous way! I chose to give you a gift of My righteousness when you made a decision to follow Jesus. The righteousness that is Who I am is available to you, and to all who choose My way of life. Some say there is too much to give up to follow My way, but I say that no one truly knows or understands what life is all about until they taste of My *Zoë* life, which opens up the wonder of righteousness.

Because I am righteous, you can be righteous also. It is not by your actions that you are righteous, but by your decision to follow Me. You cannot earn righteousness, but you can experience righteousness as you seek after Me – the righteous and faithful One, Who will never leave you or forsake you. I continuously want to reveal more and more of Who I am so that your daily life will be transformed into a reflection of Me and My righteousness, wherever you go.

Righteous are You, O Lord, and upright are Your judgments.
Psalm 119:137

The wicked are overthrown and are no more,
but the house of the righteous will stand.
Proverbs 12:7

8   AUGUST

MY WAY OF MERCY

Come to Me. Come to the merciful One, for I am always holding out mercy to you. You have experienced much hurt and anger, and it is not easy for you to accept My mercy. I want you to know that I have always held out mercy to you, even in the times that you have hurt so deeply and in the times that you thought no one cared. I am full of compassion and forgiveness. There is nothing in your life that I cannot forgive. I am waiting for you to come to Me and receive My gift of mercy that will wipe away the things of the past, and will bring you to the place that you will be able to forgive those who have hurt you. Then you will be able to extend mercy to them.

I am drawing you into a place where your understanding of My nature expands. As you know me in a deeper way, you will see yourself becoming more like Me day by day. Come and experience the wonder of receiving, and then sharing My mercy with others.

The Lord is merciful and gracious, slow to anger, and abounding in mercy. . .For as the heavens are high above the earth, so great is His mercy toward those who fear Him.
Psalm 103:8,11

Blessed are the merciful, for they shall obtain mercy.
Matthew 5:7

9 AUGUST

JESUS THE MEDIATOR

You can come boldly before My throne because of Jesus, the Mediator, and His sacrifice for you. Think about this: Jesus, My Son, was sent to earth to live a perfect life, free of sin. He then went to the cross to pay the price for your sins, and the sins of all those who have lived and those who will live until He comes again. He is the mediator of the New Covenant, which sets you free to live a life of righteousness and to walk by My Spirit in holiness.

Every area in your life that has you bound, that keeps you from walking and living in the freedom and liberty that was obtained for you through the cross, no longer has any power over you. The price was paid! You may be asking how you can experience that freedom. Trust Me, seek Me and cling to Me and My word. Hold on to My promise, as you draw into My presence, and <u>expect</u> to experience freedom, because I have promised you freedom!

And for this reason He is the Mediator of the new covenant, by means of death, for the redemption of the transgressions under the first covenant, that those who are called may receive the promise of the eternal inheritance.
Hebrews 9:15

Therefore if the Son makes you free, you shall be free indeed.
John 8:36

10 AUGUST

SHINE FORTH

Bask in My glory as you come in adoration before Me. Soak in all that shines forth from My throne as you seek Me and all that I am. Receive My holiness, My light, My purity and My righteousness. Receive My love, compassion, mercy, grace and forgiveness. As you come into My presence, the very essence of Who I am shines forth upon you. Receive from Me, for I am your God, and I have come to reveal Myself to you. I have come to bring transformation to you.

I look at you, My beloved, and I see you as the creation that I made you to be. I want you to receive and accept how I see you. I am drawing you into a place where you can see and understand, and be who I created you to be. You are My beloved, and you bring joy to My heart as you seek Me and accept yourself as I see you.

Out of Zion, the perfection of beauty, God will shine forth.
Psalm 50:2

You are the light of the world. A city that is set on a hill cannot be hidden. Nor do they light a lamp and put it under a basket, but on a lampstand, and it gives light to all who are in the house. Let your light so shine before men, that they may see your good works and glorify your Father in heaven.
Matthew 5:14-16

11 AUGUST

LOVE NEVER FAILS

I am love! Everything I do and everything I say is based on love. Love surrounds Me and dwells within Me. As you learn more about My love, you begin to move and live and have your being in My love. Love is contagious. When you receive My love, you then desire to give My love to another. Love grows and expands. When you experience My love, you find yourself falling more and more in love with Me.

You have heard the expression "circle of life." I want you to think about the "circle of love." There is no end to My love, and the more you receive My love, you will turn around and give My love away to someone who desperately needs to feel love! I am holding out My love to you today. Reach out and receive My love, and then share My love with that special person that I will bring across your path. Love never fails.

Love has been perfected among us in this: that we may have boldness in the day of judgment; because as He is, so are we in this world. There is no fear in love; but perfect love casts out fear, because fear involves torment. But he who fears has not been made perfect in love. We love Him because He first loved us.
I John 4:17-19

Love never fails. But whether there are prophecies, they fail; whether there are tongues, they will cease; whether there is knowledge, it will vanish away.
I Corinthians 13:8

12 AUGUST

GOING DEEPER

I reveal to you secret things – those things that are deep. Because light dwells with Me, I can see and know those things that are deeply hidden. Trust Me to reveal to you what you need to know. Seek after Me with an expectation that I will give you revelation. I long for you to draw into that deep place with Me where you can understand. It is My desire to share the secrets and mysteries of the deep with you and with all My people.

Take the time to seek Me, and meditate on the wonders of going deeper with Me. I am holding out to you the wonder and awe of knowing Me better, and of walking with Me in that intimate place where I share My heart with you. Let go of the pull of the world, and know the glory of the treasures of wisdom that I have to share with you.

He reveals deep and secret things; He knows what is in the darkness, and light dwells with Him.
Daniel 2:22

O Lord, how great are Your works! Your thoughts are very deep.
Psalm 92:5

13 AUGUST

RECOGNIZE MY GOODNESS

My goodness surrounds you! You are never without My goodness. There are times that you have to search for it, but it is always there. How you perceive My goodness depends upon what you let your mind dwell upon. It is imperative for you to renew your mind with My word, and for you to stay in close communion with Me. When you focus on Me and My word, you will have no problem recognizing My goodness that continually surrounds you.

Keep your spiritual eyes open, keep your spiritual ears in tune with Me and keep your heart receptive to Me. As you go deeper with Me and draw closer into My presence, you cannot help but grow in the knowledge of My goodness. I love for My people to seek after Me, with intentionality, in order to know Me better. As you draw close, you find yourself taking on My ways. You suddenly notice that anger seems to be fading, worry and doubt do not plague as in the past, and fear almost seems non-existent. Share My goodness and all that goes with My goodness as you begin to reach out to others.

He loves righteousness and justice;
the earth is full of the goodness of the Lord.
Psalm 33:5

But do not forget to do good and to share,
for with such sacrifices God is well pleased.
Hebrews 13:16

14 AUGUST

KING OF KINGS AND LORD OF LORDS

The first time I came to earth, I came as a baby. The next time I come, I will come as King of kings and Lord of lords. The first time I came was to reveal My nature and to provide salvation for My people – to make a new covenant that will last forever. The second time I come, I am coming to rule and reign in My nature – holiness, righteousness, goodness, grace, peace and love. I have called My people to rule and reign with Me as kings and priests.

There will be a new heaven and a new earth. There will be no more tears, sorrow, sickness or death. This time will be a time of great rejoicing, as everything and everyone is made complete in righteousness. This is My promise to you. Keep your eyes focused on Me, and take hold of My promise to return as King of kings and Lord of lords. Take hold of My promise of a new heaven and a new earth, where all will be covered with My glory!

And He has on His robe and on His thigh a name written:
KING OF KINGS AND LORD OF LORDS.
Revelation 19:16

And I heard a loud voice from heaven saying, "Behold,
the tabernacle of God is with men, and He will dwell with
them, and they shall be His people. God Himself will be
with them and be their God. And God will wipe away every
tear from their eyes; there shall be no more death, nor
sorrow, nor crying. There shall be no more pain, for the
former things have passed away."
Revelation 21:3-4

15 AUGUST

I AM YOUR ROCK, FORTRESS AND DELIVERER

When you are looking for security, when you feel that you need strength and when you feel that you might be overtaken, look to Me, your fortress and your strength. I am the impenetrable One! I am the only One Who can always and forever keep you from being overcome. Look to Me to place My shield of protection around you, and to cover you with My arms of strength. Run to Me when there seems to be no other way, but run to Me before you get to the place that you think you cannot make it.

I am always here, waiting with open arms. Run into My presence, and experience the strength of Who I am for you. Yes, I am ready and willing to supply all that you need. I am ready and willing to help you, support you, and to even lift you up and carry you when you cannot walk on your own. Keep your eyes upon Me, your rock and your fortress and your deliverer!

The Lord is my rock and my fortress and my deliverer; my God, my strength, in whom I will trust; my shield and the horn of my salvation, my stronghold.
Psalm 18:2

O Lord, my strength and my fortress, my refuge in the day of affliction, the Gentiles shall come to You from the ends of the earth and say, "Surely our fathers have inherited lies, worthlessness and unprofitable things."
Jeremiah 16:19

16 AUGUST

SHARE MY WAY

There is one way – only one! I am the way! There are many religions, but I came to earth! I came to reveal My nature to you. I came to provide a way (the way) for you to be a part of My family, so I can continually pour out My love upon you. I came to earth, and some followed Me. But many rejected Me and sentenced Me to death by crucifixion, where I shed My blood for you and where I paid the price for your sins, so that you can be a part of My family.

My way brings life (My *Zoë* life) to you, and it also brings truth to you. Now you can enter My Holy of Holies and dwell in My presence. You can talk directly with Me, and you can know and hear as I speak with you. You can know the way that brings peace, joy, love and contentment that is only available through Me. You can know the wonder of being in My presence, experiencing My glory washing over you. Share My way with all that come across your path, so they can know the magnificence of being a part of the family of God!

Jesus said to him, "I am the way, the truth, and the life. No one comes to the Father except through Me."
John 14:6

Therefore, brethren, having boldness to enter the Holiest by the blood of Jesus by a new and living way which He consecrated for us, through the veil, that is, His flesh.
Hebrews 10:19-20

17 AUGUST

MOVING TOWARDS PERFECTION

It is easy for you to know that I am perfect, but it is hard for you to realize that I am perfecting you, moment by moment and day by day. When you accepted Jesus in your heart, I was able to see you as perfect. But actually, day-by-day living is a process whereby I am maturing you. Sometimes you are very much aware of this process, and other times you are not aware.

This is an ongoing process, and I know when and how this process needs to progress in your life. Sometimes this process is a joy to you, and other times it is very difficult for you. At those times, it is harder for you to recognize what is happening on the inside. You are being fine-tuned, refined, shaped and molded. Each step of this process eventually brings you such great joy and peace that you cannot keep from praising Me. The key to this process of moving towards perfection is the same as for so many other aspects of your Christian journey – and that is to stay focused on Me, entering into My presence and basking in the beauty of knowing Me better and better!

I in them, and You in Me; that they may be made perfect in one, and that the world may know that You have sent Me, and have loved them as You have loved Me.
John 17:23

The Lord will perfect that which concerns me; Your mercy, O lord, endures forever; do not forsake the works of Your hands.
Psalm 138:8

261

18 AUGUST

ENJOY MY MAGNIFICENCE

Come into My presence, and magnify My name. Come before Me with thanksgiving and praise. Exalt Me when you assemble together, and exalt Me when you are alone. Meditate on My magnificence. I want to lavishly pour out My magnificence upon you. As My beloved, I desire to show you the wonder of My splendor. I want to place upon you the magnificence of what it means to be a child of God – part of My family.

I hold out to you all that is Mine. I want you to think about what that means. I withhold nothing from you. My grace, goodness, purity and righteousness are yours. I present to you compassion, mercy, love and acceptance. I hold out to you wisdom, knowledge, justice and peace. I have placed within you joy unspeakable, patience, kindness and faithfulness. Take hold of My magnificence and splendor, and bask in the glory of being My beloved!

Oh, magnify the Lord with me, and let us exalt His name together.
Psalm 34:3

And Mary said: "My soul magnifies the Lord, and my spirit has rejoiced in God my Savior."
Luke 1:46-47

19 AUGUST

MY REDEEMING LOVE

I have redeemed you. I paid the price for your sins so that you could always live with Me. Can you even begin to imagine the width, depth, height and length of My love for you? I want you to know the fullness of My love for you so that you will want to pass My redeeming love on to others. Tell them about Me, the triune God – Father, Son and Holy Spirit. Teach them to put into practice the things that I have taught you. Teach them to reverence and study My word. Help them to understand the fullness of My love for them. Teach them to seek after My presence and to bask in My glory.

It is time for the harvest, and I am sending you into the fields to reap the harvest. Go in My name, sharing My love and compassion to a lost and hungry world. Trust Me to supply all that you will need to bring My redeeming love to the multitudes – to those that have closed their hearts for such a long time, to those that have no concept of My agape love and to those who have wandered from My fold.

Blessed is the Lord God of Israel, for He has visited
and redeemed His people.
Luke 1:68

Let the redeemed of the Lord say so, whom He has
redeemed from the hand of the enemy.
Psalm 107:2

20 AUGUST

THE GLORY OF THE LORD

My glory is like a consuming fire! When you seek Me – My presence – be prepared for My glory. My glory is like a fire. Fire brings you warmth in the cold and light in the dark. Fire burns away the dross and the debris. Fire brings refining and purifying. When you seek My presence, you are seeking to enter into My glory. My glory brings warmth and light, but it also brings you to a place of cleansing. The refining that takes place cleanses you of those things that have been holding on to you. It cleanses you of all that is not of Me. There is such joy and freedom that comes from being cleansed and refined, and from accepting the freshness of all that I bring to you. Take hold of My cleansing process, and seek Me with all of your being. Receive My glory – all that I am – and worship Me in wonder and awe!

When Solomon had finished praying, fire came down from heaven and consumed the burnt offering and the sacrifices; and the glory of the Lord filled the temple. And the priests could not enter the house of the Lord, because the glory of the Lord had filled the Lord's house. When all the children of Israel saw how the fire came down, and the glory of the Lord on the temple, they bowed their faces to the ground on the pavement, and worshiped and praised the Lord saying: "For He is good, for His mercy endures forever."
II Chronicles 7: 1-3

21 AUGUST

BLAMELESS HEARTS

Dear beloved one, do you not know that I see you as blameless? I look at your heart, and I see a heart turned toward Me – a heart that desires to please Me! I look into your eyes, and I see eyes that are filled with love for Me. Is your every thought or action perfect and without blame? Of course not, but I look at your heart!

David sinned numerous times and in many ways, and I still called him a man after My own heart. That is because when he sinned, David always came to Me with a repentant heart. He was humble and teachable! He learned from his mistakes, and most importantly he sought after Me. He hungered and thirsted to be in My presence. He wanted above all else to please Me.

Do not let your sins weigh you down; but, run into My arms, seeking My presence, receiving forgiveness and letting your heart be filled with love overflowing for Me, Who loves you with an everlasting love!

Who will also confirm you to the end, that you may be blameless in the day of our Lord Jesus Christ. God is faithful, by whom you were called into the fellowship of His Son, Jesus Christ our Lord.
I Corinthians 1:8

And may the Lord make you increase and abound in love to one another and to all, just as we do to you, so that He may establish your hearts blameless in holiness before our God and Father at the coming of our Lord Jesus Christ with all His saints.
I Thessalonians 3:12-13

22 AUGUST

I AM A MIRACLE-WORKING GOD!

Why is it so hard for you to believe in miracles? Do you not remember the many miracles that I did when I walked on this earth? Can you recall the miracles, signs and wonders that I performed through My disciples and followers? Why would you think that I would not do that today for you?

Think upon and meditate on what My life was like when I lived on earth. Think about the time that Lazarus was raised from the dead. Remember when the crowd of five thousand was fed from five loaves of bread and two fish, with twelve baskets full of leftovers. There was the time that I turned water into wine. My heart's desire is to see you and all My people willing and eager to see Me do miracles through you. That is My way – to do miracles! There is so much I long to do through you. Reach out with believing hearts and with great expectation to see Me do what I have promised you!

God also bearing witness both with signs and wonders,
with various miracles, and gifts of the Holy Spirit,
according to His own will?
Hebrews 2:4

Then He commanded the multitudes to sit down on the grass. And
He took the five loaves and the two fish, and looking up to heaven,
He blessed and broke and gave the loaves to the disciples; and the
disciples gave to the multitudes. So they all ate and were filled, and
they took up twelve baskets full of the fragments that remained.
Matthew 14:19-20

23 AUGUST

MY *ZOE* LIFE

My breath brings My Zoë life to you! When you were conceived in your mother's womb, you received natural life. When you are born spiritually – born again into the kingdom of God – you receive My *Zoë* life. My *Zoë* life is full of vitality and life that cannot be explained naturally. Fullness of My life is being made available to you as you seek more of My word and more of My presence. My *Zoë* life becomes more full within you. You love Me more, you love others more, you desire to spend time with Me and desire to be transformed into My image. You seek to know Me better so that you can express and reflect Who I am to those around you – those you are beginning to see through the eyes of My love. Life takes on new meaning, and those around you will see the difference. They will want what you have. Draw close to Me, and watch and see the changes that you begin to notice as My *Zoë* life comes alive within you.

Thus says the Lord God to these bones: "Surely I will cause breath to enter into you, and you shall live. . .I will put My Spirit in you, and you shall live, and I will place you in your own land. Then you shall know that I, the Lord, have spoken it and performed it," says the Lord.
Ezekiel 37:5,14

Now after the three-and-a-half days the breath of life from God entered them, and they stood on their feet, and great fear fell on those who saw them.
Revelation 11:11

24 AUGUST

HEALING WATERS

Jump into My healing waters, and let them flood over you. My Spirit brings living waters to wash you and cleanse you from all darkness. My living waters wash over you to bring healing to the wounds of the past. My living waters wash over you to bring healing to body, soul and spirit! Do not delay! Do not hold back, but jump into My living waters, and know the joy, peace, comfort and strength that come from Me.

You can splash in the shallow, but I am telling you to jump in full force, and let My Spirit guide you and bring you to the place of healing and wholeness. When you move into My place of healing and wholeness, you will be ready to move by My Spirit as I guide you, day by day and moment by moment. Know the exhilaration of being in My deep waters where you can only rely on Me! Then you will know what it means to place total trust in Me!

Then he said to me: "This water flows toward the eastern region, goes down into the valley, and enters the sea. When it reaches the sea, its waters are healed. And it shall be that every living thing that moves, wherever the rivers go, will live. There will be a very great multitude of fish, because these waters go there; for they will be healed, and everything will live wherever the river goes.
Ezekiel 47:8-9

In the middle of its street, and on either side of the river, was the tree of life, which bore twelve fruits, each tree yielding its fruit every month. The leaves of the tree were for the healing of the nations.
Revelation 22:2

25 AUGUST

EVERYONE NEEDS ENCOURAGEMENT

Receive My encouragement to walk in the path I have placed before you. As you receive the encouragement that I hold out to you, you will find yourself growing in the gifting of encouraging others. I want to encourage you in every area of your walk with Me. Hold on to Me, and listen for My still, small voice. Be aware of the times that scripture comes alive to you, and look for understanding of what is happening in the circumstances around you. These are ways that I use to communicate with you and show you encouragement.

Be aware of what is happening around you, and be sensitive to My Holy Spirit as He brings encouragement to you. Be aware of the people around you and their need to receive encouragement. At the right moment, I will nudge you and show you what to say to them that will meet the strongest need in their lives. Be My vessel to bring comfort, strength and encouragement to those who are deeply in need of a word or a caring act of kindness. Everyone needs encouragement!

When he came and had seen the grace of God, he was glad,
and encouraged them all that with purpose of heart they should
continue with the Lord.
Acts 11:23

That their hearts may be encouraged, being knit together
in love, and attaining to all riches of the full assurance of
understanding, to the knowledge of the mystery of God,
both of the Father and of Christ, in whom are hidden all the
treasures of wisdom and knowledge.
Colossians 2:2-3

26 AUGUST

THE LORD WILL PROVIDE

Yes, I will provide. I am always providing. There are times that you are aware that I am providing, and there are other times you are unaware. Sometimes, your expectation of how I will provide is different from what I know you really need. I provided for the Israelites that were slaves in Egypt. I sent Moses to set them free, parted the Red Sea so they would have a way of escape, and then brought the waters back together upon the Egyptian army that was chasing them. Yet after the mighty miracles I did to set them free, they murmured and complained about food and about many other things. I always provided, but they were not satisfied.

Recognize My provision in your life, and praise Me for what I do for you. As you look to Me, and draw deeper and deeper in your relationship with Me, and as you study My word and believe what I say, you will find faith growing within you to believe even as Abraham believed. He knew I would provide a lamb to sacrifice in place of his son, and he knew that he and his son, Isaac, would return home together. Trust Me in all things, for I desire to reveal to you the magnitude of provision that I hold out to you!

And Abraham said, "My son, God will provide for Himself the
lamb for a burnt offering." So the two of them went together.
Genesis 22:8

27 AUGUST

I AM THE GOOD SHEPHERD

I am the good shepherd, and I care for My flock with a father's love. Each and every one of My flock is covered with My love. I look out for them, and they learn to trust Me. When they are thirsty, I lead them to living fountains of water. When they are hungry, I lead them to nourishment, and when one is lost, I go and seek that one out until he returns to the fold. Sometimes My sheep wander off. Sometimes they get in trouble when danger is present. I go after them, and I protect them.

I am always watching over My flock to make sure they are following Me. I guide them and help them find their way, and I work with them and help them to become complete in doing My will. My sheep bring Me great pleasure. I gather My sheep in My arms, and I hold them close to Me. Come, little lamb. Come and rest in My arms!

For the Lamb who is in the midst of the throne will shepherd them and lead them to living fountains of waters. And God will wipe away every tear from their eyes.
Revelation 7:17

Now may the God of peace who brought up our Lord Jesus from the dead, the great Shepherd of the sheep, through the blood of the everlasting covenant, make you complete in every good work to do His will, working in you what is well pleasing in His sight, through Jesus Christ, to whom be glory forever and ever. Amen.
Hebrews 13:20-21

28 AUGUST

HOPE IN ME!

Place your hope in Me, and you will always come through victorious. I am your hope, and I hold out to you the riches and treasures that are a part of Who I am. Your hope is in Me, and I am all that you need. I choose to supply all that you need. I have treasures that are so wondrous and majestic that you cannot even begin to imagine the greatness of what I am holding out to you.

Take hold of hope – the hope of Who I Am and all that I hold out to you! Walk in amazement and awe as your hope in Me rises stronger and stronger. I pour out My blessings upon you as you place your hope in Me. Draw close, and let Me reveal to you the wonders and mysteries of the ages. Rest in the knowledge that there is not one thing that can overtake you as you put your trust and hope in Me. Study My word, and experience the wonder of faith, hope and trust rising up strong. Let My word and My presence minister Who I Am for you!

Now may the God of hope fill you with all joy and
peace in believing, that you may abound in hope by
the power of the Holy Spirit.
Romans 15:13

Blessed is the man who trusts in the Lord,
and whose hope is the Lord.
Jeremiah 17:7

29 AUGUST

LIVING BY FAITH

Faith in Me believes what you cannot see and what has not happened, but what I have said. Faith is reaching out into My invisible world and placing Me far above what you can reason with your mind, what you see around you and what the world tells you. When you live by faith, many will scorn you and ridicule you. There is no greater joy than to KNOW what you believe in the face of persecution. You may ask how you can have joy in the midst of adversity, and I tell you that joy comes from knowing Me and My truth, and placing Me above that which you can see.

There are many in chapter eleven of Hebrews that have the testimony of living by faith, even though their circumstances seemed impossible. Receive more of Me in your life! Open up more of yourself to Me, and be amazed at what comes about as you listen to Me, hear Me and choose to believe Me. Look to and hold on to Me. I so often seem invisible, but I become more real each time you reach out to Me.

Now faith is the substance of things hoped for,
the evidence of things not seen.
Hebrews 11:1

By faith he forsook Egypt, not fearing the wrath of the king;
for he endured as seeing Him who is invisible.
Hebrews 11:27

30 AUGUST

LONGSUFFERING WITH JOY

Because I am longsuffering with you, I know that you can be longsuffering as well. Longsuffering is a word that many people do not understand. It means patience, and being able to wait and endure for the long-term result. The long-term result is worth all that you must endure as you wait. This does not come easily in the culture of today. Everyone expects answers quickly. They expect quick service in just about every area of life.

You will live longer, be happier and be more at peace if you will slow down, trusting Me to bring the results that are needed. Do not let the things of the world rush you into quick decisions, or cause you to respond to others impatiently or in anger. Turn to Me, and focus on Me. I will help you to endure joyfully to the end.

The Lord is not slack concerning His promise, as some count slackness, but is longsuffering toward us, not willing that any should perish but that all should come to repentance.
II Peter 3:9

Strengthened with all might, according to His glorious power, for all patience and longsuffering with joy.
Colossians 1:11

31 AUGUST

WALK IN ALL SUFFICIENCY!

I, the All-Sufficient One, supply all that you need. I supply all wisdom, all strength, all love, all mercy and all of your physical needs. I am the One you need to look to in all things. When you have lost your job, look to Me. I will bring the right position at the right time. When your income will not pay for all of your bills, look to Me. I will bring a way of provision. That may include a larger paycheck, or it may be a provision of wisdom to show you how to live on what you make.

My provision is not limited to material resources. My greatest provision comes in providing a closer walk with Me. I love to pour out abundant blessings upon you so that you can be all sufficient in being able to provide for the needs of those around you. It blesses My heart to see my people taking care of one another by giving to the poor, providing prayer and comfort to those who are grieving, providing fellowship with the lonely, and showing My love and compassion to the outcast. Receive all that I pour out upon you. In turn, pour out to others in need the provision that I have made available to you.

Not that we are sufficient of ourselves to think of anything as being from ourselves, but our sufficiency is from God, who also made us sufficient as ministers of the new covenant, not of the letter but of the Spirit; for the letter kills, but the Spirit gives life.
II Corinthians 3:5-6

And God is able to make all grace abound toward you, that you, always having all sufficiency in all things, may have an abundance for every good work.
II Corinthians 9:8

SEPTEMBER

1 SEPTEMBER

RESURRECTION POWER IS REAL!

The miracle of resurrection is real! My Son, Jesus, was resurrected and walked and talked with His disciples, He ascended into heaven and sits at My right hand. His resurrection shows My people that they, too, will experience resurrection.

Just as My servant Paul prayed, I want you to know Me better and experience the same resurrection power of Jesus being poured out upon you. Jesus called forth Lazarus from the dead. He raised Jairus' daughter from the dead, and that same power resides within you today. Do not hesitate, and do not doubt! Believe Me when I say that some will and have been resurrected from the dead on earth, and multitudes will experience the resurrection when My Son, Jesus, returns to earth. Be bold, move out in My resurrection power and be ready to believe for My resurrection power to be at work on earth through you. Yes, even through you, many will come to know that the resurrection power of Jesus is real and alive today!

That I may know Him and the power of His resurrection, and the
fellowship of His sufferings, being conformed to His death, if by
any means, I may attain to the resurrection from the dead.
Philippians 3:10-11

For since by man came death, by Man also
came the resurrection of the dead.
I Corinthians 15:21

2 SEPTEMBER

SALVATION BY GRACE

My grace holds out salvation to those that will receive. When you accept My gift of salvation by faith, you have accepted My invitation to be a part of My family and to live forever in My Kingdom. It also means that you are made whole, while you are living upon this earth.

When you reached out and accepted My gift, your transformation began. Others looked at you and saw the changes that began to occur in your life. They saw you expressing love and forgiveness, even as I express love and forgiveness. They also saw you putting away the things of darkness, and walking more and more in My light. I placed you on earth, and I called you to receive My salvation so that you could enter into the process of being transformed, and reflecting Who I Am in this earth. The closer you draw into My presence, the More you will express Who I Am. Share My salvation wherever you go!

For by grace you have been saved through faith,
and that not of yourselves; it is the gift of God, not
of works, lest anyone should boast.
Ephesians 2:8-9

For the grace of God that brings salvation has appeared to all
men, teaching us that, denying ungodliness and worldly lusts, we
should live soberly, righteously, and godly in the present age.
Titus 2:11-12

3 SEPTEMBER

VENGEANCE IS MINE!

I am a God of love, mercy and grace. But when evil persists, I am a God of vengeance. I am the One who subdues your enemy and delivers you from the evil one and his schemes. Keep your eyes upon Me, and let Me take care of you. Look past the evil, and seek My face, for I am a mighty Warrior. I will always provide for you at all times. When you find yourself surrounded by darkness and it seems there is nowhere to turn, I will set you free! I am your protector, and the battle is mine.

Trust Me, believe Me, and watch and see how I will bring you out of what seems to be an impossible situation. I have warring angels that I send out to surround you and fight for you. I am jealous for you, and I will bring vengeance against your enemy, for My wrath is towards him. Call out to Me in the day of distress, for My ear is always turned to the needs of My beloved.

Beloved, do not avenge yourselves, but rather give place to wrath; for it is written, "Vengeance is Mine, I will repay," says the Lord. Therefore "If your enemy is hungry feed him; if he is thirsty, give him a drink; for in so doing you will heap coals of fire on his head."
Romans 12:19-20

And shall God not avenge His own elect who cry out day and night to Him, though He bears long with them?
Luke 18:7

4 SEPTEMBER

THE GREAT PROPHET

When My Son, Jesus, walked upon the earth, He said that He only said what He heard Me, His Father, saying. And He only did what He saw Me doing. When He came as a baby to this earth, He came as the Great Prophet! There were many prophets before He came, and there have been and are prophets since He ascended into heaven to sit at My right hand. The prophets of old, and the more recent prophets, were and are imperfect human beings. I have given them the gift of prophecy to bless, enrich and encourage My people.

The Great Prophet, Jesus Christ, is perfect – the only prophet Who always spoke My truth. I have placed prophets in your midst to relay to you what you need to know. Receive a prophet in My name, but always test what is being spoken. Does it line up with My Word? There are many prophets, but there is only One Who is known as The Great Prophet! Test all that you hear by My Son and how He lived His life and by the words He spoke while He was on this earth.

Then fear came upon all, and they glorified God,
saying, "A great prophet has risen up among us";
and "God has visited His people."
Luke 7:16

For Moses truly said to the fathers, "The Lord your God will raise
up for you a Prophet like me from your brethren. Him you shall
hear in all things, whatever He says to you."
Acts 3:22

5 SEPTEMBER

SAFE IN MY PRESENCE

I will keep you safe when you are surrounded by trouble. When adversity is swirling around you, come to Me, your hiding place. I will surround you with My arms. I will hold on to you and keep you safe. There is nothing that can hurt you when you are safe in My presence. Run, run into My dwelling place, and I will hold you. I will sing to you. I am your shield and your fortress – a high tower. No one can reach you or harm you when you have sought Me to be your defender. There is none that can stand against Me.

I empowered David when he fought Goliath. I empowered Elijah when he faced the prophets of Baal. I empowered Daniel when he was in the lion's den, and it was Me who walked with Shadrach, Meshach and Abednego in the fiery furnace. Seek Me, and obey what I say. You will always be safe in My arms!

You shall hide them in the secret place of Your presence
from the plots of man; You shall keep them secretly in a
pavilion from the strife of tongues.
Psalm 31:20

You are my hiding place; You shall preserve me from trouble; You
shall surround Me with songs of deliverance.
Psalm 32:7

6   SEPTEMBER

GREATEST FRIEND OF ALL

I laid down My life for My friends. I want you to understand that when you accepted Me as your Savior, you became My friend as well as a part of My family. And I became your friend. Let's look at Abraham. He was My friend because he believed Me, and he obeyed Me. He trusted Me, and even in circumstances that seemed so unsure, he followed My directions to him. I am looking for people who will trust Me in the midst of the direst circumstances, and I have found multitudes that believe Me and trust Me. They are My friends, and I am their friend. I am the greatest friend of all!

I love unconditionally. I am always present and listening, and I never, never quit or give up. I call you My friend, and I always desire to spend time with you and to hear your heart. I want to share My heart with you! Walk in the depth of friendship with Me, friendship that is unlike any you have ever known before. Receive the fullness of My friendship that I am holding out to you continually, My beloved!

Are you not our God, who drove out the inhabitants of this land before Your people Israel, and gave it to the descendants of Abraham Your friend forever?
II Chronicles 20:7

You are My friends if you do whatever I command you. No longer do I call you servants, for a servant does not know what his master is doing; but I have called you friends, for all things that I heard from My Father I have made known to you.
John 15:14-15

7 **SEPTEMBER**

PROCLAIM WHO I AM!

Proclaim Who I Am! All through the years, I have had a remnant of people that truly believed My truth, who were passionate for Me, and who did not give in to the ways of the world. They followed Me with hearts burning with the fire of My power. This is the time for My church to awaken and proclaim Who I truly am! This is the time to know Me with all that is within you. This is the time to follow after Me and My ways so that you begin to reflect My ways upon the earth.

The earth, the nations of the earth and the tribes of the earth are hungry, starved and desperate to know Who I Am! Awaken, My people! Awaken to the truth of Who I Am. Share this truth everywhere you go, by word of mouth and by reflecting My nature through your actions. This world has no concept of Who I truly am, but I am sending you forth to reflect the light and glory of Who I Am!

For I proclaim the name of the Lord: Ascribe greatness to our God. He is the Rock, His work is perfect; for all His ways are justice, and a God of truth and without injustice; righteous and upright is He.
Deuteronomy 32:3-4

But you are a chosen generation, a royal priesthood, a holy nation, His own special people, that you may proclaim the praises of Him who called you out of darkness into His marvelous light.
I Peter 2:9

8   SEPTEMBER

FLOODS OF MY LIVING WATERS

I am ready to pour out floods of My Living Waters upon My people. My Spirit, the Holy Spirit, is ready to flood those who long to be drenched in the wonder of My Sprit in their day-by-day lives. Get ready to flow with Me, for I am able to bring you to the place of trusting Me with your whole being.

All of you who are thirsty, call out to Me, and I will give you living waters to quench your thirst. All of you who feel you are in a dry place, seek after Me, and expect to be flooded with rivers of My Living Water, pouring over and through you. Prepare and get ready to be My instruments to reflect the greatness of Who I Am in your lives, so that others will see and want to jump into My flowing waters of grace and love.

For I will pour water on him who is thirsty, and floods on the
dry ground; I will pour My Spirit on your descendants, and My
blessing on your offspring; they will spring up among the grass
like willows by the watercourses.
Isaiah 44:3-4

He shall be like a tree planted by the rivers of water, that brings
forth its fruit in its season, whose leaf also shall not wither; and
whatever he does shall prosper.
Psalm 1:3

9   SEPTEMBER

LISTEN FOR MY VOICE

Listen for My voice. The world will tell you that you cannot hear Me speak. But I tell you that it is My great pleasure to speak with you, telling you of My wonders and listening to you as you talk to Me. I created you to have fellowship with Me; both speaking and listening to each other is vital to our fellowship. You live in a busy atmosphere, and it is imperative for you to be able to get quiet and still yourself, and listen! Listen for a small, still voice – My whisper! Listen for an idea to come to you. Listen for Me to nudge you by My Spirit.

Once you make the effort, and you begin to hear from Me, you will find yourself desiring this time in My presence where you will find yourself coming alive to My Word. You will find yourself being changed as you spend time with Me and begin to know Me better!

And I heard a voice saying to me, "Rise, Peter; kill and eat." But I said, "Not so, Lord! For nothing common or unclean has at any time entered my mouth." But the voice answered me again from heaven, "What God has cleansed you must not call common."
Acts 11:7-9

That you may love the Lord your God, that you may obey His voice, and that you may cling to Him, for He is your life and the length of your days.
Deuteronomy 30:20

10 SEPTEMBER

SOUND OF HEAVEN

Have you ever heard the sound coming from heaven? Have you ever thought that it would be possible to hear the sound of heaven? I am telling you today to listen – listen with your spiritual ears – and you can hear the sound coming from My throne room. At times, some have even heard with their physical ears that beautiful sound that comes from the glory of My dwelling place in heaven.

There is the sound of the saints and the angels singing together praises to Me. The sound that comes forth is so beautiful that you never want it to stop. Sometimes, the sound that comes forth is loud and majestic. There is a sound that comes from heaven like a mighty rushing such as occurred at Pentecost. There will be a trumpet sound that will come forth when Jesus comes again. Listen for the sound of heaven, and join in with the songs of praise that the saints and angels are singing!

And I heard a voice from heaven, like the voice of many waters, and like the voice of loud thunder. And I heard the sound of harpists playing their harps. They sang as it were a new song before the throne, before the four living creatures, and the elders.
Revelation 14:2-3a

11 SEPTEMBER

OPEN DOORS

Place your trust in Me about your future. It is so easy to get caught up in trying to plan your future, trying to make things happen the way you want them to happen. How much do you trust Me? Are you willing to let Me open the doors to the path that I have for you? I have known you before you were ever conceived. I have had a plan for you all along the way. I know you better than you know yourself, and I am the One Who opens doors and shuts doors. Go through those doors of opportunity that I have opened for you, but do not try to push open doors that I have closed.

My plan for your journey with Me far exceeds anything that you could imagine for yourself. It is not always easy for you to understand why a certain door has closed and why another has opened. But as you trust Me, you will find joy unspeakable rising up within you. There is no greater joy than being obedient to the calling that I place on your life. Go through the doors I open for you, and bask in the wonder of who I created you to be!

And to the angel of the church in Philadelphia write: "He who is holy, who is true, who has the key of David, who opens and no one shuts, and who shuts and no one opens says this: 'I know your deeds. Behold, I have put before you an open door which no one can shut, because you have a little power, and kept My word, and have not denied My name.'"
Revelation 3:7-8 NAS

12 SEPTEMBER

THAT GREAT AND AWESOME DAY

Be aware of the times in which you are living! I have shown you, through My word, what will occur and what will happen before the great and awesome day of the Lord. Awaken to the magnitude of what is ahead for the church, and what will occur upon the earth as the whole earth prepares for the return of My Son, Jesus! Words cannot describe what is ahead, but you must focus on the promise of His return. When He returns, all evil and darkness will be overcome. Every knee will bow and every tongue will confess that Jesus is Lord! There will no longer be any debating, any doubt or any unbelief, because all will see and know Jesus is Lord. Those who have accepted Jesus will rejoice. Those who have turned their backs on Him will be dismayed.

When that great and awesome day occurs, there will be an end to all sorrow, tears and destruction. Jesus will rule and reign as King of kings and Lord of lords, and all will see the wonder of His everlasting love. For those who have turned their backs on Jesus, now is the time to reach out to Him, and accept the love and forgiveness He holds out to those who choose to follow Him!

The sun will be turned into darkness and the moon into blood,
before the great and glorious day of the Lord shall come.
Acts 2:20

Let them praise Your great and awesome name; He is holy.
Psalm 99:3

13 SEPTEMBER

RAIN DOWN FROM HEAVEN

I will rain down righteousness from heaven upon you. I will rain down My presence upon you, so that you can see and experience the glory of My presence surrounding you. Think what it is like when the ground is so dry that it is parched. The one thing that parched ground needs is rain to bring moisture to loosen the dirt and prepare the ground for seed. When your life becomes so dry and parched, you need the rain of My righteous presence to bring relief, to water your soul and to quench the thirsting of your heart.

Look to Me, for I am your God! I am your God that sets you free from drought. I have come to give you abundant life, full of moisturizing rain to soak your whole being. When the earth has not experienced rain for a very long time and then rain begins, what do you do? Most often, you will run outside and lift your face and your hands toward heaven, and praise Me. Expect to receive the rain of My presence coming down upon you, causing your spirit to flourish afresh by My Spirit!

O God, when You went forth before Your people, when You marched through the wilderness, Selah. The earth quaked; the heavens also dropped rain at the presence of God; Sinai itself quaked at the presence of God, the God of Israel.
Psalm 68:7-8

Drip down, O heavens, from above, and let the clouds pour down righteousness; let the earth open up and salvation bear fruit, and righteousness spring up with it. I, the Lord, have created it.
Isaiah 45:8 NAS

14 SEPTEMBER

I AM YOUR SANCTUARY

Wherever I am, I am a sanctuary. Wherever you are, I am a sanctuary for you. Find your place in Me every day and all day long. Expect to be in My presence while you are at work, while you are driving, while you are exercising – during whatever you may be doing. Find that special time to be still and enter My presence, but keep in My presence as you go about your daily routine.

I am your sanctuary – the place for you to abide in order to find respite and solace. I want you to enter into a glorious place of peace, and rest as you seek to surround yourself with My presence. Let Me enfold you in My arms and whisper of My love to you. Place your head upon My shoulder, and know that I am always with you. I have turned My ear towards you to listen and hear your heart, day by day and moment by moment. Turn your heart towards Me so that you can hear My heart beating for My beloved!

One thing I have asked from the Lord, that I shall seek: that I may dwell in the house of the Lord all the days of my life, to behold the beauty of the Lord and to meditate in His temple. For in the day of trouble He will conceal me in His tabernacle; in the secret place of His tent He will hide me; He will lift me up on a rock.
Psalm 27:4-5 NAS

Thus I have seen You in the sanctuary, to see Your power and Your glory. Because Your lovingkindness is better than life, My lips will praise You.
Psalm 63:2-3 NAS

15 SEPTEMBER

THE LIGHT OF MY COUNTENANCE

As you focus on the light of My countenance, you will find that your countenance will begin to change. You cannot come into My presence, into My light and glory, without it having an effect on you. When you are down and weary, lift up your eyes to look upon Me. Seek Me and linger in My presence as I reveal the wonder of My light, glory and grace to you. Say "no" to the temptations of the world that would keep you from spending time with Me.

I desire to pour out My countenance, which shines with My holy nature, upon you. As I pour out My light upon you, you will begin to see darkness flee. You will also begin to see each circumstance in your life through My eyes. I am drawing you into a place where you will see through the eyes of heaven. I want you to see as I see, and I want you to understand the depth of My unconditional love for you. I long for us to fellowship together in such a way that you will be transformed into My image. Come into My presence, and let My glory shine forth upon you.

There are many who say, "Who will show us any good?" Lord, lift up the light of Your countenance upon us.
Psalm 4:6

Blessed are the people who know the joyful sound! They walk, O Lord, in the light of Your countenance.
Psalm 89:15

16 SEPTEMBER

ABIDING

I have called you to abide in Me, and I will abide in you. What do you think it means for you to abide in Me? It means that you will be closer to Me than you are with anyone else. It means that you will share all of yourself, all of your life, with Me. It means that you will want to spend time with Me, talking with Me, listening and hearing what I have to say. It means that you will want to know Me better, and you will want to laugh with Me, cry with Me and rest in Me. It means letting go of worry, doubt, fear and anger, as you get to know Me and My ways better.

Me abiding in you means that I am always and forever available to you. I am so available to you that I sent My Spirit to dwell within you. You are never without Me. You can call on Me during your darkest hour. I will comfort and encourage you as I provide victory in what seems there could be no victory. I will rejoice with you in your finest hour, and I am always holding out the depth of My love to you. Reach out, and receive the fullness of My love for you today and always.

I am the vine, you are the branches. He who abides in Me, and I in him, bears much fruit; for without Me you can do nothing. . .As the Father loved Me, I also have loved you; abide in My love.
John 15:5,9

And we have known and believed the love that God has for us. God is love, and he who abides in love abides in God, and God in him.
I John 4:16

17 SEPTEMBER

EYES TO SEE AND EARS TO HEAR

It is important that you have eyes to see and ears to hear. When you stay close to Me, studying My Word and being in communion with Me, your spiritual eyes will be open to see My truth. Your spiritual ears will be open to hear My truth. There is so much deception in the world today that it is important for you to see and hear clearly. You need My discernment to know what decisions and choices to make so you can be a light in the midst of darkness. Have you ever wondered why so many people seem to be deceived and cannot see situations as you do? That is My discernment working within you. Do not hold back in sharing truth as you receive it from Me.

There are people all around you, longing to know truth. Live truth before them, and speak truth to them. Let My light shine forth so brightly from you that those around you will be able to see and hear. They will begin to receive with great joy as they suddenly find themselves understanding what seemed so cloudy and unclear before. Be My instrument to help open eyes and ears of many!

But blessed are your eyes for they see, and your ears for they hear.
Matthew 13:16

The eyes of those who see will not be dim,
and the ears of those who hear will listen.
Isaiah 32:3

18 SEPTEMBER

LION OF JUDAH

The time is near for the Lion of Judah to roar. When He roars, it will be heard around the world. It is time for My people to rise up as lions of Judah, and speak forth from their mouths My truth with such strength and fervor that none will be able to stand against them. Rise up, as My young lions, and move in My strength as I place within you a knowing and understanding of the time that is at hand. It is time to speak truth that comes forth with My anointing.

Listen to Me, study to show yourselves approved and go forth not in your own strength, but in My strength and My power. Go in My Spirit, and let the world know that I am Lord! Let the world know that it is time for repentance and time to turn to Me, for I am always forgiving and holding out My unconditional love. My arms are wide open to receive the masses that will call on My Name and choose to join My family.

They shall walk after the Lord. He will roar like a lion. When He roars, then His sons shall come trembling from the west.
Hosea 11:10

So I wept much, because no one was found worthy to open and read the scroll, or to look at it. But one of the elders said to me, "Do not weep. Behold, the Lion of the tribe of Judah, the Root of David, has prevailed to open the scroll and to loose its seven seals."
Revelation 5:4-5

19 SEPTEMBER

MY VOICE THUNDERS

My voice thunders in the heavenlies and reaches down to the earth. Pay attention to the sound of My voice as I speak things that you cannot even begin to imagine. I have looked down upon the earth, and I see many people who love Me. Their hearts are turned to Me, and I am pleased with My people. I also look down and see multitudes, masses of people, who are living in darkness and evil. My voice thunders as a wake-up call to My church.

Time is short. It is time to come together in unity and agreement. It is time to express to the world Who you serve. It is time for the world to see Me in you. You need Me as never before, and I am waiting for you to say, "Yes, Lord, here am I – send me! Speak through me, love through me, and may I express Who You are to those around me. May I be so filled with Your nature that they will see and hear You when they look at me! I am ready, Lord, and I do not want to hold back anything. I want to be fine-tuned by Your Spirit so that others will know that I have truly been in Your presence, and am truly representing you."

He had a little book open in his hand. And he set his right
foot on the sea and his left foot on the land, and cried with
a loud voice, as when a lion roars. When he cried out,
seven thunders uttered their voices.
Revelation 10:2-3

20 SEPTEMBER

BOW DOWN BEFORE ME!

Bow down before Me, for I am your God! I am your holy God, Who is filled with justice, peace, righteousness, splendor and majesty. I am your God Who created the heavens and the earth, and there is no one else like Me! My creation is so awesome that many have tried and tried to understand and explain how I did all I have done, but none can understand. Oh yes! I have given glimpses and let My people understand certain things to encourage you, but no one knows or can explain the magnitude of Who I Am and all that I have created. My majesty and splendor is beyond your comprehension. But one day, you will bow down before My throne in heaven, and you will then know and understand the magnitude of Who I Am!

Take heart today, and know that I am able to do all things well. I can take care of your every need. I can take care of the needs of everyone easily. Trust Me, listen to Me and obey Me! Bow down in humility before Me, knowing that I am more than enough. I am the Alpha and the Omega, I am the beginning and the end, and I am the all-sufficient One Who is worthy to receive your praise, honor and worship.

For this reason I bow my knees to
the Father of our Lord Jesus Christ.
Ephesians 3:14

Oh come, let us worship and bow down;
let us kneel before the Lord our maker.
Psalm 95:6

21 SEPTEMBER

BEHOLD WHO I AM

It is time to behold Who I Am! It is time to look, see and understand the depth of My fullness! Behold, for I am the Lamb of God! I came to save the world. I came to bring forgiveness and salvation to the masses. I came to reveal My true nature to each and everyone who will receive. I came to hold out the most precious gift to all that will take My gift and live with Me.

My gift is a gift of salvation, being a part of My family, receiving My Holy Spirit within you and being transformed into My image! Who could ask for anything more? I am offering all I am to you! I am the God of all creation; there is none other, there is no one to compare! I am offering Myself to you. All you have to do is give Me yourself, dying to self, and living a resurrected life with Christ in you!

Take hold of what I am telling you. Go forth with this good news, and share with all with whom you come in contact. Get up on a high hill, and shout to those below this glorious news! Do not hide your light under a basket, but shine brightly for all to see. There is a hungry and dying world out there, and I am sending you to radiate My glory wherever you go!

Again, the next day, John stood with two of his
disciples. And looking at Jesus as He walked, he
said, "Behold the Lamb of God!"
John 1:35-36

22 SEPTEMBER

BURNING HEART

When you draw into My presence, read My word and My Spirit flows within you, your heart burns with the fire of My presence and power! Do you wonder why I keep calling you into My presence? It is because you need Me, My Spirit, and My Word rising up within you to accomplish all that I have for you to do. Let your heart burn with desire for more of Me. Let your heart burn to know Me better. Let your heart burn to receive My Word and live My Word. Come before Me often. Come before Me with longing, and come before Me knowing you will not give in to temptation to be distracted. Make a determination to seek after Me, to follow Me and to worship and love Me with your whole being!

There is nothing else as important as spending precious time with Me. When you spend that time with Me, you are being changed. You are taking on My ways, and beginning to think and act as I do. You love as I do, reaching out to those in need, loving unconditionally and so much more. Draw into My presence on a daily basis, until you find yourself communing with Me as you go about your day! You will find the fire of My power rising up within you, as you become My witness upon the earth!

Then their eyes were opened and they knew Him; and He vanished from their sight. And they said to one another, "Did not our heart burn within us while He talked with us on the road, and while He opened the Scriptures to us?"
Luke 24:31-32

23 SEPTEMBER

HEAVEN'S BEAUTY

One day you will be before My throne, and you shall see what is truly beautiful. Before My throne, there is holiness! My throne and heaven are consumed with holiness. You have only seen glimpses of beauty on earth. You have seen the beauty of the mountains, the ocean, the sky, the flowers and trees, as well as the beauty of majestic animals, the creatures of the sea and of a wondrous newborn baby. I placed beauty within the earth to give My people just a taste of what eternal life in heaven will be.

Beauty in heaven will be flowers of perfection unlike you have ever seen. The greenery is so lush, you never want to take your eyes off of it. The colors are vibrant – more vibrant than anything on earth. But the most beautiful of all are My people surrounding Me. My beloved ones, who no longer experience any pain, sorrow or tears, are overflowing with My holiness. The beauty and fragrance of heaven cannot be described; it can only be experienced. One day, you will experience the beauty that awaits you!

Give unto the Lord the glory due to His name;
worship the Lord in the beauty of holiness.
Psalm 29:2

In that day the Lord of hosts will be for a crown of glory and a
diadem of beauty to the remnant of His people.
Isaiah 28:5

24 SEPTEMBER

STAND IN AWE OF ME

Stand in awe of Me as I reveal Myself to you. There are myriads of things that are awesome, but there is none to compare with what happens in your life when I reveal Myself to you! If only you could grasp the impact that I can have in your life, if you would yield more to Me. If you embrace a closer, more intimate relationship with Me, you will find that your days will go smoothly, and your life will be much more of an adventure.

I am the God of all that exists, and I want you to know Me better. I want to hear your heart. I want to teach you, transform you and love you unconditionally. There are many times that you choose the mundane things of the world over spending time with Me. I want you to grasp the AWESOMENESS of Who I Am! I want you to surrender yourself to Me afresh and anew. As you do and as you make more room for Me, you will find your life becoming totally awesome!

By the word of the Lord the heavens were made, and all the host of them by the breath of His mouth. He gathers the waters of the sea together as a heap; He lays up the deep in storehouses. Let all the earth fear the Lord; let all the inhabitants of the world stand in awe of Him. For He spoke, and it was done; He commanded, and it stood fast.
Psalm 33:6-9

25 SEPTEMBER

WORD OF LIFE

I hold out My word of life to those that are in need. There are so many in need – in desperate places – at this time. You have taken My word of life, and you are learning to apply it to your everyday life. I want you to go a step further. I want you to be willing to share My word of life with others. Be aware of the opportunities to share what I bring your way.

Do not fret, and do not plan how you will do this. Simply draw close into My presence on a daily basis, and expect to be used by Me. My Holy Spirit dwells within you, and all you have to do is speak what My Spirit prompts you to speak. Reach out in ways that I guide you to be a life preserver in other people's lives. You can be a life preserver, by saying what comes up out of your spirit that I know that person needs to hear. You can be a life preserver, by giving someone a hug and offering to fulfill a need in his or her life. As you spend time with Me daily and stay in My word daily, you will be amazed at how My word of life comes forth from you to bless someone in need.

That you may become blameless and harmless, children of God without fault in the midst of a crooked and perverse generation, among who you shine as lights in the world, holding fast the word of life, so that I may rejoice in the day of Christ that I have not run in vain or labored in vain.
Philippians 2:15-16

But Simon Peter answered Him, "Lord, to whom shall we go? You have the words of eternal life."
John 6:68

26 SEPTEMBER

WORTHY IS THE LAMB

The time is coming when the Lamb of God will be preparing for war. When that awesome day arrives, the enemy will be destroyed. And the Lamb of God will rule and reign on earth for a thousand years. He is worthy to be praised! He gave His life to bring salvation to the world. He was resurrected and ascended into Heaven to sit at My right hand, and to send the Holy Spirit to live within My people.

Give praise to the Lamb of God, for He is worthy to be praised! He leads His people to fountains of living waters, and I will wipe away every tear. This is the time for which those who know Me and know My word are waiting. Jesus, the Lamb of God, is worthy of praise! Bow your knees to Him, and sing praises to Him. Glorify His holy name – that name, which is above every name! The earth groans, and My people cry out for this day to arrive. Give glory to Him Who is worthy to receive worship from you!

These will make war with the Lamb, and the Lamb will overcome them, for He is Lord of lords and King of kings; and those who are with Him are called, chosen, and faithful.
Revelation 17:14

For the Lamb who is in the midst of the throne will shepherd them and lead them to living fountains of waters. And God will wipe away every tear from their eyes.
Revelation 7:17

27 SEPTEMBER

NAME ABOVE ALL NAMES

There is a name that is so beautiful – such a sweet sound coming from your lips – and that name is Jesus! His name is above all names, and nothing and no one can compare to Him. Who else gave His life and shed His blood to pay for your sins? Who else revealed My nature to human beings that had trouble putting their minds around Who I Am? Those of you that have accepted Jesus as your Lord and Savior have derived your name from Him. Give honor to the name of Jesus!

Many today scorn the name of Jesus, but one day, every knee will bow and every tongue will confess that Jesus is Lord. Hold on to Me, hold on to My word and hold on to My family in the days ahead. You will experience times that I make Myself so real to you that you will stand in awe! We are entering a season to prepare for that time, when every knee shall bow and every tongue confess Jesus. It is a time of putting your trust in that precious name of Jesus!

Therefore God also has highly exalted Him and given Him the name which is above every name.
Philippians 2:9

For this reason I bow my knees to the Father of our Lord Jesus Christ, from whom the whole family in heaven and earth is named.
Ephesians 3:14-15

28 SEPTEMBER

HIGH EXALTED ONE

Yes, I am high and exalted over all! Keep your focus on Me. Lift up your eyes, and look at Me – the High Exalted One. As you keep your focus on Me, you will overcome every problem, every obstacle and all those things that look so impossible! Since I am high and exalted over all, there is nothing that I cannot overcome. That means that you, My beloved, can overcome in your life every difficulty, adversity, problem and obstacle. Trust the One, True, Living God. Trust Me with every single thing that would try to bring worry, fear or doubt into your life.

Look at these challenges as opportunities to trust Me. Look at these things as a way to see your Heavenly Father at work in your life. Draw close to Me. Spend time with Me. Get to know Me better, so you will have an awareness of not only My massive power, but also of My huge desire to see you overcome in all things! Take My hand, and let us walk your journey together.

For You, Lord, are most high above all the earth;
You are exalted far above all gods.
Psalm 97:9

That they may know that You, whose name alone is the Lord, are
the Most High over all the earth.
Psalm 83:18

29 SEPTEMBER

THE ONE WHO OVERCOMES

Sometimes, your problem seems so difficult that you think there is no way out. Take heart, My beloved, for I am with you, and I am guiding and directing you every step of the way. The more difficult the problem seems, the greater the possibility of growth in your life becomes. Consider what I am saying, yield to Me and place your trust in Me, as you watch your life become an adventure. Remember, I am always right beside you and even within you. I am the One Who Overcomes, and I am in charge. There is nothing that can overtake Me!

You are never alone. You have the One Who Overcomes on your side, fighting your battle. Place your faith in Me, for I love you with an everlasting love that will continue throughout eternity. Reach out and take My hand, and let us face each obstacle, each circumstance, together. As you walk side by side with the One Who Overcomes, and you look into My eyes of unending love, you will walk in the peace that surpasses all understanding!

For whatever is born of God overcomes the world. And this
is the victory that has overcome the world – our faith. Who
is he who overcomes the world, but he who believes that
Jesus is the Son of God?
I John 5:4-5

30 SEPTEMBER

MY PROMISE

As you have lived upon this earth, you have experienced great joy, peace, love and compassion. But you have also shed many tears. There have been times you have experienced pain, suffering and grief. I want you to know that there is a day that is coming when I will wipe away every tear. The day is coming when all pain, suffering and grief will be gone. This is My promise to you. Take My promise, and hold on to the knowledge that what I say, I will do! Even in times of anguish when you are hurting and experiencing despair, I am with you! I have wept with you, and I am always holding out My presence to you, in order to bring comfort in these difficult times.

Hold tight to Me, and cling to Me, for I am your strength and your fortress. Hold on to My promise, and keep it before you. Let your mind dwell upon My comforting words. Let My presence bring reassurance to you that the God of the entire universe – all that exists – is with you now and forevermore!

He will swallow up death forever, and the Lord God will
wipe away tears from all faces; the rebuke of His people He
will take away from all the earth; for the Lord has spoken.
And it will be said in that day: "Behold, this is our God; we
have waited for Him, and He will save us."
Isaiah 25:8-9a

And God will wipe away every tear from their eyes; there shall
be no more death, nor sorrow, nor crying. There shall be no more
pain, for the former things have passed away.
Revelation 21:4

OCTOBER

1   OCTOBER

TREMBLE BEFORE ME

Tremble before Me, for I am holy and righteous! Come before Me with thanksgiving. Come before Me with praise. And even as you come before Me, you will find yourself falling before Me trembling. There is none like Me. I am the God of all, and one day all will bow down before Me! There are those that ignore Me, and there are those who ridicule Me. There are those that reason with their mind that I could not possibly exist. I do not fit into their way of thinking. There are even those that blaspheme Me.

One day, every knee shall bow and every tongue confess that Jesus Christ is Lord! One day, each one who has had an opportunity to know Me, but turned away, will see and understand that I am truly Who My word says I am. They will then know that I am all that matters, and they will be in despair. Even as I look upon the earth, it trembles. Share the good news of Who I am with everyone so all can have an opportunity to know Me as Lord!

Oh, worship the Lord in the beauty of holiness!
Tremble before Him, all the earth.
Psalm 96:9

He looks on the earth, and it trembles;
He touches the hills, and they smoke.
Psalm 104:32

2 OCTOBER

LIFT UP YOUR HEAD

When you feel as if nothing is going right, and everything is crashing in on you, lift up your head and look at Me! Look until you can see Me with your spiritual eyes, and look into My eyes! Place your focus on Me, and you will see My greatness, My goodness and My strength. You will know that there is not anything too difficult for Me. You will see the magnitude of My love for you – the fullness of My love! You will begin to realize that My desire and My will are to bring you to a place of overcoming.

As long as you look down and around you, focusing on the circumstances that are bringing you to a place of despondency, you will not experience triumph. Victory and triumph come with close communion with Me. This closeness allows you to see that My purpose for you is that you thrive and prosper. It also allows you to see that I can and will overcome every circumstance that comes against you. Lift up your head, and see Me in the fullness of Who I Am for you!

Now when these things begin to happen, look up and lift up your heads, because your redemption draws near.
Luke 21:28

But You, O Lord, are a shield for me, my glory and the One who lifts up my head.
Psalm 3:3

3   OCTOBER

KING OF GLORY

I am the King of glory! I am strong and mighty for you, My beloved. I long to reveal to you the depth of My love for you. I hold out to you all that I am. I long for you to know and understand that I am here for you. All you have to do is open up yourself to Me. Do not hold back, but share your heart with Me. Be open to receive the wonders that I hold out to you.

I am eternal, and I have prepared eternity for you. I am immortal, and I have made the way for you to live with Me forever. Take hold of Who I Am, draw close to Me and seek Me with all your being. I have made the way for you to live and dwell with Me throughout eternity. Your eternity began the day you accepted Me as your Lord and Savior. That means that even now, while you are still on earth, you can taste and experience the wonder of Who I Am. My desire is that you know Me so well that you reflect Who I Am, wherever you go and to all that are around you.

Who is this King of glory? The Lord strong and mighty, the Lord mighty in battle. Lift up you heads, O you gates! Lift up, you everlasting doors! The King of glory shall come in.
Psalm 24:8-9

Now to the King eternal, immortal, invisible, to God who alone is wise, be honor and glory forever and ever. Amen.
I Timothy 1:17

4   OCTOBER

IN THE SHADOW OF MY WINGS

There is a secret place that I have for you – it is under My shadow! Abide in this special place of protection that I have for you. There is nothing that can reach you to pluck you from My special place under the shadow of My wings. There is nothing that can harm you, distract you, deceive you or even discourage you as long as you are abiding in Me.

When you take your place with Me, you will begin to see how precious and how special you are in My eyes. I look upon you as the apple of My eye. I see you as My beloved, who has chosen to live for Me. I see you as My precious child, who returns My love and walks in tune with the beauty of Who I Am. I see you as one who desires to know Me better and better. Come and live, move and have your being in the shadow of My wings!

He who dwells in the secret place of the Most High shall abide under the shadow of the Almighty.
Psalm 91:1

Show Your marvelous lovingkindness by Your right hand, O You who save those who trust in You from those who rise up against them. Keep me as the apple of Your eye; hide me under the shadow of Your wings.
Psalm 17:7-8

5 OCTOBER

IN ME ALONE

I am your everything, and I am all that you need. Look to Me in all things, and seek to surrender everything to Me. I am the all-sufficient God, and you need none other. I am the Most High God, majestic, with nothing and no one higher than I. I have placed My banner of love over you, and I am your shepherd Who watches over you, with a desire to guide you every step of the way.

I am always with you. You can rest in the knowledge that there is never a time that you are without Me. You may feel as if I am not around at times, but I am with you at all times. I am the One Who heals you. I made you in such a way that healing is always happening in your body. Yes, I gave you doctors, and at times you fight battles with sickness, but always remember that all healing comes from Me.

I have given you My righteousness, and I have sanctified you. I always provide all that you need. I am your everlasting God, and I am your everything. Know and remember, when you begin to doubt, that I am your all, and there is none other.

My soul, wait silently for God alone,
for my expectation is from Him.
Psalm 62:5

He brought me to the banqueting house,
and His banner over me was love.
Song of Solomon 2:4

6   OCTOBER

BREATH OF LIFE

I breathed life into Adam and Eve, and I have breathed life into every human that has been born on this earth. True life is about spiritual breath that comes when you are born again into the Kingdom of God. You noticed the difference when you accepted Jesus, and you suddenly felt alive within. It was as if a light came on, and all at once you understood what you were not able to understand before. Everything seemed new and fresh because My Spirit came to live within you, and you became a new person in Me.

Since that day, you have been in a process of growing in your knowledge and understanding of what it means to live and walk by My Spirit. My Spirit breathes upon and within you each time you seek to walk in obedience to Me. Acknowledge My Spirit within you, and let My Holy Spirit thrive in and through you so that others will know that the Spirit of God brings life within!

And when He had said this, He breathed on them,
and said to them, "Receive the Holy Spirit."
John 20:22

And they were all filled with the Holy Spirit and began to speak
with other tongues, as the Spirit gave them utterance.
Acts 2:4

And the disciples were filled with joy and with the Holy Spirit.
Acts 13:52

7 OCTOBER

NEW THINGS

Some people do not like change. They do not like the new, because they would prefer to keep the old. They are used to the old. You need to be prepared for new things, because I am always changing things and changing you. I never change, but I change things around you and in you.

You need to be flexible and ready for change, because as My plan progresses in your life, there will always be change! You are changing as you know Me better. During each period of time that you spend with Me, change is occurring in your life. As you begin to recognize My character and become more familiar with Who I Am, you are being transformed from glory to glory into My image.

What worked in your life several years ago will not work as time progresses and as you grow more and more in My image. Seek Me, learn from Me, listen to Me and obey Me. I always share with you truth. I always share with you what is ahead, and what you need to know to move into the new!

Behold I will do a new thing, now it shall spring forth; shall you not know it? I will even make a road in the wilderness and rivers in the desert.
Isaiah 43:19

You have heard; see all this. And will you not declare it? I have made you hear new things from this time, even hidden things, and you did not know them.
Isaiah 48:6

8   OCTOBER

FLOW WITH ME!

Do not run ahead of Me, but flow with Me! Spend time in My presence, getting to know Me better. Draw near, and incline your ear to hear My direction. Receive My love for you. It is My pleasure to spend time with you, My beloved. It is My joy to whisper in your ear the things that you need to know, and revelation regarding the things that puzzle you. It is My desire to reveal more and more of My nature to you.

As you draw near with a listening ear, with eyes to see Me in My fullness and with a heart to receive all that I hold out to you, you will find that you are being transformed into My image. You will be flowing in My living waters, which will take you in the direction of the destiny that I have placed before you. Can you imagine, or can you even begin to understand, the scope of My plan for you? Move and flow by My Spirit, as My living waters flow over and within you, My beloved!

He who believes in Me, as the Scripture has said,
out of his heart will flow rivers of living water.
John 7:38

Then he brought me back to the door of the temple; and there was
water, flowing from under the threshold of the temple toward the
east. . .Along the bank of the river, on this side and that, will grow
all kinds of trees used for food; their leaves will not wither, and
their fruit will not fail. They will bear fruit every month, because
their water flows from the sanctuary.
Ezekiel 47:1a,12

9 OCTOBER

MY HABITATION IS WITH YOU!

There was a time that My habitation was within the ark of the covenant, but you need to understand that I choose to make My habitation within you. There was the day that My people sought Me in a temple made by men, but today I have chosen to make My habitation within you, My beloved. Your body is the temple of the Holy Spirit. Open yourself to the fullness of Who I want to be and Who I choose to be in you.

Many of My people cry out for a visitation from Me, and a visitation is a good thing. But there is something much better. When I inhabit My people, there is not anything they cannot do. I choose to live within each of My people and to make Myself known to each individually, so that each one may be transformed into My image. My glory shall cover the earth through My people, as they collectively seek Me and My ways.

Lord, I have loved the habitation of Your house,
and the place where Your glory dwells.
Psalm 26:8

For we know that if our earthly house, this tent, is destroyed, we have a building from God, a house not made with hands, eternal in the heavens. For in this we groan, earnestly desiring to be clothed with our habitation which is from heaven.
II Corinthians 5:1-2

10 OCTOBER

YOUR IDENTITY THROUGH ME!

Take hold of your identity through Me! I see you in a completely different way than you see yourself. Your idea of who you are stems from your environment as you were growing up. The people around you and the circumstances in your life influenced the identity that you have of yourself. There were times that friends made fun of you, and there were times in your childhood that you were mistreated and even abused. Often you heard adults, perhaps even your parents, saying things that you did not like or understand, and those things affected your outlook.

I want you to see yourself as I see you. I made you to be My child, and to exhibit and reflect Who I am. I have always seen you as My beloved, who can do all things well through Me. I have seen you as a loving child, who holds on to Me, draws close to Me and displays My character to those around you. Seek Me, and seek My Word. Let My image rise up within you as you live heaven to earth, and grow in your knowledge of your identity in Me.

For whom He foreknew, He also predestined to be conformed to the image of His Son, that He might be the firstborn among many brethren.
Romans 8:29

But we all, with unveiled face, beholding as in a mirror the glory of the Lord, are being transformed into the same image from glory to glory, just as by the Spirit of the Lord.
II Corinthians 3:18

11 OCTOBER

LIVING HEAVEN TO EARTH

When you focus on the things of the world, on darkness, and on the negativity that is within this world, you are living earth to heaven. You are seeing things from earth's perspective. When you focus on Me, My Word and My truth, you are living heaven to earth. You begin to see My perspective as you draw close to Me. As you spend more time with Me, you will come to know Me so well that you see things the way I see them.

This is a process that takes time day by day. Do not neglect your time with Me, but look forward to it. And as you enter more and more into My presence, you cannot help but desire My presence in your life on a daily basis. You will find yourself growing into the place of a moment-by-moment time with Me. Living heaven to earth, and seeing all around you from My perspective will bring such change in your life that you will truly know the joy, peace and love that radiates from Who I Am!

In this manner, therefore, pray: Our Father in heaven, hallowed be Your name. Your kingdom come. Your will be done on earth as it is in heaven. Give us this day our daily bread. And forgive us our debts, as we forgive our debtors. And do not lead us into temptation, but deliver us from the evil one. For Yours is the kingdom and the power and the glory forever. Amen.
Matthew 6:9-13

And I will give you the keys of the kingdom of heaven, and whatever you bind on earth will be bound in heaven, and whatever you loose on earth will be loosed in heaven.
Matthew 16:19

12 OCTOBER

ENCOURAGE ONE ANOTHER

Everyone needs encouragement, and it is My way to always encourage. You know that as you draw near to Me, you cannot help but be encouraged. Even as I encourage you, I want you to go forward and encourage those around you. Do not point out their faults, but encourage them in the things that they do well. Encourage them to step out, and begin to walk in ways they have never walked before.

As you listen to Me and know Me better, you will be sensitive to what I am showing you to do and what I am telling you to speak in order to be the encourager that they need. Look at My Son, Jesus, as He walked the earth. He only did what He saw Me doing, and He only said what He heard Me saying. You, too, can see and hear Me as you seek to be My encourager to those I bring across your path!

That their hearts may be encouraged, being knit together
in love, and attaining to all riches of the full assurance of
understanding, to the knowledge of the mystery of God,
both of the Father and of Christ, in whom are hidden all the
treasures of wisdom and knowledge.
Colossians 2:2-3

That is, that I may be encouraged together with you
by the mutual faith both of you and me.
Romans 1:12

13 OCTOBER

DREAM BIG

There are times that I give you dreams when you are asleep. And there are times that I give you thoughts that are dreams for your future. Often, when I give you these dreams or thoughts, you dismiss them as impossible. I want you to dream big! I can do all things! Do not look at your idea of your abilities, but look at My abilities. Look and dream about what you can do through Me! Seek Me, and find out My will for you. Then, do not let anything stand in the way of what I show you to do.

I plan to accomplish great and mighty things through you. I will open doors for you to go through that you would never imagine! Just watch and see what I have ahead for you, My beloved. I am taking you to My heights, and I am bringing forth My fullness through you!

Then, being divinely warned in a dream that they should not return to Herod, they departed for their own country another way.
Matthew 2:12

The great God has made known to the king what will come to pass after this. The dream is certain, and its interpretation is sure.
Daniel 2:45b

The king answered Daniel, and said, "Truly your God is the God of gods, the Lord of kings, and a revealer of secrets, since you could reveal this secret."
Daniel 2:47

14 OCTOBER

MADE IN MY IMAGE

Do you not know? Do you not understand that I made you in My image? Think for a moment. How can you, a human being, be made in My image – the image of God of all Who lives in another realm that you cannot even see? I can do all things.

I chose to send My Son, Jesus, to earth, so He could live a perfect life without sin. When you chose to accept Him as Savior and Lord, the Holy Spirit came to dwell within you – Christ in you! As you deny your flesh (for the old man is dead) and live by My Spirit that dwells within you, you are accepting the identity that I have given you.

As you seek after Me and enter My presence daily, you will discover that you are responding to people and circumstances around you as I would. You are living day to day from My perspective – living heaven to earth. What joy awaits you as you move more and more deeply into living in My image!

So God created man in His own image; in the image of God He created him; male and female He created them.
Genesis 1:27

For whom He foreknew, He also predestined to be conformed to the image of His Son, that He might be the firstborn among many brethren. Moreover whom He predestined, these He also called; whom He called, these He also justified; and whom He justified, these He also glorified.
Romans 8:29-30

15 OCTOBER

EMBRACE ALL THAT I AM!

You know what it means to take a loved one in your arms and to embrace that person. I want you to embrace all that I am. I hold out so much to you that you cannot fully understand at this point. Study My Word. Seek Me, and stay in My presence. Experience My fullness as you draw close to Me. Embrace Me and My ways. Hold on to Me, and cling to Me.

Be intentional about understanding My ways. My ways are laid out for you in My Word, but you need to experience My ways by My Spirit. What I am sharing with you will take time. You must make Me a priority! You must determine to set aside time to worship Me and to enter into My Holy of Holies. You need to be still and wait upon Me, and seek My face. As you seek My face, look into My eyes, because My eyes reflect Who I Am – My character. The more you see My character, the more you will be changed and transformed into My image. Do not hold back. Embrace the fullness of Who I Am!

Exalt her [wisdom of God], and she will promote you; she will bring you honor, when you embrace her.
Proverbs 4:8

These all died in faith, not having received the promises, but having seen them afar off were assured of them, embraced them and confessed that they were strangers and pilgrims on the earth.
Hebrews 11:13

16 OCTOBER

MY SPIRIT COMPELS YOU

Be sensitive to My Spirit that dwells within you, for He will guide and direct you. And at times, He will compel you to move in a direction that will further My kingdom on earth. Do you remember the times that Paul was compelled by My Spirit to go to certain places or to say certain things? There are times that My Spirit will nudge you more strongly. There will be times that you will sense a greater importance of moving, according to My Spirit's leading.

There are many times that My people are compelled in a certain way, and because of their obedience, people are saved, healed and set free, with signs and wonders occurring. When you experience that nudge and you feel compelled, do not hesitate to move out in obedience to Me. As you walk by My Spirit, you will see Me at work through you in ways that you have dreamed about, and in ways that you have longed to be used. Make a commitment today to walk and live by My Spirit. Draw close, and seek more of Me and more of My Spirit at work in you!

When Silas and Timothy had come from Macedonia,
Paul was compelled by the Spirit, and testified to
the Jews that Jesus is the Christ.
Acts 18:5

For the love of Christ compels us, because we judge thus:
that if One died for all, then all died; and He died for all,
that those who live should live no longer for themselves,
but for Him who died for them and rose again.
II Corinthians 5:14-15

17 OCTOBER

BEING RENEWED

Being renewed is a continual process. Once you are born again into My kingdom, there is a daily renewal that takes place as you are learning to live in My image. You have opportunities each day, sometimes many opportunities a day, to live as a new person in Christ Jesus. The old person is dead, but you need to be intentional about living by My Spirit!

The process becomes easier the more you focus on Me rather than on the negative things of the world. It takes intentionality to choose to live My way. Take My Word, and be nourished each day by reading, studying and meditating on it. Also, take time each day to seek My presence through worship. Sing praises to Me, and enter into a time of stillness, expecting to hear from Me. Entering into My gates with thanksgiving is a beginning place. Entering into My courts with praise brings you closer to Me. Keep seeking until you enter the Holy of Holies, where you will be basking in My presence! As you seek Me daily and bask in My presence, you will find yourself in a place of renewal.

And whatever you do, do it heartily, as to the Lord and not to men.
Colossians 3:23

Enter into His gates with thanksgiving, and into His courts with praise. Be thankful to Him, and bless His name.
Psalm 100:4

18 OCTOBER

NEWNESS OF LIFE

My Spirit gives newness of life. Even when you have been My child and have walked with Me for years, My Spirit is continually bringing newness of life to you. Each time you read a scripture, and something jumps out at you, My Spirit is bringing newness of life to you by bringing a greater awareness of what that scripture means.

There are times you are listening to a message, and the one speaking brings forth an example or explanation that causes you to KNOW that was specifically meant for you. Other times, you may be in a praise-and-worship service and the anointing is so strong that you enter into My Holy of Holies and have a special time with Me.

Then, there are times you desire to draw closer to Me because you are seeking direction, or having questions concerning the circumstances surrounding you. As you determine to be still and listen, you find yourself in a place where you can hear Me and receive from Me! Every time you have an encounter with Me, you are experiencing newness of life!

Who also made us sufficient as ministers of the new covenant, not of the letter but of the Spirit; for the letter kills, but the Spirit gives life.
II Corinthians 3:6

But if the Spirit of Him who raised Jesus from the dead dwells in you, He who raised Christ from the dead will also give life to your mortal bodies through His Spirit who dwells in you.
Romans 8:11

19 OCTOBER

CREATIVITY

I am a creative God, and I have placed creativity within you. In the beginning, I created the heavens and the earth. Look around you at the beauty and diversity of My creation. Look at the sky, the sun, moon and stars. Look at the mountains, with each mountain range being so different and so beautiful in their own way. Look at the ocean with all its vastness, strength and majesty.

Look at the people that I have created. Each tribal group is different, but all are beautiful. Look at the diversity of each individual. There are different colors and shades of skin, and there are different colors of hair and eyes. Each person has a remarkable beauty. Each individual is unique – not only in looks, but also in personality. Look for the unique beauty in each one that you meet.

Because I am creative, I have made you creative also. Be aware of the creative gifting that I have placed within you, and take every opportunity that I bring your way to share that creativity with others.

In the beginning God created the heavens and the earth.
Genesis 1:1

Lift up your eyes on high, and see who has created these
things, who brings out their host by number; He calls them
all by name, by the greatness of His might and the strength
of His power; not one is missing.
Isaiah 40:26

20 OCTOBER

THE LORD REIGNS

I am the Lord God Almighty, and I reign forever and ever! Whatever is happening around you, do not focus on that, for I always reign. There is darkness, pain and suffering on the earth, but there also is light (My light shining through My people), healing and joy. Each time you find yourself in sadness, grief or dismay, look to Me! I will bring peace, joy and comfort.

There is a day that is coming when all pain, sorrow and sickness will be gone. Keep your eyes upon Me. Comfort one another with My Word and My promise of the great day of the Lord's return. Yes, My Son will be returning to earth, and all will see and know that the Lord reigns. Take every opportunity to point others to Me. Share with them the good news that Jesus is alive! Tell them of His story – how He loves each one and gave His life that everyone will have an opportunity to say "Yes!" to Him!

The Lord reigns; let the peoples tremble! He dwells between the cherubim; let the earth be moved! The Lord is great in Zion, and He is high above all the peoples.
Psalm 99:1-2

The Lord shall reign forever – your God, O Zion, to all generations. Praise the Lord!
Psalm 146:10

21 OCTOBER

I WILL RESCUE YOU

Do not fear, for I am always with you. When you are in trouble, when things are looking desperate, and when you do not know what to do, put your trust in Me. I will rescue you! I will rescue you from danger, and I will rescue you from worry. Take My hand, hold on tight, and walk with Me. Let Me show you the depth of My love for you. There is nothing that can come against you that is too much for Me!

Darkness trembles before Me. Evil turns and runs at My presence. I am too much for your adversaries. They cannot stand in My presence. Look up! Look up, and keep your eyes upon Me. As you look to Me, you will experience peace, trust and faith that cannot be overcome. Walk and live in the knowledge that your God loves you, watches over you, and is always ready to rescue you!

He trusted in the Lord, let Him rescue Him;
let Him deliver Him, since He delights in Him!
Psalm 22:8

He delivers and rescues, and He works signs and
wonders in heaven and on earth, Who has delivered
Daniel from the power of the lions.
Daniel 6:27

22 OCTOBER

HAVING DONE ALL – STAND!

I want to encourage you to stand firm in faith, believing that what I have promised, I will do! There are times that circumstances around you get very difficult. Sometimes you get worn down. It is hard for you to keep strong in faith. I want you to know that you can always, always trust in Me. I do not make statements or promises, and then fail to keep them. I always fulfill My Word.

When I speak a promise to you, you can rest assured that I will fulfill it. It may not be easy, and it may take some time. But, trust Me to work it out in My timing. Stand firm in My Word. Be strong in Me. Stay in My Word. Stay in My presence, and there will be no doubt in your heart. You will know that I am all you need. You will know, regardless of how long you must stand, that I will bring you victory. Stand strong in Me! Stand tall in Me!

Watch, stand fast in the faith, be brave, be strong.
I Corinthians 16:13

Therefore take up the whole armor of God, that you may be able to withstand in the evil day, and having done all, to stand.
Ephesians 6:13

23 OCTOBER

MY PURPOSE FOR VISIONS

Sometimes I communicate with you through words, other times through visions. When I give you a vision, you will see in your mind's eye a picture. It may be a still picture, or it may be like a video. You may see a sequence of scenes. When I give you a vision, it is to encourage you. It also may be a directive for how to pray about a situation. If as you are praying you see a vision, spend time in My presence seeking understanding about what you see.

My Word is full of visions. Ezekiel, Paul, the Apostle John and many others had visions. The whole book of Revelation is a description of a vision that John had while he was on the Isle of Patmos. Do not discount visions; test them out with trusted believers. When you are sure that the vision is from Me, take hold of it, and let it bring encouragement and/or direction to you.

And in a vision he has seen a man named Ananias coming in and putting his hand on him, so that he might receive his sight.
Acts 9:12

And a vision appeared to Paul in the night. A man stood and pleaded with him, saying, "Come over to Macedonia and help us."
Acts 16:9

24 OCTOBER

ENTER MY REST

Entering into My rest is a vital part of your journey with Me. As you find and experience the secret of entering into My rest, you will know and experience peace that surpasses all understanding. Are you longing, hungering and thirsting after that deep and satisfying rest and peace, that goes beyond all that you can think or imagine? Enter into My rest by believing Me in all things. Until now, you have believed Me in some things, but there have been other things that have been difficult for you to believe. If I said it, believe it! I will do and accomplish all that I say!

You may be saying, "How do I come to the place of believing all that You say?" Focus on Me at all times. Enter into My presence, and let Me wash over you with all My majesty, wonder, goodness and wisdom. I have so much to reveal to you. I long for you to enter into that place of My presence, where I can share the glories of Who I am. Come, My beloved, and set aside the things that bring stress into your life. Enter into My rest!

Therefore, since a promise remains of entering His rest, let us fear lest any of you seem to have come short of it.
Hebrews 4:1

Let us therefore be diligent to enter that rest, lest anyone fall according to the same example of disobedience.
Hebrews 4:11

25 OCTOBER

SEEK MY FACE

You will find all that you need in My presence. Seek after Me with diligence and fortitude. Be relentless in seeking Me, even as I am relentless in My pursuit of you. Let nothing stand in your way of building your relationship with Me. Spend time with Me, and open up and share with Me. Let Me know of your questions and the things that puzzle you. Let Me know of the things that hurt you and cause you to feel neglected and discouraged.

Come into My presence, and seek My face. When you meet with Me face-to-face, you will begin to see all hurt and discouragement fade away. Whatever may be troubling you cannot exist in My presence. My presence brings joy, peace, love, acceptance and all good things to you.

Make a diligent determination today that you will do what it takes to make the time to spend with Me. I will pour out My glory, strength and joy upon you as you seek My face forevermore!

Glory in His holy name; let the hearts of those rejoice who seek the Lord! Seek the Lord and His strength; seek His face evermore!
I Chronicles 16:10-11

This is Jacob, the generation of those
who seek Him, who seek Your face.
Psalm 24:6

26 OCTOBER

OPEN HEAVEN

Are there times that it would seem as if heaven is closed to you? Are there times that you feel your prayers are not being heard? Do you sometimes feel as if you cannot connect with Me? Persevere in your pursuit of Me! Look to My Word to receive reassurance of My presence with you.

When you are having difficulty connecting with Me, it is simply an opportunity for you to draw closer to Me and trust Me. I have an open heaven for you. I want you to grow to the place in your journey with Me that you become aware of My open heaven.

Many times throughout scripture, you can see and understand how My people would seek Me and experience an open heaven. Even as I saw heaven open, as I was baptized in the river Jordan by John, you will also experience times that you KNOW heaven is open over you. And, one day you will see heaven open when the time is right for Me to return again. Seek Me, spend time with Me, know Me better and know My ways. Be ready for My return!

When all the people were baptized, it came to pass that Jesus also was baptized; and while He prayed, the heaven was opened. And the Holy Spirit descended in bodily form like a dove upon Him, and a voice came from heaven which said, "You are My beloved Son; in You I am well pleased."
Luke 3:21-22

27 OCTOBER

COME UP TO MY MOUNTAIN

Come and visit Me up on My mountain. Come and seek My face, and spend time with Me! Each time Moses would come to My mountain, He had an encounter with Me. I revealed Myself to him, and we began to build a relationship. We would talk together, and he would begin to recognize and understand Me and My ways. Each time he spent time with Me, he would desire more. He longed to know Me better.

When My Son, Jesus, walked the earth, He preached, taught, healed and brought freedom to many. He performed many miracles, but after spending time with the multitudes, He would often withdraw to the mountain to pray. He spent time with Me, being filled to overflowing with My presence.

I am inviting you to come to My mountain! I want to share with you My splendor and My majesty. I want to share with you holiness, righteousness, purity and humility. I want you to take hold of My character and My nature so you can reflect Me, even as My Son, Jesus, reflected Me as He walked the earth.

So Moses arose with his assistant Joshua,
and Moses went up to the mountain of God.
Exodus 24:13

Immediately He made His disciples get into the boat and
go before Him to the other side, to Bethsaida, while He sent
the multitude away. And when He had sent them away, He
departed to the mountain to pray.
Mark 6:45-46

28 OCTOBER

KNOW MY WAYS

Seek after My ways, for they will bring peace, joy, contentment and love into your life. The things of this world will pass away, but My ways are everlasting. My ways will guide you into fulfilling My will and My purpose for you. Live each day, seeking to know Me and My ways better.

Look at how I lived when I walked on earth. Study My Word to begin to see and understand My ways better. Look at how I taught, and what I taught, when the multitudes would gather around Me. Look at how My love and compassion brought healing to many. Be aware of the questions I asked people, and how they responded. Reflect on how I treated people who needed deliverance and on the freedom that I brought to them. Look at My life and My words. And, pursue My ways with fervor and zeal as you determine to walk in the victory that comes from following My ways.

He is the Rock, His work is perfect; for all His ways are justice, A God of truth and without injustice; righteous and upright is He.
Deuteronomy 32:4

They also do no iniquity; they walk in His ways.
Psalm 119:3

29 OCTOBER

SEEK THE LIGHT OF MY GLORY

Seek after Me and My glory! Desire the light of My countenance to shine upon you in such a way that others will see and know that there is something special that has happened to you. They will know that you are changed, and they will desire to experience what you have experienced.

Know Me better so you will reflect the wonder of Who I am to those around you. The world is hungry to see and know that there is a God who is real. They want to know that I am a God who can literally transform their lives.

Reach out to Me. Seek Me. Spend time with Me, and communicate with Me. You will find that as you grow closer and closer to Me, My glory will become real in your life. You will shine and reflect My glory in such a way that many lives will be touched and changed! Seek the light of My glory as I shine My face upon you!

Restore us, O God; cause Your face to shine,
and we shall be saved!
Psalm 80:3

God be merciful to us and bless us, and cause His face to shine
upon us, Selah. That Your way may be known on earth, Your
salvation among all nations.
Psalm 67:1-2

30 OCTOBER

I AM COMING!

I am coming to bring vengeance and recompense to a world that needs Me. I am coming with a desire to see My family come together with My love, grace, mercy and goodness. I am coming for a family who is reflecting My light, glory, wisdom and humility. I know there is a longing in the hearts of My beloved family for Me to return.

I would say to you, My family, to come together by My Spirit in unity and in one accord! It is only when you are one in the Spirit that the world will truly see and understand Who I Am! Then they will know that I am all that they need.

Yes, I am coming one day in all My strength and My power. But while you are waiting for My return, I want you to come together and reflect My ways so that multitudes will be added to My kingdom. I am coming back for a large family that knows Me and is walking by My Spirit in My ways. Prepare for My coming!

Say to those who are fearful-hearted, "Be strong, do not fear!
Behold, your God will come with vengeance, with the recompense
of God; He will come and save you."
Isaiah 35:4

And the Spirit and the bride say, "Come!" And let him who hears
say, "Come!" And let him who thirsts come. Whoever desires, let
him take the water of life freely.
Revelation 22:17

31 OCTOBER

I AM THE LORD GOD ALMIGHTY

I am the Lord God Almighty, Who was, is and is to come. I am the One Who will bring you to a place of transformation. I am the One Who created the heavens and the earth. I created all the beauty around you, and I created beauty that you have never seen. But one day, you will.

I am the One Who has protected you throughout your life. I am the One Who has cried with you and laughed with you. I am the One Who opened doors for you to go through that brought you great joy. I am the One Who has been at work in your life since the day you were conceived. I created you with a plan and purpose for your destiny. Sometimes you have veered off My path, but I have always drawn you back.

Let go of your doubts and unbelief. Take hold of My hand – the hand of the Lord God Almighty – and walk the path I have placed before you. There is no other path that will bring you satisfaction, joy, peace and wonder. Take My hand and walk with Me, for I am the Lord God Almighty!

The four living creatures, each having six wings, were full of eyes around and within. And they do not rest day or night, saying: "Holy, holy, holy, Lord God Almighty, Who was and is and is to come!"
Revelation 4:8

They sing the song of Moses, the servant of God, and the song of the Lamb, saying: "Great and marvelous are Your works, Lord God Almighty! Just and true are Your ways, O King of the saints!"
Revelation 15:3

NOVEMBER

1 NOVEMBER

MAKE YOUR DWELLING PLACE WITH ME!

My dear beloved, I enjoy your visits, but I want you to dwell with Me. Come to My dwelling place, and enter into My presence. Choose to dwell with Me and spend time with Me. Let us build a relationship together that will last throughout eternity. Do not be satisfied with a visit, but choose habitation with Me.

My arms are wide open, inviting you and waiting for you to choose Me! Choose and return to your first love. Know the joy and wonder of spending precious time with Me, your Father. Look forward to the times when I will share with you the mysteries of My wisdom. Seek to know Me, and receive of the magnitude of My knowledge. Enjoy our time together as you know Me better, and grow in your understanding of My nature.

Look forward to the change and transformation that will come as you seek Me, and as we communicate with one another. Yes, My beloved, come and make your dwelling place with Me!

Because you have made the Lord, who is my refuge, even the Most High, your dwelling place, no evil shall befall you, nor shall any plague come near your dwelling.
Psalm 91:9-10

In whom the whole building, being fitted together, grows into a holy temple in the Lord, in whom you also are being built together for a dwelling place of God in the Spirit.
Ephesians 2:21-22

2 NOVEMBER

LIFT UP YOUR HANDS!

Lift up your hands, My beloved. Lift up your hands in worship of Me. Lift up your hands as an act of surrender to Me and My will. Let the lifting of your hands be an expression of sacrifice, and also an act of showing your love for Me.

When I see your hands extended upward towards heaven, I know that you are coming to Me as a small child comes to a parent – a child holding up hands to receive an embrace and to be held in the arms of a loving parent. Picture a parent with such an expectant young child. The parent lifts up the child and whirls the child around, and maybe even dances with the child. And even as a parent delights in the innocent display of love, I delight in your display of love to Me of lifting your hands to Me. It makes Me want to reach down, take you in My arms, and whirl around and dance with you. You bring Me great joy when I see you worshipping Me with such an expression of love and trust.

Let us lift our hearts and hands to God in heaven.
Lamentations 3:41

Because Your lovingkindness is better than life, My lips
shall praise You. Thus I will bless You while I live; I will lift
up my hands in Your name.
Psalm 63:3-4

3   NOVEMBER

COME INTO MY HOLY PLACE

I am calling you into My holy place. I am inviting you into My dwelling place; the place where you can spend time with Me and communicate with Me. It is in My holy place that you will experience times of Oneness with Me. It is a place where I can share with you, and you can share with Me.

As you come into My holy place and experience My presence, you will be surrounded by My glory. Radiant light will flow all around you. You may see a cloud, feel "goose bumps," tingle all over or even tremble in My presence. You may feel as if flowing waters are washing over you. Most importantly, you will experience My love in such a depth that you will want to spend time in My presence – My holy place – as often as possible. Come, My beloved, and accept My invitation to meet with Me in My holy place.

There is a river whose streams shall make glad the city of God, the holy place of the tabernacle of the Most High.
Psalm 46:4

And it came to pass, when the priests came out of the holy place, that the cloud filled the house of the Lord, so that the priests could not continue ministering because of the cloud; for the glory of the Lord filled the house of the Lord.
I Kings 8:10-11

4   NOVEMBER

PRINCE OF PEACE

The world needs to know the Prince of Peace! The world is starving for peace. The turmoil, the violence and the desperation that seem to be everywhere makes the people of this world hunger and thirst for peace. There are desperate attempts to try to bring about peace, but there is only One Who can truly bring peace. His name is Jesus – the Prince of Peace.

The world is looking for solutions through government and through acquiescence. But the Prince of Peace brings the kind of peace that not only prefers others over self, but also loves with an everlasting, unconditional love. My Son gives peace to all who give their hearts to Him. The kind of peace that comes in those persons' lives is indescribable. A calm comes on them, and there is a feeling of being complete or of total well-being. This kind of peace does not depend on circumstances, but on relationship – relationship with Jesus! Thus, there is peace at all times, regardless of what is happening around them.

When you know the peace of Jesus, your trust is in Him rather than in others. And you take on His character. When others are around you, they do not want to fight with you or cause you harm, because they can sense and feel peace that comes from Him. Be a reflection of the Prince of Peace wherever I place you.

For unto us a Child is born, unto us a Son is given; and the government will be upon His shoulder. And His name will be called Wonderful, Counselor, Mighty God, Everlasting Father, Prince of Peace.
Isaiah 9:6

5   NOVEMBER

I AM OPENING EYES!

There are many mysteries, but I am opening eyes to see, understand and discern the times. Just as the eyes of two of Jesus' followers were opened on the road to Emmaus, I am opening eyes of My believers today to see the mysteries that are happening around them – to see through My eyes!

It is much easier for you to see things through the eyes of the world, because you are bombarded daily with negative news and conversation. Therefore, I am opening your eyes to see from My perspective. I want you to see from heaven's perspective so you can live life by My Spirit. I want you to live life trusting and resting in Me!

Many of you are already aware of what I am sharing with you. You know when I have "opened your eyes." You have begun to see circumstances and situations in a much different way. As you see through My heavenly perspective, you see solutions. You become aware of the good that I am bringing out of what has seemed so bad. Rejoice, as I open your eyes and share My good news with all!

Open my eyes, that I may see wondrous things from Your law.
Psalm 119:18

Then their eyes were opened and they knew Him;
and He vanished from their sight.
Luke 24:31

6 NOVEMBER

HEAR MY VOICE!

There are many that say you cannot hear My voice, but I say to you to listen and wait upon Me. I will and I do speak to My people, by My Spirit. Most often, you do not hear My audible voice through your physical ears, but you "hear" My still, small voice (like a whisper) through your "spiritual ears." All through the Bible, there are records of My people hearing from Me. Remember when Samuel kept hearing Me call to him, and he thought it was Eli, the priest?

I am calling to you today. I love to talk to you. I love to tell you how much I love you. I love to let you know the greatness of My grace and mercy that I pour out upon you. I love to answer your questions and to give you direction. You may be thinking, "I do not know how to hear through spiritual ears!" I want you to know that you need to pursue Me. You need to determine to spend however much time it takes to hear Me. Learn to wait upon Me with expectation. Wait upon Me, and rest in Me. Be still, and know that I am God. It is My desire to speak to you. I often speak, but you do not hear because you do not take the time to hear. Hear My voice!

Now the Lord came and stood and called as at other times,
"Samuel! Samuel!" And Samuel answered, "Speak, for
Your servant hears."
I Samuel 3:10

Be still, and know that I am God; I will be exalted among the
nations, I will be exalted in the earth!
Psalm 46:10

7   NOVEMBER

WATCH FOR THE BRIDEGROOM!

All heaven waits for the time when the bridegroom will come for His bride! The time is coming, and coming very soon, when He will appear. This is the time for which all My family is waiting. The trumpet will blow, a shout will be heard and then I will appear. Look up. Look up, and watch for your bridegroom.

I am coming to receive My bride. I will wipe away every tear; there shall be no more death, sorrow or pain. The time for which you have been waiting will be here. There will be everlasting light, love and glory. There will be majesty, splendor and magnificence, unlike anything that you can now comprehend.

When this glorious day comes, your understanding will be transformed. You will see as I see, you will hear as I hear and you will bask in the wonder of My glory. Prepare for the time the Bridegroom will come. Prepare by listening, hearing and obeying Me. Prepare by choosing to walk in the fullness of My love! Seek your first love, and do not let anything distract you. Place your focus on the soon-coming Bridegroom.

And at midnight a cry was heard: "Behold, the bridegroom is
coming; go out to meet him!"
Matthew 25:6

8 NOVEMBER

I LONG TO APPEAR TO YOU!

It is My desire to make Myself known to you. Just as in times past, when I appeared to My people, I choose to appear to you so that you can take hold of Who I Am for you. I want you to have expectation that I will make Myself known to you. My greatest desire is for our relationship to grow and deepen. As you seek Me and choose to spend time with Me, you will find that you know Me better. You will grow in your understanding of the depth of My love for you.

When I appear to you, receive the wonder of Who I Am. Receive all that I hold out to you. Bask in the glory of My presence, and the anointing that comes when I reveal Myself in greater measure. Reach out for more of Me. Seek the fullness of Who I Am. Share with others the awesomeness of being in a place of intimacy with Me. As I reveal My glory, holiness and majesty to you, you will find yourself experiencing some of what Moses encountered upon the mountain. Be prepared to share as others see My glory upon you.

Then the Lord appeared again in Shiloh. For the Lord revealed Himself to Samuel in Shiloh by the word of the Lord.
I Samuel 3:21

And whenever the children of Israel saw the face of Moses, that the skin of Moses' face shone, then Moses would put the veil on his face until he went in to speak with Him.
Exodus 34:35

9 NOVEMBER

THE FIRE OF MY SPIRIT

Do you remember feeling your heart burning? That was Me touching your heart as you drew close to Me. Even as your heart has burned, as My anointing, revelation and understanding has come upon you, expect to receive the fire of My Spirit burning within you more and more. I am pouring My fire upon you in greater increase! Do not draw back, but reach out and receive all that I have for you.

This is a season for My power – the fire of My power – to move mightily through you and each of My followers, who are willing to run with Me. You are privileged to live in this season, and to know and experience the might of My overcoming strength and power. When you feel as if there is nothing that you can do because of the circumstances surrounding you, reach out and take My hand! As you take My hand, you will experience the fire of My Spirit! That is all you need! Do not fear! Do not worry! Trust Me completely, for I will not let you down. I Am that I Am! Hold on to Me and cling to Me, for I will amaze you as you reach out and take My hand!

And they said to one another, "Did not our heart burn within us while He talked with us on the road, and while He opened the Scriptures to us?"
Luke 24:32

His brightness was like the light; He had rays flashing from His hand, And there His power was hidden.
Habakkuk 3:4

10 NOVEMBER

I AM RISEN!

I am risen! I am risen, indeed! Because I am risen, you will rise! The same power that resurrected Me will give life to your mortal body. The same power that resurrected Me is at work in you. It is My desire for you and all My believers to know and understand what I have placed within you. I placed My Spirit within you. You have all that I am available to you, so you can shine forth Who I Am to those around you!

Take hold of Me and My resurrection power. Trust My Spirit within you to be all that I have called you to be. Take hold of Me, and move down the path that I have placed before you towards your destiny. Fulfill My calling on your life, because I have provided everything that you need. I have absolutely provided all that is needed. You cannot accomplish My call on your own, but you can excel in completing all My plan and purpose for your life as you walk in My resurrection power. Watch and see what I will do through you as you trust and believe!

He is not here; for He is risen, as He said.
Come, see the place where the Lord lay.
Matthew 28:6

But if the Spirit of Him who raised Jesus from the dead dwells in you, He who raised Christ from the dead will also give life to your mortal bodies through His Spirit who dwells in you.
Romans 8:11

11 NOVEMBER

THE WONDER OF JESUS

There is no one else like My Son, Jesus. He is full of wonder. When He was on earth, His every word was wonderful. His every act exemplified wonder! Multitudes followed Him because He was filled with wonder! Everywhere He went people gathered to hear what He would say, and they gathered to see what He would do. They gathered, because they had never heard of anyone like Him. They simply wanted to be around Him.

They heard Him share about the wonder of My character. They saw Him exhibit the wonder of My love and compassion, as He would bring healing and deliverance into the lives of the sick and those in bondage. They heard Him reprove the religious leaders of the day, and they saw Him run the moneychangers out of the temple. They saw Him so lovingly forgive a prostitute of her sins, and they also heard about Him talking to a Samaritan woman at the well in such a way that her life was changed. Be open to, look for and experience the wonder of Jesus in your life!

Men of Israel, hear these words: Jesus of Nazareth, a Man attested by God to you by miracles, wonders, and signs which God did through Him in your midst, as you yourselves also know.
Acts 2:22

The woman then left her waterpot, went her way into the city, and said to the men, "Come, see a man who told me all things that I ever did. Could this be the Christ?"
John 4:28-29

12 NOVEMBER

UNCONDITIONAL LOVE

It is all about Me! I am the All-Sufficient One! I have all that you need, and I am all that you need. Lay down the things of the world. Lay down all that besets you. Take hold of Me, your heavenly Father, Who loves you with an everlasting love. My love expands to such a great magnitude that it is hard for your mind to even comprehend it.

My love was willing to send My Son to earth to pay the price for your sins. My love, even now, holds out to you life on earth and life eternal. If you will accept and take hold of My life on earth, you will begin to understand things through My perspective. As you begin to focus more and more on Me, you see and understand that all things can truly work for good, regardless of how they look now. Take My hand, walk with Me, and bask in the wonder of My unconditional love that always seeks the best for you!

That Christ may dwell in your hearts through faith; that you, being rooted and grounded in love, may be able to comprehend with all the saints what is the width and length and depth and height – to know the love of Christ which passes knowledge; that you may be filled with all the fullness of God.
Ephesians 3:17-19

And we know that all things work together for good to those who love God, to those who are called according to His purposes.
Romans 8:28

13 NOVEMBER

OVERCOMING WAVES OF MY SPIRIT

There are two kinds of waves. There are stormy waves of adversity that come against you and try to knock you down. But, there are waves of My living waters that wash over you bringing cleansing, renewing and freshness. The waves of My Spirit also bring the fire of My power, which empowers you to go forth in My fullness.

When the apostles were in the boat with Jesus during a storm that was brewing, they became afraid. Jesus was asleep, and they woke Him when the boat began to fill with water. He then rebuked the wind and the tumultuous water. Jesus asked, "Where is your faith?"

Today, remember you are never alone in the storm, for you have My Spirit dwelling within you. When the storms and waves of adversity are flooding over you, seek My presence. And as you keep your focus on Me, there is nothing that can harm you. Enter into that secret place with Me, where you can experience the waves of My Spirit that will wash over you and empower you to overcome.

And they came to Him and awoke Him, say, "Master, Master, we are perishing!" Then He arose and rebuked the wind and the raging of the water. And they ceased, and there was a calm.
Luke 8:24

Deep calls unto deep at the noise of Your waterfalls; all Your waves and billows have gone over me.
Psalm 42:7

14 NOVEMBER

FULLNESS OF TIME

You are living in a time and a season when the fullness of time will be manifested on the earth in a way that the world will see and know that I am truly alive! I came to earth when the fullness of time had come, and many in the earth have received Me as Lord and Savior. But there is a time, and it is now, when you, My believers, are becoming so in love and in intimacy with Me that now the world will begin to see My believers truly reflecting Who I am. They will see you bringing a taste of heaven to earth, as you walk together in unity and in love.

In the past, they have seen a church divided and not really much different from the unbelievers. But I am revealing Myself in such love, and humility that My church is growing and will continue to grow in My image. You will reflect the fullness of My character of love with such magnitude that the world will see, understand and run into My arms!

But when the fullness of the time had come, God sent forth His
Son, born of a woman, born under the law.
Galatians 4:4

That in the dispensation of the fullness of the times He might
gather together in one all things in Christ, both which are in
heaven and which are on earth – in Him.
Ephesians 1:10

15 NOVEMBER

BURN WITH THE FIRE AND
PASSION OF MY SPIRIT!

I am causing your hearts to burn with the fire and passion of My Spirit! The world needs to see a church so on fire for Me that there will be no compromise, no wavering, no doubt or unbelief. Instead, My church needs to reflect to the world what total commitment is all about – My people standing firm with perseverance, expressing My love and truth!

The world is hungry for steadfastness, stability, truth and commitment instead of negativity, disunity and conflict. Rise up, My people, and draw close to Me. In this world, you will experience tribulation, hurt, conflict and grief. But as you draw into My presence, full of worship, praise and honor for Me, you cannot help but become more and more like Me. As you draw near, My fire and My passion will consume you in such a way that you will be transformed from glory to glory into My image. When the world sees My people reflecting My image and My character, they will begin to live with passion as they seek Me and give their lives to Me!

And they said to one another, "Did not our heart burn within us while He talked with us on the road, and while He opened the Scriptures to us?"
Luke 24:32

Then I said, "I will not make mention of Him, nor speak anymore in His name." But His word was in my heart like a burning fire shut up in my bones; I was weary of holding it back, and I could not.
Jeremiah 20:9

16 NOVEMBER

PERFECT LOVE OVERCOMES FEAR

I placed you on this earth to walk free of fear. I hear you asking Me, "How can that be possible?" You already know the answer: all things are possible with Me! But I understand your questioning. Fear can loom so easily and seem so strong. I have provided all that you need to overcome fear in your life. All that is necessary is that you draw into My place of love. Perfect love casts out fear.

When you sense fear rising up in you, come to Me! Come into My presence through worship, praise and thanksgiving. Read My Word, study My Word and apply it to your life. Keep your focus on Me. And when your mind begins to wander to negative thoughts and thoughts of the world, renew your mind by worship and My Word. Do not give in to the ways of the world. Do not give in to the ways of today's culture. Stay focused on Me. Reach out to Me. As you come into My presence, you will find faith rising up within you as My overcoming love sets you free personally to be a witness to others!

There is no fear in love; but perfect love casts out fear,
because fear involves torment. But he who fears has not
been made perfect in love.
I John 4:18

And do not be conformed to this world, but be transformed by the
renewing of your mind, that you may prove what is that good and
acceptable and perfect will of God.
Romans 12:2

17 NOVEMBER

MY GOODNESS PRODUCES UNENDING LOVE

Take hold of My hand, and walk with Me. I want to show you what it is like to understand the depth of My goodness. Whatever definition there is on earth of goodness will never describe the magnitude of the character of My goodness! Walk with Me, hold My hand, and let Me explain My goodness to you.

My goodness goes beyond your vocabulary. When you are seeking Me and entering into My presence, you will begin to experience My goodness. You will experience the massive love that I have for you. You will also begin to understand the persevering kind of love that I poured out when I allowed My Son to go to the cross for you. You have heard the story so often that sometimes you forget to meditate on the depth of that action of love. That action caused pain – physical pain, emotional pain and even spiritual pain. But that pain has produced a love within the lives of My people from that day until now that the world does not understand. They do not understand, but they are drawn to My goodness, which produces unending love!

*He loves righteousness and justice; the earth is full
of the goodness of the Lord.
Psalm 33:5*

*They shall utter the memory of Your great goodness,
and shall sing of Your righteousness.
Psalm 145:7*

18 NOVEMBER

MY ENCOURAGEMENT THROUGH YOU TO OTHERS

I am walking with you, step by step and moment by moment. I am teaching you to walk in the newness and freshness of this season. As you listen, hear and begin to move in the truth of My Word as I bring it alive to you, the people around you will see My reflection. My reflection will grow stronger and stronger in you as you continue to grow in the knowledge of My love and My nature.

Reach out to those around you with My love. Shower My kindness and goodness upon them. Look to Me and seek to see each individual through My eyes. Then they will see My reflection through you, and they will be drawn to Me. They cannot escape the wonder of My love as they experience seeing your love for Me, and thus for them. Some will be hard to love. But as you seek Me, I will reveal My potential that I have placed within them. Enjoy the privilege of being a part of My encouragement to others.

And sent Timothy, our brother and minister of God, and our fellow laborer in the gospel of Christ, to establish you and encourage you concerning your faith.
I Thessalonians 3:2

That our hearts may be encouraged, being knit together in love, and attaining to all riches of the full assurance of understanding, to the knowledge of the mystery of God.
Colossians 2:2

19 NOVEMBER

• ## THE LIGHT OF MY JOY

Have you ever noticed how the entrance of My light brings joy? When I shine the light of My countenance upon you, you will find joy rising up within you. You may be going through great difficulty, or perhaps even grief over a loved one's coming home to Me, yet My joy will arise as I shine the light of My countenance upon you.

Do not make the mistake of turning away from Me when your sorrow overtakes you. Instead, turn towards Me, seek My face and cling to Me. I am your help and your comfort. Draw into that secret place with Me, and I will bring joy and gladness. Joy and gladness reside in My presence. Joy and gladness are a part of Who I am. Even in the darkest times, I will pour out My love, comfort and, yes, even My joy! Begin to lift your voice in praise to Me. It will start out as a sacrifice of praise, but it will soon turn into a joyful sound. Persevere and do not give up! Cling to Me, and I will pour the light of My joy upon you!

Blessed are the people who know the joyful sound! They walk, O Lord, in the light of Your countenance.
Psalm 89:15

Light is sown for the righteous, and gladness for the upright in heart. Rejoice in the Lord, you righteous, and give thanks at the remembrance of His holy name.
Psalm 97:11-12

20 NOVEMBER

SING UNTO ME

Lift up your voice, and sing unto Me! I love to hear you sing – yes, even you who think you cannot sing. Everyone can sing. You simply open your mouth and sing from your heart to make a joyful noise unto Me. It brings Me great pleasure when you choose to sing to Me, because it gives you an opportunity to express your heart to Me.

Singing unto Me also sets you free! It sets you free from the bondage of thinking about self and of being prideful. It releases within you the freedom to pour out your love to Me. It also frees you from the fear of man, from caring more about what others think than what I think.

Lay down your inhibitions, and lift your voice. Sing unto Me! I love to hear you sing. Rejoice in My presence with singing, and watch how pride and fear begin to fade away. Sing unto Me, and see how your heart is filled with joy. Sing unto Me, and experience freedom!

I will sing to the Lord as long as I live; I will sing praise to My
God while I have my being.
Psalm 104:33

Make a joyful shout to the Lord, all you lands! Serve the Lord with
gladness; come before His presence with singing.
Psalm 100:1-2

21 NOVEMBER

SOAR LIKE AN EAGLE

When you are weary, and you feel as if you have done all you can do, wait upon Me. Be still, and know that I am God. I will renew your body, soul and spirit, so you can soar like an eagle. You will rise up with new strength. You will be strong and courageous. There will not be anything that can bring you down. You are My beloved, and I take care of you. I provide all that you need.

Picture the beauty of an eagle soaring through the sky. The eagle has extremely keen eyesight. When you rise up and soar as an eagle, you will be able to see with a keen sense of discernment. I am calling you to soar as an eagle, as you let Me renew your strength. Receive My courage and boldness to move into heights that you have never reached before. Step out in My strength and My power to soar like an eagle, as I fill you afresh and anew with all that you need to fly with Me.

But those who wait on the Lord shall renew their strength; they shall mount up with wings like eagles, they shall run and not be weary, they shall walk and not faint.
Isaiah 40:31

Who satisfies your mouth with good things, so that your youth is renewed like the eagle's.
Psalm 103:5

22 NOVEMBER

WALK IN MY EXCELLENCE

Excellence is My name. Everything I do is done in excellence. Think on this. If all I do is excellent and I dwell in you, My excellence is in you and always available to you. You do not have to strive or struggle for excellence, because I have made it available to you.

Look at My creation – the majesty and beauty of the mountains and the wonder of the roaring ocean with waves consistently coming to shore. Look at the beauty of flowers, trees, lakes, the galaxies in the sky and so much more. Look at the excellence of how I created mankind and the way I created the human body to heal. Consider all the medical and scientific discoveries. Where did they originate? They originated from Me, as I have guided people to walk in excellence.

There is no reason to settle for mediocre or less. In all that you do, trust Me! Let Me guide you in all of your endeavors. Do not even consider moving into areas that are not of Me. I will help you live a life of excellence as you seek Me, trust Me and follow My ways.

O, Lord, our Lord, how excellent is Your name in all the earth,
Who have set Your glory above the heavens!
Psalm 8:1

As for the saints who are on the earth, "They are the excellent
ones, in whom is all my delight."
Psalm 16:3

23 NOVEMBER

MY ANGELS HAVE CHARGE OVER YOU

Because My angels are of My realm, you are rarely aware of them, because you cannot usually see them. But, I want you to know angels are around you. I give them charge over you. There are incidents every single day that go unnoticed where My angels have protected My people. Only on occasion do I give someone a vision or a knowing that one of My angels has intervened in his or her life.

Trust Me to take care of you. You have no concept of the number of My angels that are available to take care of My people. Keep your focus on Me. During the times when something comes up that could harm you or cause problems for you, it is important that you know and acknowledge My desire to protect you.

Daniel was adamant in his worship of Me. Because he would not bow his knee to another, he was thrown into the lions' den. Because of Daniel's living such a committed life, the king and all of the people saw a mighty miracle. I sent an angel to shut the lions' mouths. I protected Daniel, and the king wrote a decree for all to fear Me.

For He shall give His angels charge over you, to keep you in all your ways. In their hands they shall bear you up, lest you dash your foot against a stone.
Psalm 91:11-12

My God sent His angel and shut the lions' mouths, so that they have not hurt me, because I was found innocent before Him; and also, O king, I have done no wrong before you.
Daniel 6:22

24 NOVEMBER

LIFE-CHANGING TESTIMONY

What is your testimony? Do you realize the importance of your testimony? Your testimony of your relationship with Me can change the lives of others. As you share what I have done in your life and what a difference I have made in your life, people's lives will be transformed! Your testimony points to Me and My Word. Your testimony is a historical and spiritual account of reformation – how your life has been reformed by My atoning blood and by My life rising up within you.

People around you have been seeing the changes in you. They want to know and they need to know what brought those changes. There are masses of hungry and needy people starving for answers. They long to know if there is any way to overcome all the chaos, discouragement, adversity and darkness. Do not hold back, but share with them, putting your trust in My Spirit to bring forth the message of your testimony in such a way that many lives will be touched, saved and transformed!

And they overcame him by the blood of the Lamb and the word of their testimony, and they did not love their lives to the death.
Revelation 12:11

Even as the testimony of Christ was confirmed
in you so that you come short in no gift, eagerly
waiting for the revelation of our Lord Jesus Christ.
I Corinthians 1:6-7

25 NOVEMBER

HEART, ARISE!

I am calling you to come before Me. I want you to come and be still, so you can receive all that I have for you. You have been through times of despair and desolation, and I want to speak to your heart. I am telling your heart to arise with My life! Heart, listen to My words and receive My truth. It is time for your heart to arise so full of Who I am that there will be nothing that can overcome you.

The only way that your heart can arise with My fullness is to receive My love through My Word. Every word I speak is full of life. Every word I speak brings My truth, My Word and My love to you. When you find yourself discouraged and weary, come to Me. Listen for Me to share with you My truth. Read My Word, and soak in My Word. Sing praises to Me, and you will discover joy rising up within you. Your heart will begin to beat with the rhythm of My heartbeat. Come and listen to Me for the truth of My heartbeat and arise!

For it is the God who commanded light to shine out of darkness, who has shone in our hearts to give the light of the knowledge of the glory of God in the face of Jesus Christ.
II Corinthians 4:6

And so we have the prophetic word confirmed, which you do well to heed as a light that shines in a dark place, until the day dawns and the morning star rises in your hearts.
II Peter 1:19

26 NOVEMBER

I KNEW YOU!

Do you know how much I love you? Do you know that I knew you before you were ever conceived? I planned for you to be born. I purposed for you to grow, and discover Me and My plan for your life. It brought me great pleasure to bring you into this world. Even as your mother and father rejoiced at your birth, I rejoiced even more! I watched as you grew, and I surrounded you with angels to protect and minister to you. I have guided you, and there have been times I have waited for you to get back on the path that I have placed before you.

My plan for your life brings abundant life. I charted a course for you so you could begin to step out of your comfort zone in preparation for your destiny. Seek Me, and seek to know and understand the path I have set before you, for it will bring you great peace, joy, comfort and strength. It will also bring you My fire and passion! Be prepared to take the journey of a lifetime with Me, your Heavenly Father, Who has inscribed you on the palms of My hands.

Before I formed you in the womb I knew you; before you were born
I sanctified you; I ordained you a prophet to the nations.
Jeremiah 1:5

See, I have inscribed you on the palms of My hands;
your walls are continually before Me.
Isaiah 49:16

27 NOVEMBER

EXCEEDING, ABOUNDING GRACE

My grace is a free gift, and I choose to give My grace in excess. I desire to pour out exceeding, abounding grace upon My people. The gift of grace is not easy for you to understand, because the world does not accept grace. Grace comes from Me, and as I distribute it to My people, it changes lives. Grace is a part of My nature, so human beings cannot understand grace until they receive and accept Me.

When My exceeding, abounding grace became a part of your life, you began to let My grace flow through you to others. My grace is contagious because it is surrounded with My love. My love expresses grace. When My grace is received, you begin to be an expression of My grace to others.

The world is hungry for My grace. Be a reflection and conduit of My grace, showering others with an abundance of My love, kindness and goodness.

But as you abound in everything – in faith, in speech, in knowledge, in all diligence, and in your love for us – see that you abound in this grace also.
II Corinthians 8:7

And by their prayer for you, who long for you because of the exceeding grace of God in you. Thanks be to God for His indescribable gift!
II Corinthians 9:14-15

28 NOVEMBER

I WILL BRING YOU VICTORY!

I see your dilemma, and I know you believe there is no way out. But I want you to hear Me today when I say to you, "Do not look to the circumstances of the world around you. Look up! Lift up your eyes and look to Me, for I am ready. Yes, I am always ready to reveal to you the answers that you need. I am wisdom, and I have a solution to everything that troubles you."

My wisdom overpowers the works of darkness. As you seek Me, trusting and waiting upon Me, I will show you each step to take. My great desire is to give you revelation and understanding about the complexities around you. I know that you look at your problem, and you do not see that there could possibly be a solution. Have faith in Me! I am greater than he who is in the world. Nothing is impossible with Me! Look beyond your senses and trust Me. I am your great and mighty God, and it is My delight to bring you victory!

But thanks be to God, who gives us the victory
through our Lord Jesus Christ.
I Corinthians 15:57

For whatever is born of God overcomes the world. And this is the
victory that has overcome the world – our faith.
I John 5:4

29 NOVEMBER

RISE UP, MY VALIANT ONE!

Rise up, My valiant one! I see you as a person of valor, who can bring down strongholds because I have placed My valor within you. Do not look at yourself through your eyes, but see yourself through My eyes. I have placed a potential within you that has only begun to come forth.

As you read My Word, think upon My acts and My deeds. Do you see courage, boldness, bravery and determination in My life when I walked this earth? You believe that was possible for Me, but not for you. I am telling you that it is possible for you. Gideon believed it was impossible for him to be a mighty man of valor, but I had placed My valor in him. Just as I created him to be strong and courageous, I created you to walk in strength, boldness and determination.

Rise up, O valiant one, and accept and move in the potential that I have placed within you. Move out as a mighty person of valor, and go where I send you. Tear down strongholds, and expect to see Me at work through you.

[Men and women of faith] quenched the violence of fire, escaped the edge of the sword, out of weakness were made strong, became valiant in battle, turned to flight the armies of the aliens.
Hebrews 11:34

And the Angel of the Lord appeared to him, and said to him, "The Lord is with you, you mighty man of valor!"
Judges 6:12

30 NOVEMBER

THE GIFT OF FAVOR

My favor is a gift that I give to you. I pour out My favor upon those that I know I can trust to follow through with their destiny! I look to and fro across the earth to see who has a desire to fulfill My call on his or her life.

Over two thousand years ago, I looked for a young woman who would be willing to trust Me, and I found Mary. Her heart was turned towards Me, and she desired to follow Me. When I sent the angel, Gabriel, to her to tell her she had been chosen to bring Jesus, the Messiah, into the world, she responded to Me, "Let it be according to your Word to me." She did not let any thoughts of rejection, danger or even possible death distract her from fulfilling My will.

My favor was upon Mary because she had a heart after My own heart. She desired to be obedient to Me, regardless of the possible consequences. Forgetting all else, she said, "Yes, Lord. Your will be done through Me!" Yield yourself to My will, and My favor will flow strongly upon and through you.

Then the angel said to her, "Do not be afraid, Mary, for you
have found favor with God"...Then Mary said, "Behold the
maidservant of the Lord! Let it be to me according to your word."
And the angel departed from her.
Luke 1:30, 38

For you, O Lord, will bless the righteous;
with favor You will surround him as with a shield.
Psalm 5:12

DECEMBER

1   DECEMBER

ACCORDING TO YOUR WORD

Yes, it pleased Me when Mary said, "Let it be according to Your Word to me." It pleases Me each time you say "yes" to what I am asking you to do. It pleases Me, because I see deep love for Me. As you submit your will to Mine, you grow in your relationship with Me. You desire more of My presence and My way in your life, recognizing that My way brings joy, peace and contentment.

Let your love for and commitment to Me flow from you to others. As they see and understand what is happening in your life, they will want to walk in obedience to Me as well. My Kingdom is growing, and it is growing through relationships. Your relationship with Me grows, and others see the results. They choose to draw close even as you have. This has a ripple effect, and many enter into My Kingdom seeking to follow My way. Following My way, even as Mary, David, Paul and many others did, brings about great rejoicing, as it is seen that My Kingdom grows and increases!

Him we preach, warning every man and teaching every man in all wisdom, that we may present every man perfect in Christ Jesus.
Colossians 1:28

2   DECEMBER

SON OF THE HIGHEST

When Gabriel revealed to Mary her calling to bring My Son into the earth, he explained to her that her Son would be the Son of the Highest. My Son, Jesus, was born of this virgin named Mary, and He lived a life on earth for thirty-three years, expressing on earth My qualities.

I sent My Son, the Son of the Highest, to earth so My people could begin to understand Who I am. Their concept of Me had grown stale. Many were living a religious life, but they did not know Me. The Son of the Highest not only revealed My nature, but He also paid the price for all sin forever. He made the way for My creation to become a part of My family.

When Jesus came to earth, He came to establish My Kingdom of which there will be no end. Every earthly kingdom will fade away, but My Kingdom will rule and reign forever with the Son of the Highest as King. Rejoice forevermore, for there never has been a time like this when the earth is preparing to receive the Son of the Highest – this time as King!

He will be great, and will be called the Son of the Highest; and the Lord God will give Him the throne of His father David. . .And the angel answered and said to her, "The Holy Spirit will come upon you, and the power of the Highest will overshadow you; therefore, also, that Holy One who is to be born will be called the Son of God." Luke 1:32, 35

3 DECEMBER

NO END TO MY KINGDOM

My Kingdom is an everlasting Kingdom. Heaven is full of rejoicing, because My Kingdom is reality in heaven. There are tastes of My Kingdom on earth, and those tastes are increasing with great acceleration. The time is coming soon where My Kingdom will be large banquet places – places of feasting in the wonder of My Kingdom. As My beloved ones begin to taste of the goodness of My Kingdom, they will be compelled to share Me with everyone around them. Many will come running to the banquet halls (churches), wanting to be part of the goodness and glory of Who I am.

As My Kingdom increases, the governments of the world will decrease. Regardless of what the circumstances are wherever you are, My Kingdom is increasing and will never end. Hold on to Me and cling to Me with everything that is within you, and you will see My Kingdom increase around you. Look up! Look up! Your redemption draws near. There will be a shout and the trumpet will sound as I meet you in the air!

For unto us a Child is born, unto us a Son is given; and the government will be upon His shoulder. And His name will be called Wonderful, Counselor, Mighty God, Everlasting Father, Prince of Peace. Of the increase of His government and peace there will be no end.
Isaiah 9:6-7a

4   DECEMBER

BE OVERCOME WITH JOY AND GLADNESS

Be overcome with joy and gladness, for I have made a way where there seems to be no way. I have provided My living water to cleanse and refresh you. The wind of My Spirit blows upon you, bringing My life alive within you. The fire of My power burns within you and enables you to be a reflection of Who I am. This is a time of rejoicing. Even when everything around you seems to be crumbling, rejoice!

As you rejoice and praise Me in the midst of deep darkness, joy will begin to bubble up within you. You will know that I am more than enough to see you through! You will know that I will turn your circumstances around and bring good to you.

Share My goodness with others. So many do not realize the depth of My goodness. They have heard so many negative things about Me that it is hard for them to accept My goodness. As you walk in rejoicing and gladness, they will see your love and trust for Me. They will not be able to turn away from the joy and gladness permeating your life.

The Jews had light and gladness, joy and honor. And in every province and city, wherever the king's command and decree came, the Jews had joy and gladness, a feast and a holiday.
Esther 8:16-17a

But be glad and rejoice forever in what I create; for behold, I create Jerusalem as a rejoicing, and her people a joy.
Isaiah 65:18

5 DECEMBER

TURNING HEARTS OF THE FATHERS AND CHILDREN

Even as it was said of John the Baptist that he would turn the hearts of the fathers to the children, I say to you today that this is the season of turning the fathers' hearts to the children and the hearts of the children to their fathers. It is time for fathers to rise up and see their children through My eyes. My eyes reflect love unending, wisdom, understanding, discernment and compassion.

There has often been harshness in the way fathers have treated their children, because they have mistakenly thought harshness would bring about obedience. Both parents often have mistakenly thought if they criticize misbehavior, their child would behave. Always encourage and give positive input rather than criticizing or being negative. Wake up, fathers and mothers, and see the giftings and potential that I placed within your child.

As you encourage your child lovingly, you will see a lot of the rebellion and anger cease. You will begin to see the hearts of children turn back to their fathers. That is what I am doing in this season. It is time to see My people – all My people – come together in love, unity and oneness.

He will also go before Him in the spirit and power of
Elijah, "to turn the hearts of the fathers to the children,"
and the disobedient to the wisdom of the just, to make ready
a people prepared for the Lord.
Luke 1:17

6   DECEMBER

GLAD TIDINGS

Share the glad tidings that Jesus has come! The King of all creation very humbly came as a baby, a baby Who was born in a stable. What started out to look like a very simple beginning has been heralded all over the world as glad tidings!

He lived a simple life, and yet He led an awesome life. When the time was right, His ministry began at age 30. He taught, preached, healed, set free and expressed a love unlike the world had ever seen. My Son came to set the record straight. He came to reveal My love and to make a way for all of humanity to receive salvation, to become a part of My family and to live throughout eternity with Me.

Many rejected Him, and many received Him. Today, many reject Him still, and many receive Him. The disciples spread the glad tidings of Jesus across the known world after His resurrection and ascension to heaven. The time for you and all My believers to share the glad tidings with great joy across the world is today!

And the angel answered and said to him, "I am Gabriel, who stands in the presence of God, and was sent to speak to you and bring you these glad tidings."
Luke 1:19

How beautiful upon the mountains are the feet of him who brings good news, who proclaims peace, who brings glad tidings of good things, who proclaims salvation, who says to Zion, "Your God reigns!"
Isaiah 52:7

7   **DECEMBER**

IMMANUEL – GOD WITH YOU!

I am with you! The name that was prophesied for the Messiah hundreds of years before He was born means, "God with you!" Immanuel was born in a stable in Bethlehem. There were a few that knew the significance of My Son's birth, but for most the night He was born was no different from others.

There were a group of shepherds in a field, watching over their sheep, when a host of angels appeared to them. There was a great light, and the angels began to tell them about My Son, the Messiah, having been born and lying in a manger. Can you imagine the surprise and wonder that the shepherds were experiencing? They sought out the place of His birth with great rejoicing.

My Son's coming as a baby is a time for rejoicing for all, then and down through the ages, that have come to know and understand that He came to reveal the depth of My love. He reveals to all that will receive the good news that I, God of all creation, am continually with My people. I am always available and present for all who will accept and receive My love through Jesus.

Therefore the Lord Himself will give you a sign: Behold, the virgin shall conceive and bear a Son, and shall call His name Immanuel!
Isaiah 7:14

"Behold, the virgin shall be with child, and bear
a Son, and they shall call His name Immanuel,"
which is translated, "God with us."
Matthew 1:23

8   DECEMBER

HIS STAR IN THE EAST

Some wise men from the east saw a star that led them to Jerusalem to search for the Child that had been born to be the King of the Jews. The birth of Jesus was so important to them that they traveled a great distance to pay homage, bring gifts and worship Him. They believed He was of great importance!

Wise men in the east saw a star; shepherds in a field in Bethlehem saw a great light and a host of angels. I was letting My people know that My Son, Jesus the Christ, the Messiah, that they were anticipating had come to earth as a baby. He came humbly to earth as a baby that was dependent on His earthly mother and Joseph, who raised Him as a son.

A shining star, a great light and My glory shining forth brings you, My beloved, to a place of receiving more of Me in all My glory. But never forget the humble beginnings of My Son, the Messiah, as He came to earth to die for your sins and to live humbly as He reflected My nature!

[The wise men] saying, "Where is He who has been born
King of the Jews? For we have seen His star in the East
and have come to worship Him."
Matthew 2:2

I see Him, but not now; I behold Him, but not near; a Star will
come out of Jacob; a Scepter shall rise out of Israel, and batter the
brow of Moab, and destroy all the sons of tumult.
Numbers 24:17

9   DECEMBER

LOWLY BEGINNINGS

Even as Jesus was born in a lowly stable and lay in a manger in Bethlehem, He grew up in the small town of Nazareth. Nazareth was a town of little significance. At one point, Nathanael said, "Could anything good come out of Nazareth?" Why did I allow My Son to be born in such humble surroundings, and be raised in a town without significance? I wanted My people to learn and know what is truly important.

The King of all creation walked in humility and submission to Me first, and to those around Him, to be an example of My nature. He always exhibited My love, compassion, mercy, caring and forgiveness. He did not come the first time to rule and reign. He came to show you, My beloved, the wonder of being just, loving mercy, and of walking humbly with Me. Once this principle comes alive within you, then you will be able to handle the wonder of My glory, My anointing, My greatness and My power, which also resides within you. Then you will be ready to receive Him when He comes the second time to rule and reign!

And Nathanael said to him, "Can anything good come out of Nazareth?" Philip said to him, "Come and see."
John 1:46

He has shown you, O man, what is good; and what does the Lord require of you but to do justly, to love mercy, and to walk humbly with your God?
Micah 6:8

10 DECEMBER

BRING THE MULTITUDES HOME TO ME

When Jesus was twelve, He went to the temple in Jerusalem with His family. After they had started back home, Joseph and Mary discovered He was missing. After searching for three days, they found Him in the temple, listening to and asking questions of the teachers. They all were astonished at His understanding and questions.

Even as a boy, My Son, Jesus, was aware of His calling. He lived an obedient life with His earthly parents. But there was always the knowing that, at the right time, He would move into that calling. He knew His calling was to share about My goodness, to help people understand Who I am and to provide for them My way of salvation. His desire was to see Our family grow. His desire was that none would perish.

He was willing to go to the cross and pay the price for every sin ever committed. He was willing to take every sin upon Himself, and suffer separation from Me. He was willing to suffer anguish, pain and torment so multitudes would be saved. Share the glad tidings of Jesus, and help bring the multitudes home to Me!

Now so it was that after three days they found Him in the temple, sitting in the midst of the teachers, both listening to them and asking questions. And all who heard Him were astonished at His understanding and answers. So when they saw Him, they were amazed; and His mother said to Him, "Son, why have You done this to us? Look, Your father and I sought You anxiously." And He said to them, "Why did you seek Me? Did you not know that I must be about My Father's business?"
Luke 2:46-49

11 DECEMBER

BAPTISM OF MY SON

When the time was right, Jesus came to John the Baptist, who was preaching repentance and baptizing people in the river Jordon. When Jesus saw John, He came forward to be baptized. John protested because He recognized Jesus as the Messiah. He felt he needed to be baptized by Jesus. But Jesus explained that He needed to be baptized to fulfill all righteousness.

Of course, when My Son was baptized, My Spirit descended upon Him, and I said, "This is My beloved Son in Whom I am well pleased." My Son was prepared for His calling, and it was time for Him to go forth in ministry to the people.

There was never a time before, nor has there been a time since, where My people literally physically experienced My Son walking, living and being with them as both human and God. What an awesome time! My Son, the Son of God, came to earth, walked, talked and lived with mankind! Reach out to those around you who do not know, who live a life of despair, who are in bondage and who need a Savior. You have what so many others need. Share My Son, Jesus, with a hurting and desperate world!

But Jesus answered and said to him, "Permit it to be so now, for thus it is fitting for us to fulfill all righteousness." Then he allowed Him. When He had been baptized, Jesus came up immediately from the water; and behold, the heavens were opened to Him, and He saw the Spirit of God descending like a dove and alighting upon Him. And suddenly a voice came from heaven, saying, "This is My beloved Son, in whom I am well pleased."
Matthew 3:15-17

12 DECEMBER

SHARE MY TRUTH

With every opportunity that arose, Jesus went about teaching. He went up on the mountain to teach the Beatitudes. He taught along the seashore, and He taught in the temple. He spoke My Word, and many listened and received. There were others that rejected Him, taunted Him and ridiculed Him. Did that stop Him? NO! He continued to share My good news.

I have placed you, My beloved, on this earth to share My good news. All My loved ones are called to share about My goodness. Look for opportunities. Study My Word, and stay prepared by entering into a place of intimacy with Me. In My special place with you, I will draw you close to Me. I will share the glory of Who I am with you. This will be our time together to open up and share our hearts together. As your heart begins to beat with My heartbeat, you will discover people all around you who are longing for the good news of Jesus Christ! Come unto Me, and go forth by My Spirit!

Then He opened His mouth and taught them, saying: "Blessed are the poor in spirit, for theirs is the kingdom of heaven. Blessed are those who mourn, for they shall be comforted. Blessed are the meek, for they shall inherit the earth. Blessed are those who hunger and thirst for righteousness, for they shall be filled.
Matthew 5:2-6

13 DECEMBER

MOVED WITH COMPASSION TO HEAL

Jesus went about healing those suffering from sickness and disease. He had great compassion and love that brought about healing. There was a centurion that asked Him to heal his servant. He had such great faith, recognizing the authority and power that Jesus had, and knew that Jesus could heal him from afar. Another time Jesus was in Peter's home, and his mother-in-law was sick with a fever. He simply touched her hand, and the fever left. He also healed a leper as He reached out His hand to touch him.

There are so many accounts of Jesus healing the sick. Just as He went about praying for healing, I am calling My people today to reach out and pray for those that are sick. Be a reflection today of the compassion for healing that was so strong in My Son, Jesus, when He walked on this earth. Healing is still very much a part of Who I am! Look to Me, seek Me and walk in My power to heal. My will is to bring healing into the lives of My people and those that have not accepted Me yet. Healing draws unbelievers to seek to know more about Me. Move out in faith, and trust Me to heal through you!

And when Jesus went out He saw a great multitude; and He was moved with compassion for them, and healed their sick.
Matthew 14:14

Then Jesus went about all the cities and villages, teaching in their synagogues, preaching the gospel of the kingdom, and healing every sickness and every disease among the people.
Matthew 9:35

14 DECEMBER

LIBERTY TO THE CAPTIVES

Jesus came to set the captives free. He came to loose the bonds of oppression and set My people free. When He was in the synagogue at Nazareth and stood up to read, He was handed the scroll of Isaiah. He purposefully turned to the place where it is written, "The Spirit of the Lord is upon Me because He has anointed Me to. . .proclaim liberty to the captives." This scripture says so much more, and I want you to grasp the significance of what He was reading. He was sent to set the captives free, preach, teach and heal.

There are so many people in bondage today. There are addictions to drugs, alcohol, tobacco, spending, pornography and so much more. The world today needs to know that I have an answer for them.

I can set you free, and then you can go forth to see others set free, because I came to set all that suffer bondage free. I am sending you today! Christ dwells within you. That same power that brought freedom back then is alive within you today. Reach out to Jesus, and go forth in His name and power so that He can set others free!

The Spirit of the Lord God is upon Me, because the Lord has anointed Me to preach good tidings to the poor; He has sent Me to heal the brokenhearted, to proclaim liberty to the captives, and the opening of the prison to those who are bound.
Isaiah 61:1

Then He closed the book, and gave it back to the attendant and sat down. . .And He began to say to them, "Today this Scripture is fulfilled in your hearing."
Luke 4:20a-21

15 DECEMBER

SENDING YOU OUT!

When Jesus was on the earth, He called His disciples to Him. He anointed them to go out in His name, heal the sick, cast out demons and bring freedom to the captives. He trusted His followers to go forth and do the works that He did.

Just as Jesus sent them out then, I am sending you out today. Do not protest. Do you not know that I trust you? You are mine, and I am yours. You have given Me your life, which is dead! You have new life, My life, within you. I trust you to go forth in My name, strength and power to meet the needs of those who are oppressed, discouraged and desperate. My answer for them dwells within you. My answer for them is, "Christ in you, the hope of glory." I am bringing them hope as I send you to them. I am strong and mighty! And yet, I am merciful, loving and kind! Go forth, and be an expression of Who I am! I am sending you because I trust you, My beloved!

And when He had called His twelve disciples to Him, He gave them power over unclean spirits, to cast them out, and to heal all kinds of sickness and all kinds of disease.
Matthew 10:1

And through the hands of the apostles many signs and wonders were done among the people. And they were all with one accord in Solomon's Porch. . .Also a multitude gathered from the surrounding cities to Jerusalem, bringing sick people and those who were tormented by unclean spirits, and they were all healed.
Acts 5:12,16

16 DECEMBER

LOVE YOUR ENEMY

I know the concept of loving your enemy is hard to understand. But as you live by My principle of love, you will receive a greater degree of understanding! I do not tell you to love your enemy to make it hard on you. My purpose is to help you grow in your likeness of Me. As you experience the amazing results of loving your enemy, you will begin to be eager to put this principle into practice more often.

Yes, loving your enemy is like pouring coals of fire on his head, but that does not bring you satisfaction. What brings you satisfaction is seeing Me at work – seeing how love overcomes darkness and causes anger, hurt and frustration to literally melt away from your heart. Expressing love in the face of judgment, defiance, criticism or just downright ugliness brings a peace to you. At the same time, it also causes coals of fire on your enemy's head, and your enemy will not know how to react to your kindness. Eventually his heart will be changed, or he will simply give up. Love conquers! Love wins!

Let your light so shine before men, that they may see your good works and glorify your Father in heaven.
Matthew 5:16

Therefore if your enemy is hungry, feed him; if he is thirsty, give him a drink; for in so doing you heap coals of fire on his head. Do not be overcome by evil, but overcome evil with good.
Romans 12:20-21

17 DECEMBER

RAISE THE DEAD!

There are times that I will show you to pray for the dead to arise! When Jesus walked the earth, there were numerous times that the dead arose. Jesus was revealing even then what was to come when He went to the cross. Just as Jesus arose from the dead, there have been many times down through the ages when the dead have come back to life.

This will only happen as I choose for it to happen. There is so much you do not and cannot understand at this time. I am all-knowing, and I know when and who will be raised from the dead. Be aware that this is real. Be aware that even as Lazarus, Jairus' daughter, and the widow's son were raised from the dead, there have been and will be many more raised from the dead. It will not happen by might, nor by power, but by My Spirit. It will only happen when I know the time is right. Death has lost all its sting.

Death for those who love Me is simply moving from the earth's realm to My realm of glorious life forevermore!

The blind see and the lame walk; the lepers are cleansed
the deaf hear; the dead are raised up and the poor have
the gospel preached to them.
Matthew 11:5

Then He came and touched the open coffin, and those who
carried him stood still. And He said, "Young man, I say
to you, arise." So he who was dead sat up and began to
speak. And He presented him to his mother.
Luke 7:14-15

18 DECEMBER

LEAST AMONG YOU!

When the disciples asked Me who among them would be the greatest, I took that opportunity to answer them: "Those who come to Me as a little child." Whoever comes to Me as a little child is greatest in My Kingdom. Whoever is least will be greatest in My Kingdom.

Do not try to be greatest. Do not dwell on who is better than another, but seek Me and My Kingdom. When you seek Me, you discover the wonder of My nature. My nature brings about humility, preferring others to yourself, submitting one to another and loving those that hate you. My way and My Kingdom are not based on the world's principles. My principles make no sense to the world, but they lead you to a life of peace, joy, love and the kind of contentment that does not exist in the world's ways.

Lay down pride, and lift up others. See what an amazing effect this will have on you, as well as the people around you. Share humility, mercy, grace and forgiveness, drawing others unto Me!

And [Jesus] said, "Assuredly, I say to you, unless you are
converted and become as little children, you will by no means enter
the kingdom of heaven. Therefore whoever humbles himself as this
little child is the greatest in the kingdom of heaven."
Matthew 18:3-4

To me, who am less than the least of all the saints, this
grace was given, that I should preach among the Gentiles
the unsearchable riches of Christ.
Ephesians 3:8

19 DECEMBER

DIVISION OR PEACE

I am the Author of peace. My peace rules and reigns in the hearts of My people – those that know Me, love Me and walk with Me. I came to make My peace available in the hearts and lives of those who accept Me.

The world does not know peace and will never know true peace until I return. My love brings division in the hearts of those that walk in darkness. Men may try every form of governing. But until they turn their hearts and lives over to Me, all that they do will be of no avail.

I have called My people to be shining lights in the midst of a dark world. Do not be discouraged, and do not give up. But lift your eyes, your focus, your heart and your whole being to Me. Seek Me, stay in My presence and enter into a time of worship that can only come from Me. Let go of all that is swirling around you to enter into My Holy Place. There, you will be encouraged and lifted up; there, you will experience My glory and My peace! Let My glory shine so brightly through you that others will be amazed!

Do you suppose that I came to give peace on earth? I tell you, not at all, but rather division. For from now on five in one house will be divided: three against two, and two against three.
Luke 12:51-52

But the multitude of the city was divided: part sided with the Jews, and part with the apostles.
Acts 14:4

20 DECEMBER

MY KINGDOM IS LIKE A MUSTARD SEED

My Kingdom is like a mustard seed – the smallest of seeds; but it grows to be a very large tree. The beginning is small, but the end result is huge. Just as the mustard tree grows large so the birds can nest in its branches, My Kingdom is a place where My people can rest in My presence. It is a place where they will know the joy and peace of letting go of all fear, worry and anxiety. They can rest in Me, because they know My love for them never ceases; and it covers them like a blanket on a cold night.

They know and understand that I am the God of all creation, and there is none other. My strength, power, majesty and greatness protect them and bring victory in their lives. My Kingdom is a place of refuge where they can gather with Me and one another. They have a sense of belonging that gives them the confidence, courage and boldness to be all that I created them to be. My Kingdom is forever, and My family will rejoice forevermore!

Another parable He put forth to them, saying: "The kingdom of heaven is like a mustard seed, which a man took and sowed in his field, which indeed is the least of all the seeds; but when it is grown it is greater than the herbs and becomes a tree, so that the birds of the air come and nest in its branches."
Matthew 13:31-32

21 DECEMBER

THE KINGDOM OF GOD IS WITHIN YOU

I have told you that Christ is in you. I have also told you that My Kingdom is within you. My Kingdom is not something you can see. It is the result of My Kingdom that you see – that you have discernment. My Kingdom is not made up of land, buildings or government. It resides within you. And as My Kingdom is growing within you, the people around you will see the changes and transformation as My image comes forth more and more in you.

My Kingdom is a dwelling place made up of My people. As you learn to dwell with Me, seeking Me and My ways, loving Me and observing Me, you will begin to notice that you are sounding more like Me. Your thoughts, feelings and speaking will be changing. You will be more aware of the goodness in the people around you. You will become less critical and negative as you see them through My eyes, and as you receive My love for you. You will begin to express My love to those around you in such a way that My Kingdom will increase and grow.

Now when He was asked by the Pharisees when the kingdom of God would come, He answered them and said, "The kingdom of God does not come with observation; nor will they say, 'See here!' or 'See there!' For indeed, the kingdom of God is within you."
Luke 17:20-21

For the kingdom of God is not eating and drinking, but righteousness and peace and joy in the Holy Spirit.
Romans 14:17

22 DECEMBER

GROWING IN ME!

Wait with expectancy! Wait on Me, for I will never let you down. I have what you need, and I wait with an expectancy to pour out My goodness upon you. I look forward to these times that are increasing in frequency. They are increasing as our relationship deepens. You are coming to know Me better, and you are developing a deeper walk with Me.

As we spend these times together, I see that you are changing. I see that you are receiving from Me so that you can be a shining light to others. I also see that you love others with a deeper love. You see their needs, and you find ways to meet that need.

I also see that your motives are changing. You are more concerned with others than yourself. You are sensitive to their wounds and hurts of the past, and you trust Me to heal them and set them free. I rejoice as I see you exhibit My nature to those around you!

Wait on the Lord, and keep His way, and He shall exalt you to inherit the land; when the wicked are cut off, you shall see it.
Psalm 37:34

My soul, wait silently for God alone,
for my expectation is from Him.
Psalm 62:5

23 DECEMBER

LIGHT OF MY FACE

When you come into My presence and enter into a face-to-face encounter, you will experience the light of My face. My glory and My light radiate from My face. Many rays of light come streaming from My face upon you. It delights Me to shine My face upon you, because My light comes like the dawning of the day. It causes all darkness to fade away and leaves the pure light of My glory to surround you.

My light brings cleansing and enlightenment. As I shine My light upon you, you begin to understand things you could not understand before. It is like when you go into an extremely dark room and cannot see a thing. But then, you turn on the light switch, and you see perfectly. My light brings revelation to you. Do not fear My presence, My glory or My light. Bask in the joy and wonder of being in the presence of the God of all creation. My beloved, enjoy Me as I pour out My love in such fullness that you are overcome with the wonder of Who I am and of My massive love for you.

And He was transfigured before them. His face shone like the sun, and His clothes became as white as the light.
Matthew 17:2

For it is the God who commanded light to shine out of darkness, who has shone in our hearts to give the light of the knowledge of the glory of God in the face of Jesus Christ.
II Corinthians 4:6

24 DECEMBER

MOMENT IN TIME

Come before Me with thanksgiving, and come before Me with praise. I am your hope. I have set everything into motion. I have outlined for you in My Word what is to come. There was a moment in time when the world was changed. The moment was over two thousand years ago, when My Son was born on earth. When that day occurred, so few had any concept of the magnitude of what had happened. To most, it seemed only as if another child had been born. Most did not know that the Savior of the world had come to earth to set mankind free, and to make a way for eternal life for all who would receive.

That precious moment of time, when Jesus was born to Mary and Joseph in Bethlehem, shines like a beacon in the hearts and minds of millions of My family across the world. However, there are still millions who have turned away. Some have scoffed, and others are too busy. Let the light of My Son, Jesus, shine forth from you wherever you go so that My family will continue to grow!

But when the fullness of the time had come, God sent forth His Son, born of a woman, born under the law, to redeem those who were under the law, that we might receive the adoption as sons.
Galatians 4:4-5

The scepter shall not depart from Judah, nor a lawgiver from between his feet, until Shiloh comes; and to Him shall be the obedience of the people.
Genesis 49:10

25 DECEMBER

JOY TO THE WORLD

Joy to the world, for the Lord has come! What a time of rejoicing! My Son was born in a lowly manger in Bethlehem. The angels had announced His arrival to shepherds who were in the field with their sheep. They were amazed and in awe, because they were being told of the arrival of the Messiah. Later, the wise men came rejoicing to worship Him and to give Him gifts.

It was not until thirty years later that many others began to understand Who He was. But many rejected him, and He was crucified and died on a cross. On the third day, He arose! That was a great time of rejoicing! His disciples and followers still were not sure what was happening, but then Jesus instructed them to wait in the upper room for the fulfillment of His promise to them. On the day of Pentecost, the Holy Spirit descended upon them, and My church was born. Rejoice! Rejoice! My Son was born and arose from the dead, and My family has received My Holy Spirit to empower them to take the joyful message of Jesus to the world!

When they saw the star, they rejoiced with exceedingly great joy.
And when they had come into the house, they saw the young Child
with Mary His mother, and fell down and worshiped Him.
Matthew 2:10-11a

But now I come to You, and these things I speak in the world, that
they may have My joy fulfilled in themselves.
John 17:13

401

26 DECEMBER

RECEIVE THE FULLNESS OF WHO I AM

Come before Me, until you are filled to such fullness that you are flowing over. Let My Spirit flow through you with such strength that you are completely renewed and refreshed. Begin to move out, letting My fountain of living waters flow through you to those around you.

Each day, as you prepare for your day, be ready to receive all I have for you. Let your hunger for more of Me guide you into that special place with Me, where I can share all the glories of My goodness with you. Be filled with My goodness. Receive My kindness. Walk in My mercy and grace. Let My compassion enfold you in such a way that others will quickly know that you are Mine.

Share with family. Take My goodness to your neighbors. Let My kindness be known at your place of work. Do not hold back any aspect of Who I am. The world is hungry for Me. Share Me with all around you.

To know the love of Christ which passes knowledge; that you may be filled with all the fullness of God.
Ephesians 3:19

Till we all come to the unity of the faith and of the knowledge of the Son of God to a perfect man, to the measure of the stature of the fullness of Christ.
Ephesians 4:13

27 DECEMBER

IMITATE ME!

When you consider how much I love you, the giftings that I hold out to you, and the fact that My Holy Spirit dwells within you, why would you have doubts, worry or fear? I know that you live in a very imperfect world and are surrounded with negativity, darkness and depravity. To overcome all of this evil and ugliness that permeates society, it is imperative that you stay in My Word, stay in My presence and keep your focus on Me.

My desire is for you to know Me so well that you imitate Me. In other words, as you seek Me, you cannot help but be changed – changed into My image! What a joy it would be for Me to see you and all My family looking like Me, speaking like Me and acting like Me. Let the ways of this world slip away, and move into My ways! When My family is imitating Me, our family will grow. Others will see and be drawn to the beauty and wonder of their heavenly Father!

Imitate me, just as I also imitate Christ.
I Corinthians 11:1

Therefore be imitators of God as dear children. And walk in love,
as Christ also has loved us and given Himself for us as an offering,
a sacrifice and us to God for a sweet-smelling aroma.
Ephesians 5:1-2

28 DECEMBER

THE LEAST OF THESE

Look at every person you see through My eyes. Look at them, and be aware of the great value that I place upon them. Look at their uniqueness. Look at their eyes. Do you see sadness or joy? Do their eyes show darkness or light? As you look at each one, let Me show you how to pray for each individual, or what act of kindness to show each one. Do not just glance and go your way, but consider who they are and what their needs may be.

There are many lonely and hurting people out there, and simple acts of kindness could lead them into My arms. My arms are wide open, as I wait for so many to respond to Me. They just need to see someone who reflects Me. A simple smile, a willingness to reach out with My goodness, can make a tremendous difference in lives. Listen to My Spirit that dwells within you, and He will show you exactly what words or what deeds would make life-changing differences.

Then they also will answer Him, saying, "Lord, when did we see you hungry or thirsty or a stranger or naked or sick or in prison, and did not minister to You?" Then He will answer them, saying, "Assuredly, I say to you, inasmuch as you did not do it to one of the least of these, you did not do it to Me."
Matthew 25:44-45

29 DECEMBER

THE FAMILY OF GOD

I have called you to imitate Me – to be like Me. I know that it is difficult for you to imagine being like Me, and you cannot in your own strength and power. You can only be like Me as you surrender to Me, yield to Me and allow Me to work through you by My Spirit.

My plan and My desire is to have a huge family that loves one another, walks together in unity and prefers the others – always wanting what is best for all. When we are living together eternally, that is what life will be like. But I want you to know this kind of life can begin on earth. Reach out to one another with no ulterior motives, but only in My love. Be there for each other, and show the world what it is like to be a part of the family of God.

Look for ways to be a blessing to My family, and also to those that have not yet chosen to come into the fold. Look for ways to shine forth My love, as you seek to reach out to those who are desperately in need of My never-ending love.

Let love be without hypocrisy. Abhor what is evil. Cling to what is good. Be kindly affectionate to one another with brotherly love, in honor giving preference to one another.
Romans 12:9-10

Fulfill my joy by being like-minded, having the same love, being of one accord, of one mind. Let nothing be done through selfish ambition or conceit, but in lowliness of mind let each esteem others better than himself.
Philippians 2:2-3

30 DECEMBER

TAKE THE GLAD TIDINGS

Take the good news and glad tidings of Jesus to all the world. Take My message of love, redemption, grace and mercy to everyone around you. Do not hold back, but share the wonder of Who I am in your life. Let your family, neighbors, co-workers and friends know of the excitement that is in your heart. Tell them of your encounters with Me, and how I have brought peace, joy and contentment unlike anything you have ever experienced in your life.

Go upon the mountain and shout to the people in the valley about the God of all creation, about how I sent My Son to earth as a baby, and how He lived among the people. Tell them about how He expressed My loving forgiveness everywhere He went. Let them know about how He healed the sick, calmed the storms and set the captives free. Share with them about how He went to the cross to pay for their sins so they could live eternally with Me, by accepting Him into their hearts.

Make sure that they hear and understand about the day of Pentecost, when We sent the Holy Spirit to live within all believers. Help them to understand that they can rely on Us – Father, Son and Holy Spirit – to always be with them forever and forever. As you share and as they receive, know the everlasting joy that comes when our family receives another loved one into the fold.

Now it came to pass, afterward, that He went through
every city and village, preaching and bringing the glad
tidings of the kingdom of God.
Luke 8:1

31 DECEMBER

SHINE FORTH MY RADIANCE

May the radiance of My glory shine forth upon you in such a way that you are aglow with My light. My countenance shines forth upon you, bringing My radiance to such brilliance that others will see and want what you have. Seek My face, for it is My face that brings the brilliance of My light to you.

Look into My eyes, which are flames of fire. As you look upon Me and meet My gaze upon you, you will experience the majesty of My presence. You will experience My fire burning through you that will bring alive passion for My way!

You will go forth with a desire to share Me – to share My radiance – with others. They will see the excitement and fervor within you, and they will desire to draw close to Me. My passion is contagious! There is a hunger for so much more than the norm. There is a hunger for a deeply meaningful relationship with Me that will spark a fire that will continue to burn! Shine forth brightly with My radiance!

Now you've got my feet on the life path, all radiant
from the shining of your face. Ever since you took
my hand, I'm on the right way.
Psalm 16:11 MSG

His head and hair were white like wool, as white as snow, and His
eyes like a flame of fire. . .He had in His right hand seven stars, out
of His mouth went a sharp two-edged sword, and His countenance
was like the sun shining in its strength.
Revelation 1:14,16

CPSIA information can be obtained at www.ICGtesting.com
Printed in the USA
LVOW12s0640181213

365751LV00001B/1/P